RUNAWAY DREAM

BORN TO RUN AND BRUCE SPRINGSTEEN'S AMERICAN VISION

LOUIS P. MASUR

BLOOMSBURY PRESS

NEW YORK   BERLIN   LONDON

For Jani
"love is wild . . . love is real"

Copyright © 2009 by Louis P. Masur

All rights reserved. No part of this book may be used or reproduced in any manner whatsoever without written permission from the publisher except in the case of brief quotations embodied in critical articles or reviews. For information address Bloomsbury Press, 175 Fifth Avenue, New York, NY 10010.

Published by Bloomsbury Press, New York

All papers used by Bloomsbury Press are natural, recyclable products made from wood grown in well-managed forests. The manufacturing processes conform to the environmental regulations of the country of origin.

LIBRARY OF CONGRESS CATALOGING-IN-PUBLICATION DATA

Masur, Louis P.
Runaway dream : Born to run and Bruce Springsteen's American vision / Louis P. Masur.—1st ed.
p. cm.
Includes bibliographical references and index.
ISBN 978-1-59691-692-0 (alk. paper hardcover)
1. Springsteen, Bruce. 2. Rock musicians—United States—Biography.
I. Springsteen, Bruce. Born to run. II. Title. III. Title: Born to run and Bruce Springsteen's American vision.

ML420.S77M37 2009
782.42166092—dc22
[B]

2009003045

First published by Bloomsbury Press in 2009
This paperback edition published in 2010

Paperback ISBN: 978-1-60819-101-7

1 3 5 7 9 10 8 6 4 2

Typeset by Westchester Book Group
Printed in the United States of America by Worldcolor Fairfield

CONTENTS

Bruce Springsteen—1991. (© TIMOTHY WHITE)

SETTING UP

The release date is just one day. The record is forever.

—BRUCE SPRINGSTEEN, 1975

FULL DISCLOSURE: I want "Born to Run" played at my memorial service (preferably in about forty years). Looking back, Bruce Springsteen said he wanted to "make the Greatest Record Somebody's Ever Heard." With me, he succeeded. And I'm not alone.

Born to Run transformed a scraggly twenty-five-year-old from Freehold, New Jersey, into a rock icon. If he was an overnight sensation, however, he was one ten years in the making, having practiced guitar eight hours a day from his early teens. He honed his gifts playing with other rock 'n' roll dreamers, several of whom became part of his E Street Band. Springsteen, though, was different. He wrote his own music. While performing, he had a presence that others lacked. Shy and awkward when standing in the shadows, onstage he was a leader, in control, directing what he wanted until everyone got it right. Appearing on the covers of both *Time* and *Newsweek* on October 27, 1975, came as a shock, but a part of Bruce Springsteen knew he deserved to be there; he was that good, better than the rest.

Born to Run mattered at the time because it filled a musical vacuum. The record industry was in decline, the vapors of psychedelic rock and pop rock had dissipated, and while punk and disco

I

punctured the airwaves, a void loomed for anyone who once felt transformed by rock 'n' roll and wanted to be again, or for those yet to be liberated by the beat. The top song of the year was the vanilla "Love Will Keep Us Together" by the Captain and Tennille. Ten years had passed since Bob Dylan revolutionized music with "Like a Rolling Stone." How quickly the scene had changed.

The album also filled a cultural vacuum because in 1975 exhaustion sapped the national spirit. A recession was in full force in 1974 with an oil crisis that had led to long lines at the pumps and shocked the country. Nixon had resigned. The Vietnam War came to an inglorious end. For anyone between fifteen and twenty-five, it felt as if everything was in decline, that little was happening, that the most exciting times were past with nothing ahead to look forward to.

I was eighteen in the summer of 1975, home after my freshman year of college. Living in my parents' two-bedroom apartment in the Bronx, I felt trapped. I was working as a waiter in a restaurant and I was pining for a girl I'd met toward the end of the school year, but she lived in Chicago. That summer I bought my first car, a used 1973 metallic-blue Dodge Dart Swinger. Any excuse I could find had me driving—to the beach, to the other boroughs, up Route 17 to the Catskills. I first heard "Born to Run" that August on my car radio, and it did two things: It spoke to my soul and it made me drive faster.

Born to Run announced a change. It sounded old, and yet unlike anything you had heard before; it spoke with romance and longing and sharp pain for dreams of love; it befriended you and suddenly you weren't alone. Those few critics who disliked the album may have only heard melodramatic stories featuring a cast of characters with names like Mary, Wendy, Terry, Eddie, the Bad

Scooter, and the Magic Rat. But those characters were us, and they were both escaping from something and searching for something.

The album was not only about freedom but also fate. In the layered sounds of guitar, piano, and sax, the pounding beat of bass and drums, it was too easy for some listeners to hear only the romance and miss the darkness that gathered like mist. "Rock 'n' roll has always been this joy. This certain happiness that is, in its way, the most beautiful thing in life," Springsteen said. "But rock is also about hardness and closeness and being alone." Who are we? What do we want? Where are we headed? *Born to Run* was connected to the times but also timeless, built to last, and so thirty years later it still speaks to those who were eighteen when it came out, and those who turned eighteen in 1985, 1995, or 2005.

Obvious, but must be said: This is an album. Springsteen designed it to be listened to in its entirety, in order. No singles to be downloaded and no filler to support a single. This is true of all of Springsteen's work, with each album painstakingly crafted musically and lyrically, as a writer might a novel, for the complete effort to come together as a whole. You could listen to one tune, but doing so would be like reading one chapter of a book.

It must also be said that these are songs, not poems. As gripping and inspirational as the words may be, they are delivered through music and any attempt to understand the power of *Born to Run* falls short without emphasizing its musical qualities. Springsteen himself made the point just after the album came out: "I'm a songwriter, I'm not a poetry man."

Finally, I write as a hardcore fan, maybe even as a true believer, but not as naïve or uncritical. I examine how Springsteen made the record and how the public received it. I've tried to understand why so many testimonials name the album, or specific songs on it, as life-changing. Almost all of the major themes of Springsteen's work and their development over time emanate from the big bang that was *Born to Run*. Springsteen has said as much: "The primary questions I'd be writing about for the rest of my work life first took form in the songs on *Born to Run*." I've quoted copiously from published interviews with him and comments that he has made onstage. It is essential that his voice come through; it offers the testimony for the story that I tell.

I am interested in Springsteen's work, not his life: the art not the artist. The exception is his childhood, when his relationship with his parents shaped in important ways the songwriter and performer he became. Fortunately, Springsteen has not been shy about discussing his life and work. He may only reveal what he wants to bare, but he has provided more than enough to study and understand.

In 1975, critics called Springsteen "an American archetype," a "true American punk." Being labeled a punk was a compliment: a little wild and alienated, but also innocent, romantic, and in important ways rooted in tradition. Rebellion in America is itself a tradition. The United States began as a revolt against authority, and any number of actual and fictional characters have added to the mythology, from Daniel Boone to Woody Guthrie, Hester Prynne to Huck Finn. Asked in 1953's *The Wild One* what he was rebelling against, Marlon Brando's character, Johnny, sporting a leather jacket like the one that Bruce will wear on his album cover more than twenty years later, answers, "What've you got?"

Born to Run is a masterpiece embedded with American themes of escaping and searching, of redemption and connection. This is why it transcends its moment. The album carries us on a journey that is jubilant and despairing, joyous and hopeless. It is an album rooted in an American geography that is both physical—highways, roads, streets—and cultural—individualism, community, salvation. For more than thirty years, Springsteen has been thinking about American identity. I try to tell that story here, the thematic story of Springsteen's American vision that begins on *Born to Run* with a piercing harmonica and a screen door slamming.

SOUND CHECK: "THE SCREEN DOOR SLAMS"

When the Born to Run *album came out, the record was so tied in with who I was, I felt like, hey, I felt like I was born. I felt like it was a birthday.*

—BRUCE SPRINGSTEEN, 1987

IN JUNE 1973, Bruce Springsteen and the E Street Band (the name came from pianist David Sancious's address in Belmar) opened for the group Chicago at Madison Square Garden. Springsteen loathed the experience. He hated playing in a huge arena, the band had no time to perform a sound check, and Columbia executives in attendance couldn't understand what all the Springsteen fuss was about.

I attended one of those shows with someone I was desperately trying to make my girlfriend. I was sixteen years old, between my junior and senior years in high school, and any excuse to leave my parents' apartment for a concert downtown was reason to go. We had floor seats and I remember two details from that night: At one point, my date sat on my lap and wrapped her hands around my neck. The other detail I remember is a man named Bruce Springsteen playing furiously and riveting my attention. Sometime that summer I bought his only album. Whatever Bruce thought of the show, he had won at least one fan.

Only a year earlier, Springsteen had signed with Columbia Records after auditioning for John Hammond, the legendary executive

6

who had discovered Bob Dylan in 1961. Springsteen's first album, *Greetings from Asbury Park, N.J.*, appeared in January 1973; it had taken him all of three weeks in the studio to complete the recording. Critics admired it. Lester Bangs, in *Rolling Stone*, dubbed him "a bold new talent" and marveled over Springsteen's use of words. But the album did not sell particularly well. Neither did the second album, released later that same year, *The Wild, the Innocent, and the E Street Shuffle*. Here again, however, reviewers extolled not only his ability to write lyrics, but his musical gifts as well.

The comparisons to Bob Dylan started to mount. It didn't help that Hammond declared that Springsteen was "much further along, much more developed than Bobby was when he came to me." In March 1973, Springsteen said he didn't like the label of "new Dylan"; in fact he resented it, because he knew how many careers had been derailed by the tag. He would declare his love for Dylan and proclaim his work "*the* greatest music ever written." At the same time, he would state that there was only a brief period when Dylan "was important to me . . . when he was giving me what I needed."

That period, 1964 to 1966, produced *Bringing It All Back Home, Highway 61 Revisited*, and *Blonde on Blonde*. No matter how troubled he may have been by the incessant comparisons to Dylan, in late 1974 and early 1975 Springsteen would regularly perform Dylan's "I Want You." " 'I want you'—that's it," Springsteen declared. "That's the ultimate statement you can make to anybody. What else can you say? And that's the greatest lyric in the song, those three words, in the whole damn song! I put that on, man, and I get blown away. I get blown down the street, 'cause there's no hoax there. It was real, real as hell."

At the same time, he reminded anyone who would listen that

he came from a totally different scene and was influenced by a range of artists including "Elvis, Otis Redding, Sam Cooke, Wilson Pickett, the Beatles, Fats, Benny Goodman, a lot of jazz guys." "You can hear them all in there if you want," he said in September 1974. He might easily have added Dion, the Ronettes, the Stax artists, Van Morrison, the Doors, the Who, the Animals, the Yardbirds, the Stones, and the Band.

In April 1974, Springsteen said to *Time* reporter Jay Cocks that "the best thing anyone can do for me is not to mention Bob Dylan." Cocks pointed out that the "scattering intimations of Dylan" collided with "the fierce rhythms of Springsteen's own wild fusion of rock, jazz, and folk music." Springsteen put the difference simply: "I like to write songs you can dance to."

Most of Springsteen's early fans became converts after hearing him perform live, and none was more important than Jon Landau, who, though only twenty-six, served as music critic for *Rolling Stone* and had experience as a record producer. Landau heard him perform in April and again in May 1974, in Cambridge, Massachusetts. In the *Real Paper*, a Boston weekly on par with New York's *Village Voice*, Landau wrote a review of the May 9 late show at the Harvard Square Theater—a dazzling piece of writing and reflection that begins with a long autobiographical confession about the joy Landau took from the "spirit of rock 'n' roll" in the sixties and how, sadly, fewer and fewer artists seemed to be making any sort of impression. Then he wrote the following:

> But tonight there is someone I can write of the way I used to write, without reservation of any kind. Last Thursday, at the Harvard Square theatre, I saw my rock 'n'roll past flash before my eyes. And I saw something else: I saw rock and roll future

and its name is Bruce Springsteen. And on a night when I needed to feel young, he made me feel like I was hearing music for the very first time.

One of the songs Landau heard that night was "Born to Run." It was the first time Springsteen had performed it live. Landau described it as having "a 'Telstar' guitar introduction and an Eddie Cochran rhythm pattern." "Telstar" was a reference to a 1962 instrumental hit by the Tornadoes; it was named after the communications satellite and had the sound of a rocket blasting off. And Eddie Cochran was a rising star who had died in a car crash at the age of twenty-one in 1960, but who already had to his credit such hits as "Summertime Blues" and "C'Mon Everybody," songs that relied on studio overdubbing to achieve their effect. Landau's brief comment shows just how astute he was as a music critic.

Springsteen was already in the studio trying to capture on tape what he heard in his head. The process had begun in January 1974. It took six months to record "Born to Run." The album would not be finished until July 1975. In the meantime, Columbia Records seized on Landau's column and marketed Springsteen as the future of rock 'n' roll.

For five nights in August 1975, fans packed the streets outside the Bottom Line at Bleecker and Mercer streets in New York's Greenwich Village. Lines had started to form at five and snaked around the block. Critics and fans were there to hear Bruce Springsteen and his band perform. The twenty-five-year-old had been leading groups for at least a decade. There had been the Castiles and Steel Mill and other incarnations of a collection of friends and musicians who rocked every bar and club and college that would book them. There had been good notices, too, including one reviewer who called a show by

Steel Mill in Berkeley in 1970 "one of the most memorable evenings of rock in a long time." But the band did not last.

When Bruce Springsteen and the E Street Band took the stage at the Bottom Line in August 1975, the stakes were high. Columbia's publicity machine had gone full throttle to promote the new record, *Born to Run,* set to be released on August 25. The company bought nearly one thousand of the four thousand available tickets and spread them around to the media. One disc jockey explained Columbia's philosophy: " 'Go see him. If you don't like him, don't play him—don't write about him.' "

A poster for the show contains the essential elements of the iconic figure that Springsteen soon would become. It shows him full-figure, facing away. His hair is long and he is wearing a leather jacket that says WILD & INNOCENT. His guitar dangles behind his back, and attached at the neck of the instrument is a pair of sneakers. It is pure attitude evoking Elvis Presley, James Dean, Marlon Brando, and Bob Dylan, among others. One writer said he was "the kind of artist Walt Whitman and Jack Kerouac and Otis Redding would have joined hands over."

For two years now, Springsteen had felt conflicted over the hype, which was not limited to Landau's sanctification. He wanted to shape his own identity and, Landau's prediction notwithstanding, the only future he was interested in was his own. But he also knew that he had the goods: the talent, the charisma, the experience, the attitude, the ambition, the work ethic, the gift. He would later call "Born to Run" "my shot at the title. A 24 yr. Old kid aimin' at the greatest rock 'n roll record ever."

WNEW-FM in New York broadcast the early show on Friday, August 15. If you lived in the New York area and cared about rock, WNEW at 102.7 was the only station that mattered. Their disc

Poster for August 1975 shows at the Bottom Line.

jockeys were minor celebrities who shaped the musical tastes of a generation. Scott Muni, Dennis Elsas, Pete Fornatale, Dave Herman, Richard Neer, Jonathan Schwartz, and Alison Steele, who called herself "the Nightbird," put together long sets of music by the known and unknown. If record companies pressured them to play certain artists, it was hard to tell from the eclecticism of the music. But until that night, WNEW had been slow to respond to the rising chorus of critics raving about Springsteen's music. In what amounted to a public apology, Dave Herman said on air that he regretted being turned off from Springsteen by all the hype coming out of Columbia Records. Seeing him live at the Bottom Line, however, converted him. Springsteen was "totally unique, totally fresh." Richard Neer agreed: "Bruce has to be seen to be believed."

Neer served as host for the radio broadcast. Before Springsteen took to the stage, he grabbed Neer's microphone and joked that he was feeling really good at the weigh-in and that he was ready to fight. "For the heavyweight championship of the world," Neer remarked, "we turn you over to the stage and Bruce Springsteen."

Bruce and the band came out together. Danny Federici, on organ, had been with Bruce the longest, back to before the days of Steel Mill in 1970. When Springsteen finally was signed by Columbia, Federici rejoined the new Springsteen band. Garry Tallent, on bass, had played with Bruce at the Upstage in Asbury Park. He studied oldies as if they were sacred texts, and he joined Springsteen in 1971. Clarence Clemons, "the big man," whose sax solos became a staple and off whom Bruce frequently played onstage, came along in 1972. Piano virtuoso Roy Bittan and explosive drummer Max Weinberg became members in September 1974 after answering an ad placed in the *Village Voice*. Weinberg was the fifty-fifth drummer who auditioned and he won the position when Bruce put up his arm and Max hit a rim shot. Bittan and Weinberg replaced David Sancious and Ernest "Boom" Carter, who decided to pursue other opportunities, but not before recording "Born to Run." Finally, just several months earlier, Steve Van Zandt, a Jersey Shore regular who was working with Southside Johnny and had been with Bruce in his earlier bands, including Steel Mill, rejoined the band.

For two hours, Springsteen and the E Street band led those in the club, and those listening to the radio, on a rock 'n' roll journey. His voice controlled the room and the airwaves: Gravelly, whispery, explosive, sincere, imploring, joyful, visceral, playful— it conveyed the spectrum of feelings and ideas embedded in the music and lyrics. He told stories. He played with the audience, at one point dancing on top of the tables at stage front until his microphone cord disconnected. He and the band rocked the house.

He opened with "Tenth Avenue Freeze-Out," a song on the new album, *Born to Run*, and first performed live less than a month earlier. It served its purpose: Even though no one knew it, the R&B number had the audience clapping a minute into the song. He kept the energy flowing with "Spirit in the Night," dedicating it to the people down at the shore. Adjusting for gender, and with bells ringing in the background, he covered the Crystals' "Then He Kissed Me," one of many Phil Spector–produced hits. The pace slowed with "Growin' Up," followed by two other songs from the first two albums, including "The E Street Shuffle," before which Bruce told a long, comical story about meeting Clarence Clemons. He also covered the Searchers' "When You Walk in the Room." Then came three consecutive songs from the new album: "She's the One," "Born to Run," which he introduced as "Tramps Like Us," and a quiet "Thunder Road" at piano. He brought the energy back to a boil with "Kitty's Back" and "Rosalita" and left the stage. As encores he first slowed the pace with the ballad "4th of July, Asbury Park," and then the band brought everyone to their feet by closing with Gary U.S. Bonds's "Quarter to Three." He ended by screaming, "I'm just a prisoner of rock 'n' roll."

This was the art of "rock 'n' roll hysteria" at its best. Not five minutes after the show ended, Neer and Herman predicted that Springsteen at the Bottom Line ranked alongside the shows first given by the Beatles and Dylan in small clubs. Critics reviewed the Bottom Line shows with a breathlessness that almost matched the performances themselves. John Rockwell, music critic for the *New*

York Times, called Springsteen the next Mick Jagger and proclaimed that the shows he saw "will rank among the great rock experiences." And Dave Marsh, who would soon become Springsteen's biographer, announced that A ROCK STAR IS BORN. "Like only the greatest rock singers and writers and musicians, he has created a world of his own," explained Marsh. But "Springsteen doesn't write rock opera; he lives it."

Springsteen also couldn't have been more pleased with the Bottom Line shows: "It went pretty ideally. The band cruised through them shows like the finest machine there was. There's nothin'—nothin'—in the world to get you playing better than a gig like that. The band walked out of the Bottom Line twice as good as they walked in." "Controlled spontaneity," is how Steve Van Zandt described the band's power. Max Weinberg recalled that he couldn't suppress his adrenaline: "We hit the stage and blew the people back in their chairs." Clemons thought that each night got better and better: "We would have killed them if we'd stayed at the club any longer."

Years later, Springsteen explained the mission and power of the band: "I learnt when I was very young how to build a band that would excite you, impress you, that we're putting on a show for the people, that when you come out tonight, we're not gonna fuck with you, that your ticket is our handshake . . . that this matters, that it's a circus, it's a political rally, it's a dance party, but that also the band is a group of witnesses, witnesses to our times, that our job is to make you laugh, make you cry, and to testify as seriously as we can, as seriously as we can, about the things we've seen."

In *Rolling Stone*, Dave Marsh offered a far-sighted review of the Bottom Line shows. Springsteen, he said, "is everything that has been claimed for him—a magical guitarist, singer, writer, rock &

roll rejuvenator—but the E Street Band has nearly been lost in the shuffle. Which is ridiculous because this group may very well be the great American Rock & Roll Band."

And yet, at this precise moment, late August 1975, Springsteen had critics wondering whether he could produce a record album that captured the grandeur of the live performances. John Rockwell thought that the only factor keeping Springsteen from superstardom was the "discrepancy between the impact of his live performances and his albums." He doubted whether any album would be anything but a "pale reflection" of Springsteen's "overwhelming" live performances, but success in rock was measured by album sales, not sold-out concerts in clubs, and the first two albums had hardly sold fifty thousand copies combined. The reality of the business, according to Rockwell, was that "no matter how many critics call you the greatest thing since Elvis or Dylan, you aren't a superstar unless you sell millions of records." Later in his career, Springsteen would put it this way: "I like the classic idea of hits—it was sort of like *50,000,000 Elvis Fans Can't Be Wrong.*"

Springsteen knew all this and felt the pressure to produce. Garry Tallent later recalled, "We were ready to be booted from the label." Roy Bittan remembered that Bruce "felt everything was on the line." Steve Van Zandt said if the third record "didn't make it, it seemed obvious that it was going to be the end of the record career." In October 1974, Springsteen talked about the finances of moving forward: "We got a band; we got a blue bus; we got a sound man; we got an office in New York. Those are the sort of things that influence my decisions. We have to play, because if we don't everything falls apart. We don't make any money off records."

But he remained a romantic. "To me," he said some years later, "the idea of a romantic is someone who sees the reality, lives the reality every day, but knows about the possibilities too. You can't lose sight of the dreams. That's what great rock is about to me, it makes the dream seem possible."

ONE

BEFORE *BORN TO RUN*

I was born, grew old, and died making that album.

—BRUCE SPRINGSTEEN, 1976

SPRINGSTEEN WAS SEVEN when he saw Elvis on *The Ed Sullivan Show*. Presley's third and final appearance took place on January 6, 1957; Bruce was born September 23, 1949. On that Sunday night in 1957, Elvis smiled and smirked and played with the audience. He came out wearing a bloused shirt and vest, makeup around the eyes. This was a stark contrast from the Elvis who had appeared less than three months earlier on October 26. On that occasion, Elvis sang "Don't Be Cruel," "Love Me Tender," and "Hound Dog," shaking his hips, standing on his toes, girls screaming, music reaching places you didn't know you had. And that guitar: It was a weapon and it was armor. This was the dream.

The show Springsteen saw was in many ways more sedate. The camera never peered below Elvis's waist, and Elvis held the guitar for only a moment, as a prop at the end of "Heartbreak Hotel." No band behind him, just his backup singers, the Jordanaires. No matter. The performance worked its magic.

Jimmy Iovine, who engineered *Born to Run* and rose to become chairman of Interscope/Geffen/A&M Records, summarized the significance of Elvis as well as anyone: "Elvis Presley was the big bang. He was the single most influential figure in the history of American

17

pop culture. He changed the way we looked, thought, dressed, held a guitar. He didn't invent rock 'n' roll, but he defined it in a way that everyone who followed owes him a debt . . . Elvis took the power of sexuality and rebellion and showed us how to be free."

Watching the show, Springsteen was mesmerized. "I couldn't imagine anyone not wanting to be Elvis Presley," he recalled. His mother eventually bought him a guitar and even set up lessons, but Springsteen's hands were too small, he didn't like structured instruction, and he put the instrument aside for sports ("I wanted to be a baseball player") and the other activities of childhood.

The rock 'n' roll seed, however, had been planted, and it gave Springsteen something he didn't receive in any other way: "It reached down into all those houses where there was no music or books or any kind of creative sense, and it infiltrated the whole thing. That's what happened in my house."

He grew up in Freehold, a conservative, working-class town. His parents' two-family home was located on Randolph Street, outside the downtown area. His paternal grandparents lived with him until he was six. As a child, Springsteen was always up until all hours of the night. "We had a very eccentric household," he has said. "My clock got thrown off when I was really young. Five and six, I was up until 3 A.M. I'm sure it's no coincidence I ended up a musician."

One of Springsteen's earliest memories is the smell of a single kerosene lamp and a coal stove that warmed the house. He would shoot his water gun onto the coals and watch the steam rise. Springsteen's parents then moved to a house on Institute Street. Finally, when his grandparents needed to live with them again, they moved to another house, on South Street, where Springsteen resided during his high school years.

House on South Street in Freehold, New Jersey, where Springsteen lived as a teenager.

Springsteen attended Saint Rose of Lima, where he internalized a vocabulary, if not a theology, that would appear with increasing frequency in his work as he got older. Parochial school left its marks, both emotional and physical, on a boy who from the start was an outsider perceived by others as crazy for his refusal to conform. "I hated school," he recalled in 1978. "I had the big hate." He remembered mouthing off in class in eighth grade and, as punishment, being sent by the nuns to the first-grade class and made to occupy one of the tiny desks and chairs. He sat there smirking and the sister said, "Show this young man what we do to people who smile in this classroom." "This kid," Springsteen recalled, "this six-year-old, who has no doubt been taught to do this, he comes over to me—him standing up and me sitting in this little desk about eye-to-eye—and he slams me in the face." He could still feel the sting, more humiliation than pain, just as the time the nuns shoved him into a garbage can and said he was worthless.

In 1978, he said, "I was raised Catholic and everybody who was raised Catholic hates religion . . . I quit that stuff when I was in eighth grade. By the time you're older than thirteen it's too ludicrous to go along with anymore."

By all accounts, Springsteen's parents, Douglas and Adele, both Catholic, had a good marriage, though there were severe strains in the household. At different times, his father's parents lived with them. Economic catastrophe was always an unpaid bill or two away. Springsteen recalls his parents as not overly political. One day he came home from grade school and asked his mother if they were Democrats or Republicans. She said, "We're Democrats 'cause Democrats are for the working people." That constituted his political education until he took an interest later in life.

Adele, whose background was Italian-American (her maiden name is Zirili), glued the household together. Springsteen's affection for her is unambiguous. ("Just like Superwoman, she did everything, everywhere, all the time," Bruce said.) In 1998, he described her as nurturing and supportive and freely giving of her faith and love.

From his mother he acquired his work ethic and his appreciation of the significance of working day after day—the stability, dignity, and community that comes from the commitment to one's job. "She walked with pride and strength," he said, and it gave him great comfort as a child. He recalled what she did to provide for the family:

> I always remember my mother—we had a finance company that was a hundred yards from our house. And it was just very—it

was just a part of our life. My mother would go in March and she would borrow till the summer and then she would pay it off. And when she got it paid off, she would go and borrow again and it would get us through the next—it was this constant cycle of financial struggle. And they had a pretty difficult life. And amazingly enough, we were pretty protected from most—a lot of it, I think. You know, my mother was, and remains to me, quite, you know, quite noble. And because she was the patriot of consistency, she got up in the morning, got us off to school, went to work. And this went on day after day, after day, after day.

Douglas, however, of Dutch and Irish ancestry, was something of a drifter and a drinker, struggling to hold down work: "My father struggled very hard to sustain a job and to hold on to work, and they both barely scraped by." His father, unlike his mother, associated work with pain, both literally—he lost hearing working in a plastics factory—and emotionally—the inability to find a meaningful, satisfying vocation. A veteran of World War II, he was a loner—Springsteen has recalled never having seen a friend come over, or even hearing his father laugh. "I remember when I was a kid I always wondered what my old man was so mad about all the time," he has said. Douglas would often just get in the car on Sundays and drive, family in tow, with no destination. "We would drive around the whole damned Sunday and come in the evening all exhausted," Springsteen remembers. And yet he has also noted that was the only time his father would beam with joy. The memory would inform many of Bruce's songs about people in cars, people on the move. He observed that "perhaps that kind of action was the only thing he needed after working the whole week at his machine in the plastics plant."

Something ate at Douglas, maybe disappointment that his life didn't turn out differently, a disappointment that mutated into anger and nastiness that created deep conflict between father and son. Springsteen later understood that it had to do with his father's inability to find a meaningful, lasting vocation: "I grew up in a house where there was a lot of struggle to find work, where the results of not being able to find your place in society manifested themselves with the resulting lack of self-worth, with anger, with violence." Springsteen grew up feeling isolated, alienated, and alone.

In the 1970s and 1980s, Springsteen would often use the stories he told on the concert stage about his father as a way to exorcise some of the demons, as a way, as he put it, "of having a dialogue that didn't exist": "When I was really young I don't remember thinking about it much, but as I got a little older, I'd watch my father, how he'd come home from work and just sit in the kitchen all night like there was something dying inside of him, or like he'd never had a chance to live, until I started to feel like there was something dying inside of me. And I'd lay up in bed at night and feel like if something didn't happen . . . that I was just gonna . . . that someday I'd just . . ."

He doesn't finish the sentence.

For Springsteen, his father's life, and his grandfather's, showed him the underside of the American dream: how people get trapped by no fault of their own. And he dedicated himself to breaking the cycle: "When I got to be about sixteen, I started to look around me and . . . I looked back at, I looked at my friends and tried to see what they were doing, and it didn't seem like anybody was going anyplace or had a chance of getting out of the kind of life they were living. I looked back at my dad and he was working in a plastics factory, and I looked back at his father and he worked in a rug mill in town, and it didn't seem like it was gonna be any different, any different for me." "When I was real young," he said in 1981, "I decided that if I was gonna have to live that way, that I was gonna die."

When Springsteen turned thirty, his aunt showed him a picture of his father in uniform after returning from the war: "I couldn't ever remember him looking that proud or that defiant when I was growing up. I used to wonder what happened to all that pride, how it turned into so much bitterness. He had been so disappointed, had so much stuff beaten out of him by then . . . that he couldn't accept the idea that I had a dream and I had possibilities."

Bruce's younger sister, Virginia, was born in 1950, and then came Pamela, born in 1962. Springsteen recalls her birth as "one of the best times I can ever remember . . . because it changed the atmosphere of the whole house for quite a while—the old 'Shh, there's a baby in the house.'"

But in short order the tension reemerged, deepened by Bruce entering his teen years. Springsteen felt invisible. He was thirteen or so when he bought a guitar from Western Auto Store for eighteen dollars with money he had saved from various jobs: painting houses, tarring roofs, tending gardens. After he saw the Beatles on *The Ed Sullivan Show*, practice became all consuming. Impressed by her son's dedication, Adele Springsteen took out a loan for sixty dollars and for Christmas 1964 bought Bruce his first electric guitar. He would one day pay tribute to his mother and the memory of that morning in the song "The Wish."

Music took over. "Everything from then on revolved around music. Everything," he would recall. "I was someone who grew up in isolation, emotionally. That's how I learned to play the guitar. I played for eight hours a day in my room." "My whole life," Springsteen reflected, "was this enormous effort to become visible." In

1975 he told *Time* magazine, "Music saved me. From the beginning, my guitar was something I could go to. If I hadn't found music, I don't know what I would have done." He elaborated: "Music became my purpose in life. Before that I didn't have any purpose. I tried to play football and baseball and all those things. I checked out all the normal alleys and I just didn't fit. I was running through a maze. Music gave me something. It was never just a hobby. It was a reason to live." He knew that "once I found the guitar I had the key to the highway." And it gave him his identity: "The first day I can remember lookin' in the mirror and standin' what I was seein' was the day I had a guitar in my hand," he said in 1975. And later, "Rock 'n' roll was the only thing I ever liked about myself."

In 1992, Springsteen showed keen insight into his psychological makeup and its connection to his songs and performance. "Onstage I talk a lot about community," he admitted, "but it is very difficult for me to connect up with anything. From my youth, I had a tendency to be isolated psychologically. All my music is a journey towards some sort of connection with both people at large and then a person . . . For me, the music is about trying to get closer, trying to take down the walls that I had left up."

It was hearing music on the radio, late at night, that gave him hope that his life could turn out differently than his father's and grandfather's. "I was lucky," he said onstage in 1981, "because on the radio, I used to sit up in bed at night with the radio under my pillow and it was in the music that I heard, in the early sixties, in the rock 'n' roll, that I heard there was a promise of life, there was promise that if you're born onto this earth, it's your right to be able to live with some decency and some dignity, and I always used to wish that I'd be able to go downstairs at night and tell my father, like, 'Listen to this, listen to this song by Elvis Presley or this song by the Drifters,' and hope that he could hear, he could hear in his heart what I heard in mine. But a lot of people miss that, when a lot of people hear that promise, they think it just sounds like noise or they think that it can't be true but . . . but I think it can."

Douglas Springsteen could not hear the music, not the way his son wanted him to. Instead Springsteen's guitar playing, long hair, and late nights out only amped up tensions with his father. "There were two things that were unpopular in my house," Springsteen would say onstage. "One was me, the other one was my guitar." In 1976, introducing his cover of the Animals' "It's My Life," Springsteen went into considerable detail:

My pop, he used to, every night, every night around nine o'clock, man, he used to shut off all the lights in the house . . . sit in the kitchen with a six-pack, smoke a cigarette, my mom, she used to sit in the front room, watch TV . . . till she fell asleep in the chair, wake up the next morning, just go to work . . . and she worked, she was a, she was a secretary, she was a secretary, she worked downtown . . . and my pop, he was, he was a guard down at the jail and he worked in this plastics factory for a while and . . . he worked in this rug mill till they closed it down . . . a lot of times he was in between jobs, he was just home . . . and soon . . . soon as I hit sixteen . . . I used to head out . . . I'd come back and I'd walk through town again until, until I'd end up standing in my driveway and my pop, he used to lock up the front door so that me and my sister, we couldn't come in the front, we used to have to come in round through the kitchen so he'd see us . . . I remember I'd stand in the driveway and I could look through the screen door, I could see just the light of his cigarette, sitting at the kitchen table . . .

I'd slick my hair back real tight, tight as I could, so he couldn't tell how long it was, step up on the porch . . . try and slip through the kitchen before he, before he'd stop me . . . and he'd wait, I remember the old man'd wait until I hit that bottom step, when I hit that step, he'd call my name to come back . . . come back to the kitchen table and sit down with him for a while . . . and so I remember I would sit down there at the kitchen table, he'd be telling me . . . telling me things, I could always hear his voice . . . we were sitting there in the dark . . . but I remember . . . I remember I could never see his face . . . he'd start off talking about easy things . . . then he'd start asking me where I was getting my money from . . . who I was going out with, what I thought I was doing with myself . . . and we'd end up, we'd end up screaming at each other, my mother'd end up running in from the front room . . . trying to keep us from fighting with each other, pulling him off me . . . I'd end up running out the back door, running out the back door screaming, telling him, telling him . . . how it was my life and I was gonna do what I wanted to do.

At Freehold Regional High School, Bruce was an indifferent student. He seldom read any books. "That was my problem in school," he said in 1976. "I couldn't stand reading them books. Not that I didn't like them. I just didn't have the patience to do it." Only in creative-writing courses did he receive good grades. It was here that he wrote thematic essays and also would sometimes transcribe a song—"stretch it out into a story or an essay . . . I was interested in writing and in that kind of writing."

In 1965, Springsteen joined his first band, the Castiles. The story of what he did after the tryout is indicative of his desire. Gordon "Tex" Vinyard, a man in his thirties, a factory worker with no children of his own, managed the band. Bruce came to a rehearsal and played. At the end, he asked whether he was in and Tex told him to learn a few more songs and return. "The *next* night," Tex recalls, "it must have been about eleven o'clock, there was a rap on the door. 'Hi,' he says. 'I'm Bruce Springsteen. Remember me?' I said, 'Yeah. I remember ya.' He says, 'Well, I learned a little.' . . . Well, this damn kid sat down and knocked off five songs that would blow your *ears*. Five. Leads. No amplifier, but five leads." Tex asked him who taught him. Bruce replied, "I listened on the radio."

That year, he also heard on the radio a song that consumed him: "The first time I heard Bob Dylan, I was in the car with my mother listening to WMCA, and on came that snare shot that sounded like somebody'd kicked open the door to your mind. 'Like a Rolling Stone.' My mother, she was no stiff with rock 'n' roll, she liked the music, sat there for a minute, then looked at me and said, 'That guy can't sing.' But I knew she was wrong. I sat there and I didn't say nothing but I knew that I was listening to the toughest voice that I had ever heard. It was lean and it sounded somehow simultaneously young and adult."

Springsteen spent the fall listening to *Highway 61 Revisited* again and again and again. He would sit staring at the cover, the cool, punk Dylan staring back. "When I was a kid," Springsteen recalled in 1988 in his speech inducting Dylan into the Rock and Roll Hall of Fame, "Bob's voice somehow thrilled me and scared me, it made me feel kind of irresponsibly innocent—it still does— when it reached down and touched what little worldliness a fifteen-year-old high school kid in New Jersey had in him at the time. Dylan was a revolutionary. Bob freed the mind the way Elvis freed the body. He showed us that just because the music was innately physical did not mean that it was anti-intellectual. He had the vision and the talent to make a pop song that contained the whole world. He invented a new way a pop singer could sound, broke through the limitations of what a recording artist could achieve, and changed the face of rock 'n' roll forever."

Springsteen, with Dylan's roaring sound in his head, played dances with the Castiles at various CYOs and YMCAs and at teen clubs along the Jersey Shore. They made it into the Village at times to play the Café Wha? They even recorded two songs cowritten with the band's lead singer, George Theiss, who had dated Springsteen's sister. During the summer, Springsteen would hitch rides to the beach. Girls were always attracted to him, the quiet kid who played a hot guitar. A bandmate recollects that "there was something special about him . . . put him onstage with a guitar and he lit it up. It was like somebody plugged him in." The band started to fracture, as most teen bands do: Bruce wanted to sing and wanted to do heavier rock material as well as his own songs. By the end of the summer in 1968, they were through.

One of the members of the Castiles joined the Marines (he would be killed in Vietnam). Springsteen had no intention of going the military route. He recalled how his father "used to tell me, 'Man, I can't wait till the Army gets you . . . man, when the Army gets you, they're gonna make a man out of you . . . they're gonna cut all that hair off and they'll finally make a man out of you . . . and uh, I can remember one time I had an accident, a motorcycle accident . . . and I was laid up in bed and he had a barber come in and cut my hair when I couldn't walk . . . I can remember telling him that I hated him."

In 1969, Springsteen was summoned for his physical. He hoped the concussion he had suffered from the motorcycle crash would keep him out. And he intentionally filled out the forms with gibberish. "We were scared going up on the bus," Springsteen later recalled. "I thought one thing: I ain't goin'. I had tried to go to college [Ocean County Community College], and I didn't really fit in . . . I remember being on that bus, me and a couple of guys in my band, and the rest of the bus was probably sixty, seventy percent black guys from Asbury Park. And I remember thinkin', like, what makes my life, or my friends' lives, more expendable than that of somebody who's goin' to school?"

Springsteen failed the physical. He came home and his parents asked, "What happened?" He said, "They didn't take me." And "my father sat there, and he didn't look at me, he just looked straight ahead. And he said, 'That's good.' It was, uh . . . I'll never forget that, I'll never forget that." In that instant Douglas Springsteen gave his son a gift that one day would allow for some healing and reconciliation. Not until Bruce was in his thirties, however, could he and his father express their love for each other.

Painful childhoods and tormented relationships leave lasting marks. In 1990, before introducing "My Father's House," a song about "the hard things that pulled us apart," Springsteen offered a personal revelation:

> I had this habit for a long time. I used to get in my car and I would drive back through my old neighborhood in the town I grew up in. I'd always drive past the old house I used to live in, and I'd do it sometimes late at night . . . I got so I would do it really regularly for two or three, four times a week for years, and I eventually got to wondering, What the hell am I doing? [*chuckles*] So I went to see a psychiatrist and I sat down and I

said, you know, "Doc, for years I been getting in my car at night, drive back to my town, and I pass my house late at night and, you know, what am I doing?" And he said, "I want you to tell me what you think you're doing." [*laughter*] So I go, "That's what I'm paying you for." So he says, "Well . . . what you're doing," he says, "something bad happened and you're going back thinking you can make it right again, something, something went wrong and you keep going back to see if you can fix it or somehow make it right." And I sat there and I said, "That *is* what I'm doing." And he said, "Well, you can't."

A few weeks after Springsteen's failed physical in 1969, the rest of the family moved to San Mateo, California, seeking a new start. Bruce remained behind. In 1998, Springsteen recalled his parents' journey. They had no idea where to go; they just decided that they were going to leave. A hippie girlfriend of Bruce's suggested Sausalito, and they headed there only to discover that scene was not for them. Springsteen finishes the story: "My mother said they went to a gas station and she asked the guy there, 'Where do people like us live?'—that's a question that sounds like the title of a Raymond Carver story!—and the guy told her, 'Oh, you live on the peninsula.' And that is what they did. They drove down south of San Francisco and they've been there ever since. My father was forty-two at the time—it's funny to think that he was probably seven or eight years younger than I am now. It was a big trip, took a lot of nerve, a lot of courage, having grown up in my little town in New Jersey."

When his parents left, Springsteen moved to Asbury Park. He was already a familiar face in the clubs along the Jersey Shore. In 1968 he was playing with a hard-rock trio called Earth ("a real

Hendrix/Cream" group, he recalls), and got invited over to the Upstage Club to jam. Started that year by Tom and Margaret Potter,
the café and club quickly became the center of an extraordinary
late-night music scene. The Upstage remained open until five A.M.
on weekends, and the Potters insisted that there be no drug use or
alcohol. They also encouraged musicians to mix with one another
and break out of their cliques. These musicians may have played
Top 40 covers before midnight at their various bar and dance gigs;
after, they played whatever they wanted, including their own songs,
experimenting with different styles. A back wall of speakers filled
the stage. All a musician had to do was plug in. It was there, reported *Rolling Stone*, that the "prototypical Asbury band was born,
blaring out of a wall."

But the Upstage was no democracy. Tom Potter decided who
played, and guitarists from all over came to try their hand. "The
Upstage became a kind of guitar-slinger Dodge City," recalls Tallent, who often played bass through the night. "Every guitar player
in at least a twenty-mile radius heard about this place and showed
up and tried to outdo each other."

Recollections vary as to who invited Bruce to the club and
how the scene unfolded and who was present. Margaret Potter recalls a quiet kid asking to borrow a guitar. He plugged in and
started playing. She raced down to the second floor where Vini Lopez, Steve Van Zandt, and Johnny Lyons were hanging out, playing
Monopoly. "Hey guys, there's some kid upstairs who can really
play," she shouted. Lopez recalls Danny Federici being there: "We
saw Margaret Potter at the top of the stairs. There's also Bruce and
Vinnie, that's Vinnie Roslin. So Danny and I jumped in, and the
four of us all jammed together. Afterwards we were a band. Maybe
not a real band yet, but definitely something that we were looking

to do." Roslin recalled that Springsteen "just had this enormous appetite to play. He'd play anywhere, anytime, for anybody. He was like a television set with one channel, and on the set was 'practice music.'"

Bruce has recalled, "When I walked in the first night Vini Lopez was on drums, Danny was on organ and it was a revelation because we had good musicians and there were people playing some original music. It was a shock to me. I can remember walking in and I felt like I really discovered something. It's how I began to play with many of the fellows that I played with for a long, long part of my career."

Springsteen, Lopez, Federici, and Roslin called themselves Child, and then changed the name in 1970 to Steel Mill after discovering another band had the same name. In 1971, Roslin left and Van Zandt joined as bass player. The group developed a significant following of loyal listeners who treated them as a local supergroup. They rocked hard—like Ten Years After or Cream—but also carried something of an R&B beat. Managed by Carl "Tinker" West, who owned a surfboard factory where Bruce worked and lived for a while ("the resin from the surfboards really knocked you out for a while"), the band traveled to Berkeley, California, in late 1969 and was well received. They even cut three demos for Bill Graham, the legendary rock promoter who offered a contract, but the band turned it down.

On July 4, 1970, Asbury Park exploded in racial violence that it had escaped in the mid-1960s while other cities burned. Police and state troopers were called in to suppress an explosion of rage from the West Side black community, exhausted from years of broken promises and shrinking opportunities. The riots destroyed whatever cachet that Asbury Park still had as a summer vacation resort, a haven by the sea. Springsteen watched the city burn from the top of a water tower. He would soon create in a band an integrated profile and sound that the city itself never managed to manufacture. The riots put an end to a brief but lustrous era for the cultural life of the city. "The riots changed the economics of Asbury Park overnight," says historian Robert Santelli. "It became a virtual no-man's-land. The tourist resort concept went away immediately, so the clubs started closing." Recalls Tinker West, "After the riots, it was all over."

It was over for Steel Mill as well. In San Francisco, Springsteen heard another band that was better than his and realized it was one thing to be the best local band, but he wanted to lead the best band with no qualifiers. Furthermore, Springsteen's musical tastes were changing, away from hard-rock guitar to more of an R&B sound with lots of brass. "Bruce didn't want to do Steel Mill anymore," recalls West. "He'd seen Leon Russell and Joe Cocker and that big ten-piece thing." "We would have been happy to have been Van Morrison and his band," recalls Garry Tallent. For a brief period (a couple of known shows), Springsteen led an ever-changing jam band called Dr. Zoom and the Sonic Boom that included Sancious, Federici, Lopez, Tallent, Van Zandt, and others (Springsteen's first, short-lived nickname was the Doctor). In 1971, he formed the Bruce Springsteen Band, which not only had horns but also female backup singers who provided a soul and gospel sound. The band built on Steel Mill's cult status in Richmond, Virginia, where they played the college circuit. Most of the group moved to Richmond. And then, according to Tallent, "one day Bruce was gone . . . He just disappeared and the rest of us stayed behind."

Springsteen later said, "I had some personal problems with this, that, and the other thing." He drove to California and spent time at his parents' apartment, then returned to New Jersey. "I started to think that I needed to approach the thing somewhat differently," he recalled later. "I began to write music that would not have worked in a club, really. It required too much attention, too much listening, a certain kind of focus. But I felt if I was going to take a real shot at it, I was going to have to do something very distinctive and original. I wanted the independence, the individuality of a solo career, and that's when I began to write some of the initial songs for *Greetings from Asbury Park*. I was living above this little out-of-business beauty salon with an old piano in the back, and at night I'd go down amid all the hair dryers and I wrote a bunch of the songs from that album."

Through West, Springsteen met Mike Appel and Jim Cretecous, songwriter/producers, and in March 1972 Springsteen signed the first of three contracts. He would later tell Robert Hilburn that he never got discouraged because he never hoped: "I just said, 'Hell I'm a loser. I don't have to worry about anything.' I assumed immediately that nothing was happening. But it is not the same as giving up. You keep trying, but you don't count on things. It can be a strength."

Cocky, abrasive, arrogant, Appel pushed hard for his client in whom he deeply believed and managed to get him a May 2 audition with John Hammond at Columbia. Indeed, Appel was so disrespectful to Hammond that the executive later told Springsteen that he was ready to hate him. But Hammond gave a listen. Springsteen later recalled:

It was a big, big day for me. I'd played a lot of bars, a lot of different shows. I was 22 and had come up on the bus with an acoustic guitar with no case which I'd borrowed from the drummer from the Castiles. I was embarrassed carrying it around the city. I walked into his office and had the audition and I played a couple of songs and he said, "You've got to be on Columbia Records. But I need to see you play. And I need to hear how you sound on tape." Me and Mike Appel walked all around the Village trying to find some place that would let somebody just get up onstage and play. We went to the Bitter End, it didn't work out. We went to another club. And finally we went to the old Gaslight on Macdougal Street and the guy says, "Yeah, we have an open night where you can come down and play for half an hour." There were about 10 people in the place and I played for about half an hour. John Hammond said, "Gee, that was great. I want you to come to the Columbia recording studio and make a demo tape." A demo I made at Bill Graham's studio in San Francisco in '69 was the only other time I'd ever been in a real recording studio. Columbia was very old-fashioned: everybody in ties and shirts; the engineer was in a white shirt and a tie and was probably 50, 55 years old, it was just him and John and Mike Appel there, and he just hits the button and gives you your serial number, and off you go. I was excited. I felt I'd written some good songs and this was my shot. I had nothing to lose and it was like the beginning of something.

On 1998's *Tracks*, Springsteen released the demo tapes. Listening to these versions of the songs—"Mary Queen of Arkansas," "It's So Hard to Be a Saint in the City," "Growin' Up," and "Does This Bus Stop at 82nd Street?"—you can hear the austere power of Springsteen as a solo acoustic artist, which is what Hammond thought he was signing. When Bruce called his mother in

California to tell her he got a record deal, her first question, perhaps with Bob Dylan in mind, was, "What did you change your name to?"

But when Bruce arrived at the studio in July 1972, he was no solo acoustic act. He brought a band with him: Sancious, Tallent, and Lopez. And Clarence Clemons joined for two songs recorded toward the end of the sessions, "Blinded by the Light" and "Spirit in the Night." He said in 1974, "I figured if I could get into the door alone, I could bring the band in later." "I wanted a rhythm section," Springsteen later said. "I wanted a band actually because I'd played with a group for a long time and knew that a big part of my abilities was to be able to use a band. So what we ended up doing was an acoustic record with a rhythm section, which was the compromise reached between the record company, everybody else and me." It took three weeks to record the album.

Springsteen's first album, *Greetings from Asbury Park, N.J.*, was released in January 1973, the title and postcard cover doing as much as anything to memorialize the now-vanished musical scene. The songs, Springsteen says, were "twisted autobiographies," and "I never wrote in that style again. Once the record was released, I heard all the 'new Dylan' comparisons, so I steered away from it. But the lyrics and spirit of *Greetings* came from a very unselfconscious place. Your early songs come out of a moment when you're writing with no sure prospect of ever being heard. Up until then it was just you and your music. That only happens once."

The reviews took note of the remarkable talent: "Never have I been more impressed with a debuting singer," said the *LA Free Press*. "You know the kid is good when you wake up and you're singing his songs," declared *Crawdaddy*. Columbia promoted the album with an ad that said, "This man puts more thoughts, more ideas, into one song than most people put into an album." But the sales, maybe twenty thousand the first year, disappointed expectations.

Springsteen was writing prolifically: "I wrote like a madman. Put it out. Had no money, nowhere to go, nothing to do. Didn't know too many people. It was cold and I wrote a lot and I got to feeling guilty if I didn't."

He was back in the studio that summer to record his second album, *The Wild, the Innocent, and the E Street Shuffle*, which Columbia released in September. *Rolling Stone* called him "a considerable new talent," and praised the band that "cooks with power and precision." "He deserves a much wider audience," declared one reviewer. "Incorporating touches of jazz, soul, and Latin music, this is basically get up and dance rock and roll." Perhaps the most important notice came in the *New York Times*, where Bruce Pollack wrote that "in an era of diminishing returns, false prophets, and false bottoms, where the best of our instant pop-up superstars are either choked-off, laid-back, lame or laid out flat, it is with a great sense of relief that I announce to disbelievers that Bruce Springsteen has delivered another stone, howling, joyous monster of a record." Pollack ended the review by asking, "Can you imagine what his third album will be like?"

Off the second album, "Rosalita" immediately became a signature song, with its playful beat and liberation theme of a young rock 'n' roller, fresh off signing a big advance, coming for his girl:

> *I'm comin' to liberate you, confiscate you, I want to be your man*
> *Someday we'll look back on this and it will all seem funny.*

The song, Springsteen later said, "was my 'getting out of town' preview for *Born to Run*, with more humor." As for his look into the future, he intended "not that it would all *be* funny, but that it would all *seem* funny. Probably one of the most useful lines I've ever written."

The pure joy of "Rosalita" was counterposed by "4th of July, Asbury Park (Sandy)." If the former, the next-to-last song on the album, is about new beginnings, the latter, the second song, is about an ending. The narrator says good-bye to summer romance and good-bye to the whole worn-out scene: "This boardwalk life for me is through," he sings. And of course it was literally through for Springsteen and the other musicians of the Upstage—which had closed its doors—and the arcades, where the crowds, in the aftermath of the riots, had thinned. The song was "a goodbye to my adopted hometown," he said in 1998.

The second album did not sell much better than the first, but Springsteen and the band kept playing, getting better. There were some personnel changes (Lopez out, Carter in; then Sancious and Carter leaving, and Bittan and Weinberg joining along with Van Zandt). He headed into the studio for his make-or-break third album. He had written some new songs, pretty good ones, he thought, maybe even a hit. To the question of how much of his music was autobiographical, he has provided different answers at different times.

He has said: "I really don't want to talk about it. I really don't want to touch on the songs at all, because I'll screw them up. As soon as you start talking about them, you're messing with the magic."

He has said: "Songs are not literally autobiographical. But in some way they're emotionally autobiographical. As they go by, you see your own take on the world and how it's changed since you were a kid. You create a variety of characters, and the thing they have in common is some emotional thread you've tried to use to make your own way through what can feel like a particularly imponderable existence."

And he has said: "There ain't a note I play onstage that can't be traced directly back to my mother and father."

TWO

THE MAKING OF *BORN TO RUN*

When I did Born to Run, *I thought, I'm going to make the greatest rock 'n' roll record ever made.*

—BRUCE SPRINGSTEEN, 1987

BEFORE ANYTHING ELSE, Springsteen had the title. Three words: *Born to Run.* It was spring 1974 and he was living in a small house in West Long Branch, New Jersey, a block off the beach. It was the first house he had ever lived in by himself. During the afternoon he would sit by the window in front of an Aeolian piano and compose.

In *Songs,* he recalls that "at first I thought ['Born to Run'] was the name of a movie or something I'd seen on a car spinning around the Circuit . . . I liked the phrase because it suggested a cinematic drama I thought would work with the music I was hearing in my head." But "it took me a really long time to write it. I think it took me months. I worked every day. I had this little notebook, and if you open up the first page you see the first few lines, and then page after page, and by the end of the notebook the song is intact, which is a lot for a few verses." The amount of time he spent "honing the lyrics was enormous." The notebook for the one song runs more than fifty pages.

" 'Born to Run,' " Springsteen says, "was the first piece of music I wrote and conceived as a studio production." He was looking for "a range of sound . . . to realize the song's potential," and as full-

40

Long Branch, New Jersey, house where Springsteen wrote the songs on *Born to Run*.

sounding as his band could be, it was not enough to capture what he wanted to hear. In December 1975, after the album had been released, he explained, "I don't want to have a vocal or guitar here, a piano there. I want people to hear one big sound, a rumble." "*Born to Run* was the first time I used the studio as a tool and not in an attempt to replicate the sound of when we played," he recalled in 1998. The most dynamic live performer of his era turned to the studio to make the record that would introduce his music to a vast audience.

Springsteen labored over the song and the album. Taking production seriously in a way he hadn't previously, his perfectionist tendencies came to the fore as he navigated the "twists and turns of the arrangement." "We were working on a sixteen-track board," he recalls, and "we were overdubbing and overdubbing and doubling everything and mixing everything down and it seemed like it went on forever." Louis Lahav, the engineer at 914 Studio where "Born to Run" was recorded, recalled in 1988 that "it was a sixteen-track, but it was packed, like a thirty-two-track today." "You couldn't relax in the mix for a second," remembers producer and manager Mike Appel. "The song would set the tone for the entire album and for his career from that point forward." "It was more than just cutting a song," adds Lahav. "It was this *thing* you believed in so much—like a religion." Springsteen had set a near-impossible standard: "I wanted to make one of the greatest rock records ever."

"We knew what we wanted to do," Springsteen said a few months after finishing the album. "It was just a very hard thing to do." He felt terribly the pressure that was coming from the record company and from critics. "That was the most horrible period of my life . . . *the most horrible period of my life*," he declared at year's end. When asked why, he pointed to the publicity packet that proclaimed him rock's future. He tore it in half and screamed, "THAT!" "Suddenly, I was the future of rock 'n' roll," he told one writer. "That much attention pushed me back to the time when there wasn't any. Working on *Born to Run* was a very scary thing. I was born, grew old, and died making that album."

"It was *the* most intense experience I ever had," he said shortly after the album was completed. "There was nothin' ever came close. And what was worse was, like if you can imagine being at the particular height of intensity for like *four months*. Some days when you got in there it was like murder. Some of the stuff that was in the air in that studio was *deadly*. People would *back off*."

For inspiration, Springsteen turned to various musical influences. Rock musicians are like painters: They borrow, quote, imitate, and pay homage to the masters, and quite often in doing so they transcend the roots of their art. Over the years, Springsteen has said that on the song and album he wanted to sing like Roy Orbison, play guitar like Duane Eddy, and imitate the production values of Phil Spector.

Orbison was perhaps the premier rock singer of the 1960s. His voice was operatic and emotional, had a three-octave range, and made his ballads come alive. Hits such as "Only the Lonely," "Oh, Pretty Woman," and "Crying" turned stories into operas. In 1987, Springsteen inducted Orbison into the Rock 'n' Roll Hall of Fame and told of riding for fifteen hours in 1970 to Nashville to open for the singer at the Nashville Music Festival. "When I went into the studio to make 'Born to Run,'" he said, "most of all I wanted to sing like Roy Orbison." He added that "I'll always remember what he means to me, what he meant to me when I was young and afraid of love."

Duane Eddy in effect invented the rock guitar. He took the instrument to center stage and made it a force of nature. His playing—plucking at the bass strings and rapidly repeating and re-verberating notes—became known as "twang." Between 1958 and 1963 he had a series of instrumental hits, fifteen Top 40 songs in-cluding "Ramrod," "Cannonball," and "Forty Miles of Bad Road."

The other influence was the remarkable sound created in the studio by Phil Spector, the preeminent producer of the late 1950s and early 1960s. Spector's method has been called the Wall of Sound. He built up songs with layers of multiple instruments, com-plex arrangements making each one sound like a miniature sym-phony. The form lent meaning and gravity to songs about teenage love: the Ronettes' "Be My Baby," the Crystals' "Da Doo Ron

Ron," the Shangri-Las' "Leader of the Pack," the Righteous Brothers' "You've Lost That Lovin' Feelin.'" Employing Spector's style, Springsteen wedded music to poetry to make magic.

Indeed, he had hoped to incorporate the girl-group sound even more explicitly into his music. In March 1974, he said, "I want to get girls into the band for the next album because I've got some good ideas which add up to more than just background vocals. But right now I don't have the money to do it."

Through the spring and summer of 1974, when Springsteen wasn't playing live, he was in the studio recording "Born to Run." Shows would often be canceled if time at the studio was available. And if he felt stuck in the studio, he would leave to play live or simply write. Because he was experimenting so extensively, the cost of studio time was building up—one of the reasons, Dave Marsh points out, that Bruce stayed at an inferior facility in Blauvelt, New York, when better ones in New York City were available to him.

The earliest available live version of the song dates from July 13, 1974, at the Bottom Line in New York, more than a year before his famous string of shows there. While musically the song is almost set (the opening tempo is a bit slower, but Ernest Carter's drum roll gets it started), lyrically the song is dramatically different from the final version, so much so that the meaning of the song shifts. After "runaway American dream," Springsteen sings, "At night we stop and tremble in the heat/With murder in our dreams." The song is darker. He is not singing to Wendy, whose name does not appear. The second verse opens, "So close your tired eyes little one/And crawl within my reach . . . we'll ride tonight on the beach/Out where the surfers, sad, wet, and cold/As they watch the skies/There'll be a silence to match their own."

Springsteen is working the themes of loneliness and violence to the extreme. After "boys try to look so hard," he sings, "Like animals pacing in a black dark cage/Senses on overload/They're gonna end this night in a senseless fight/And then watch the world explode." Clearly, he is trying to stay consistent with other songs that he is considering for the album; at the same show he premiered "Jungleland." The "broken heroes" of this early version of "Born to Run" have "a loneliness in their eyes," and instead of loving "with all the madness in my soul" the narrator seeks to "Drive through this madness/Oh, burstin' off the radio." Sometime between July and the end of the summer, Springsteen transformed "Born to Run." He told one writer, "I'm still fiddling with the words for the new single, but I think it will be good." The notes of alienation, loneliness, and violence yielded to love, companionship, and redemption.

The alternate mixes of "Born to Run" that are available reveal some of the ways in which Springsteen experimented musically. In one, a female chorus joins him in the background when he sings "get out while we're young," "got to know how it feels," and "walk in the sun." Musically, the strings at various points are more prominent than they would be in the final version. It's easy to see why Bruce rejected this mix: The chorus and strings make the song too ethereal and distance it from the driving force of the beat. In another mix, Springsteen's lead vocal is doubled, the chorus is still intact, and the strings at the end of the song are even more pronounced. Two other mixes play with the balance of strings and bass. At one point, the engineers experimented with different sound effects such as streetcars and drag racing.

In Thom Zimny's documentary *Wings for Wheels: The Making*

of Born to Run, Bruce is shown listening to some of these earlier versions. He smiles, shakes his head, and at times breaks out laughing. "The strings," he says, "took away some of the darkness." Every note of the song was composed. The combinations of mixes and overdubs were almost infinite, and it seems as if Bruce went through all of them until he found what he thought he wanted, and even then he kept making adjustments.

In *Wings for Wheels*, for example, he explains how in "Born to Run" he bent up to the major note in playing the central guitar lick of the song, but Steve Van Zandt couldn't hear it through all the layers. It sounded like a minor rather a major, and Bruce made the change. Similarly, when isolating Carter's drums, you can hear a syncopated jazz fusion riff at the takeoff point in the song, a riff that Max Weinberg honestly admits he could never play.

In *Songs*, Springsteen recalls that "Born to Run" was "a turning point, and it allowed me to open up my music to a far larger audience. 'Born to Run' was a long time coming; it took me six months to write. But it proved to be the key to my songwriting for the rest of the record. Lyrically, I was entrenched in classic rock and roll images, and I wanted to find a way to use those images without feeling anachronistic."

Garry Tallent, the bassist, knew only this: "When we rehearsed 'Born to Run' for the first time, in my dad's garage. Then I knew. This is it. This is the song that's going to pay the rent."

Now it all seems inevitable and we treat the final version as preordained. But working in the studio, Springsteen experimented. What seemed just right one day fizzled upon a fresh listen the next. Mix upon mix mounted and Springsteen kept sifting for the right combination to make the song sound like a force of nature. "There's a lot of stuff that's on there that you won't hear," he said, "but it's important that it's there." Its length became a source of concern: At four and a half minutes, it was considered too long to become a hit single. But there was no way to cut it down. The architecture of "Born to Run" was such that all the parts were weight-bearing. Remove one, and the song collapsed.

It took Bruce six months to record "Born to Run." Van Zandt, in *Wings for Wheels*, laughs at that: "Anytime you spend six months on a song, there's something not exactly going right. A song should take about three hours."

Bruce didn't care. He would rather sound spontaneous than be spontaneous. "Spontaneity," he said, "is not made by fastness. Elvis, I believe, did like 30 takes of 'Hound Dog.'"

Peter Knobler, a writer for *Crawdaddy*, got an early listen in Springsteen's Long Branch house. The place was cluttered with motorcycle magazines and old 45s. Over Bruce's bed, according to Knobler, was a poster of Peter Pan leading Wendy out the window. The detail is suggestive: "Wendy let me in, I wanna be your friend/I want to guard your dreams and visions."

To Knobler, the "song sounded huge, like a Spector spectacular. I still couldn't make out many words, but through a wall or on a cassette Bruce had worked up to simulate a car radio, it sounded to me like Hit City. The end was fairly pulsating and as it faded, Bruce chimed in, 'WABC!' [AM hit radio] and, honest to God, it sounded inevitable."

Dave Marsh also reported on "Born to Run" for *Creem* in October 1974: Springsteen "is better than anything on the radio, and he has a new single, 'Born to Run,' which, if we are all fortunate, will be played across the land . . . The magic of Springsteen harks back to a tradition at least as old as 'Jailhouse Rock' and 'Maybelline.' If he cleans up his production, there is no reason why the key line of 'Born to Run'—'Tramps like us we were born to run'—will not become the rallying cry of the decade."

By early 1975 any attempts to shorten or change the song would have been too late, because it had already become something of a hit. Mike Appel was anxious to get the song airtime on the radio. It had been a year since *The Wild, the Innocent, and the E Street Shuffle.* On November 3, 1974, Springsteen appeared with DJ Ed Sciaky on WMMR in Philadelphia. Sciaky was an early and boisterous supporter. He had a surprise for listeners that day: the radio premiere of "Born to Run."

Within weeks, Appel also sent tapes to Scott Muni at WNEW in New York, Maxanne Sartori at WBCN in Boston, and Kid Leo (Lawrence Travagliante) at WMMS in Cleveland. To Leo, "'Born to Run' was the essence of everything I loved about rock 'n' roll. Bruce held on to the innocence and the romance. At the same time, the music communicates frustration and a constant longing to escape." Leo played the song every Friday afternoon at five fifty-five; one fan remembers it as the start to the weekend happy hour. Nearly two dozen more stations had it by the new year. All this exposure, with no record in sight, made the record company nervous. When listeners heard something they liked, they usually wanted to buy it right away. But in this case, hearing the song on the radio helped build anticipation for the album.

That Bruce and the band had "Born to Run" down is evident from a show at the Main Point in Bryn Mawr, Pennsylvania, on February 5, 1975. Whereas the premiere performance of "Thunder Road" and performances of "She's the One" and "Jungleland"— the other songs he played that would appear on the album later in the year—only partially resemble the final recorded versions, the band rocked "Born to Run" as if they had been playing it for years.

Bruce had a lot of work ahead of him in the studio, but "Born to Run" was done.

The sessions at 914 Studios in Blauvelt, begun in January, continued on and off into October. In September, Roy Bittan and Max Weinberg joined the band as David Sancious and Ernest Carter left to pursue other opportunities. Adding two new members meant that, in effect, the band was suddenly brand-new, and much time was spent, in Springsteen's words, "tutoring the rhythm section." This placed a particular strain on bassist Garry Tallent, who had to readjust his playing for a number of reasons, not the least of which being that Roy Bittan is left-handed and therefore played the bottom end of the keyboard more vigorously. At the same time, all the band members were learning how to be a recording band that in the studio moved away from the performance "hyperactivity" for which they were known. Springsteen's writing became more taut and the band followed suit, learning that less could be more. But paring down the playing proved difficult for a band known for its excitement and spontaneity. In the studio, recording and tracking compressed the range of sound and undermined the band's freedom. The culture of the band "was as close to jazz as rock could get," recalls Tallent. Recording "went against the grain of everything we did live." The band would have to learn studio technique.

Without access to the studio log, it is impossible to know what the band worked on when. Early stabs at "Jungleland" began the recording sessions at 914, and the band first played the song in concert on July 13, 1974, but Bruce was still changing the lyrics late into the fall. Early versions of "Backstreets" and "She's the One" were also recorded at 914, only to be discarded and rerecorded later.

Springsteen also recorded songs that he left off the album. *Born to Run* marks the beginning of Bruce recording song after song in the studio, then going through the arduous process of deciding what belonged on the album. *Born to Run* had only three or four outtakes (though many more are rumored). His next album, *Darkness on the Edge of Town*, three years later, had more than twenty-five. Springsteen is a prolific songwriter, and on lists he made for "New Album #3" he included the following titles: "Angel Baby," "Architect Angel," "Thundercrack," "Vision of Fort Horn," "Two Hearts," "Here She Comes," "Glory Road," "Janey Needs a Shooter," and "Jungleland." A separate list had "American Summer," "War and Roses," "Up from the Street," "Sometimes at Night," "From the Churches to the Jails," "The Legend of Zero and Blind Terry," "The Hungry and the Hunted," and "Between Flesh and Fantasy."

In October, the band recorded "A Love So Fine," which evolved into an instrumental backing track used on "So Young and in Love." That song contains lyrics that would migrate to "Night": "the rat traps filled with soul crusaders." Early in 1975, he recorded "Walking in the Street" (also known as "Lovers in the Cold"). The song is musically and narratively similar to "Thunder Road," which he was simultaneously working on. Other songs recorded in whole or in part, but not considered, include "Lonely Night in the Park," "A Night Like This," and "Janey Needs a Shooter." "Linda Let Me Be the One" was in all likelihood the last track ruled out for inclusion on the album. Lyrically, it fits with the narrative: "The midnight boys are outside/Scraping tears up off the street." Eddie is the main character, who walks "like an angel in defeat" and talks "Fast cars and spare parts/Empty homes and hearts." But including this midtempo cut would have upset the balance of eight songs that ended up on the album.

The year was coming to a close and still there was no sign of a new album, much to the consternation of Columbia Records executives. Bruce was struggling in the studio, obsessing over details, rewriting and reworking material, laboring to get the sound in his head down on tape.

Among the songs Bruce was working on that fall, "Jungleland" seemed to occupy much of his thinking. He first performed it live in July 1974 at the Bottom Line, and in October he talked about the song with Paul Williams in *Crawdaddy*. He said the song has "been coming along. There's a verse that's not really finished. It goes . . . there's a chorus that goes . . . 'The street's alive with tough kid jets in nova light machines.'" He talked about the slow part and quoted other lyrics that would change over the next six months. He added that "Jungleland" was one of the titles that he was considering for the new album.

Included among the mixes of "Jungleland" that Bruce eventually rejected are two with strings added, one with sax solo and one without. Clemons's solo is so essential to our hearing of the song that listening to a version without it brings new appreciation for how the solo bridges the parts of the song and lends drama and spirituality. The violins and cellos allow us to daydream and seem to work against the drive of the piano; the sax focuses our attention. Springsteen's vocals here are uneven. He is still feeling his way through the song and he has yet to unearth the primal groans that end the recorded version.

In *Wings for Wheels*, Clemons talks eloquently about the sax solo and how hour after hour, in a sixteen-hour session, Bruce worked out every note and every line. But still, the song kept getting away. Clemons recalls, "I went to the bathroom a few times, but I don't think we stopped to eat. He was telling me, 'More warmth, more movement, I like that note there, let's work around that.' We had to find those passages that go to the bone . . . I've had people say to me, 'That sax solo saved my life.' So I did my job." One night they played it straight through fourteen times, bringing the session to a close at four A.M. When the sun came up, according to one contemporary account, "people were near tears."

Sometime in November, Springsteen got together with Jon Landau. It was Landau, rock critic and producer, who had heard Springsteen debut "Born to Run" in Boston. In December, Bruce played a demo of "Jungleland" and asked Landau for his opinion. Jon said he didn't think the production values showed much improvement from the first two albums. "The biggest thing Landau did," Springsteen said, "was to make me see that I was screwing up." The song, a near ten-minute epic, still needed work. Indeed, the very last song being mixed on the very last day in the studio the following July was "Jungleland." Trial and error was Springsteen's approach to try and get at what was in his head. Landau recalls, "That was a nightmare. He was finishing with Clarence in one room. The band was in another room. They were mixing 'Jungleland' without the sax, waiting to put it in, in another room. And at 7 o'clock, 8 o'clock in the morning they just rolled out of the studio, got in a van and drove up to Providence to begin the tour." Springsteen recollects that "on the last day we stumbled out after four straight days of recording, into the car to our first concert of the tour. It was like, 'Hallelujah! Thank God I'm anyplace but in that studio."

At the February 5 show at the Main Point in Bryn Mawr, Springsteen premiered "Wings for Wheels," which would evolve into "Thunder Road." The differences in lyrics are substantial. Mary is named Angelina, but more significantly, he has not yet found the poetry that would transform the song from ordinary to transcendent. After the opening, when the tempo picks up, he sings, "This 442 is going to overheat/Make up your mind, girl, I have to get her back on the street." He sings, "take a chance, take a chance," where he will eventually sing "Thunder Road." The song continues, "The season's over and I feel it getting cold/I wish I could take you to some sandy beach where we'd never grow old/But baby you know that's just jive/Tonight's busted open and I'm alive . . . maybe I can't lay the stars at your feet/But I got this old car and she's pretty tough to beat." He implores her to climb in and ends by declaring he is "born to win."

The studio versions include some minor lyrical differences from the final version (Angelina is now Chrissie). Musically, one version opens with a sax solo that invests the song with sorrow. In another, the saxophone parts are even more prominent. There is also a take in which Springsteen plays the song acoustically. It is haunting. His voice echoes. He builds the energy vocally and the appeal to Chrissie ("Leave what you've lost/Leave what's grown old") is both soulful and mournful.

Sometime in February, Landau stopped by one of the recording sessions. He listened and told Bruce what he thought the problems were. Again, a month later, conversations with Landau impressed Springsteen. Bruce was feeling stuck, and Landau seemed immediately to see what some of the problems were and offer solutions that worked. In *Wings for Wheels*, Landau explains how he helped solve the problem of "Thunder Road" by suggesting that the sax solo be moved from the middle to the end. Suddenly, a song that went on too long became a four-minute gem. The experience was eye-opening for Springsteen. Paul Nelson reported that "when Springsteen discovered he could write a song one night and successfully record it within the next few days, he was so astonished he began writing and rewriting the rest of the album with renewed intensity." Nelson called the collaboration "the ideal artistic marriage of creative madness and controlling method." Landau, who was able to help Springsteen capture on tape sounds that were in his head, became coproducer of the album.

The relationship between the two became fraternal. In 1978, Springsteen discussed what Landau did for him: He was "a big help to me. He helped me see things—to see *into* things—and somehow it would come out in the songs. It's hard to explain. There's a certain little consciousness barrier that gets broken down." Bruce talked about how he came from a home with little in the way of books or music or culture whereas Landau, an honors graduate from Brandeis, was marinated in those things. Conversations with Landau made Springsteen appreciate all the more what he had to offer intellectually as well as musically.

In April, after one session at Blauvelt, Landau moved the project to the Record Plant in Manhattan, which had superior facilities. This was where John Lennon, among other rock superstars, recorded. Jimmy Iovine, who would go on to a distinguished career as a producer, became the engineer. Between April and July, Springsteen would struggle to bring this third album to fruition. "Springsteen is one of the hardest people to record," Iovine told an interviewer in November 1975. "His vocal is distorted and you've got to constantly deal with that. I didn't try to make a clean album. I let Bruce do his thing and made the best record around that." "It was really hard," Iovine recalled years later. "God it was hard. We worked very slowly, and he had a picture in his head of what he wanted. But all of us were young and inexperienced, so we had to go the long way to do anything."

Each song presented its own challenges. Bruce had the Bo

Diddley three-pause-two-beat down for "She's the One." When he played the song in concert at Avery Fisher Hall in April 1974, he joked, "About twenty years ago somebody discovered that . . . good girls get bad when they hear this beat and bad girls get worse."

The beat remained steady, but the lyrics kept changing. In a version performed live at the Main Point, and an alternate take from the studio session, the song went on for more than six minutes. He sings how he hated her and hated himself and hated the lies. The litany of hates goes on and on; they would eventually find their way, in abbreviated form, onto "Backstreets." By removing the hatreds from "She's the One," the song becomes a testament to desire rather than betrayal. Similarly, lines from "Santa Ana," a song intended originally for the second album, made their way to "She's the One" ("French cream won't soften them boots/And French kisses will not break that heart of stone"). And where literal lines didn't migrate, themes certainly did. Here is the closing couplet of "Seaside Bar Song," recorded but left off the second album: "He knows you're out on the run/But I don't care, I wanna live a life of love while the night's still young."

In 1999, Springsteen commented on the evolution of his material: "If you have a good line, you don't like to throw it [away]—you don't write that many. If I came up with a line that I liked I always tried to use it because writing was hard and, for one reason or another, things would begin here and end up there." At the same time, Springsteen has always written easily and prolifically. Danny Federeci recalls that with Steel Mill in 1970, "Bruce was writing about a song per day. It was crazy. It got so I didn't want to go to rehearsal, because every time there'd be this mess of new songs to learn."

But *Born to Run* was different. "Writing it was very difficult," Springsteen recalled in an interview in 1999. And recording it, "getting a sound that approximated to what I wanted," seemed nearly impossible. But it was precisely that artistic struggle that in the end provides *Born to Run* with narrative coherence and lyrical intensity. The very process of writing and recording the album mirrors the core themes of searching and moving that permeate the record.

Born to Run marked a change in Springsteen's writing style. Shortly after the album appeared, he said that he "took a different approach to some of the lyrics in the songs." Previously, he "wrote everything in a few minutes, you know, ten minutes. And then once I took six months to write one song, 'Born to Run.' And then I sort of went back . . . to like three, four days working on something." He spent as long as he did on the words to "Born to Run" because, as he explains in Zimny's documentary, "I was very aware that I was messing with classic rock 'n' roll images that easily turned into clichés." His subsequent writing became simpler, more compressed and visual. The move to the Record Plant seemed to invigorate him, and he recalled writing most of the songs in a three-week period—but recording them remained hard.

He not only took a different approach to the lyrics, but also to the composition. He began "Born to Run" on guitar but finished it on piano. The orchestral sound he desired and found came from writing the songs on the piano. "It was on the keyboard," he recalled in *Songs*, "that I could find the arrangements needed to accompany the stories I was writing." Bittan points out in *Wings for Wheels* that "you can discover things on piano you wouldn't necessarily discover on guitar." Not everyone in the band was equally thrilled. After all, Bruce had made his early reputation as a guitar slinger, often with Steve Van Zandt at his side. Decades later, Van Zandt would confess that "my whole problem with the whole album was the piano, which I despise. You immediately go from rock 'n' roll to Broadway. But over the years I've grown to appreciate the theatricalness of the music."

The openings of "Jungleland" and "Backstreets" were especially theatrical. With its twists and vocal intensity, "Backstreets" offered endless opportunities for experimentation, and there are numerous alternate versions with varying string arrangements. In one, Danny Federici's organ plays behind the piano and the strings come pouring in before the opening lyrics. Bruce seems to rush the lyrics, but his agonized vocals are in peak form. The problem is that his voice and the strings rub against each other to opposite effect. At some point, Bittan's piano would work its magic, but it is not there yet. Another take has the sound, but Bruce still hasn't settled on the lyrics. He bluffs through them with such lines as "I found her where she fell/Just another busted sister of the Heartbreak Hotel," and "dancing in the dark to the sounds of the King." Only the final verse is intact. "We were recording epics at the time," recalls Bittan. "I mean 'Jungleland' and 'Backstreets' are not easy songs to record. It's like trying to drive a Grand Prix course: every time you go around one turn, there's another."

The horns on "Tenth Avenue Freeze-Out" also presented a problem. No one could figure out how to get the R&B sound to fill out Clemons's sax parts. Michael Brecker and Randy Brecker were hired to play trumpet, flugelhorn, and tenor saxophone, but they were awaiting instructions on what to play. Steve Van Zandt was in the studio visiting. Van Zandt played guitar with Southside Johnny and the Asbury Jukes, and he and Bruce went back to the beginning of the Jersey Shore scene. Springsteen asked Van Zandt to help. According to Van Zandt, "I was hanging around the studio, and what he was doing just wasn't working. I knew how to make it work, and I was too naïve to know my place and stay there and shut up. I didn't give a fuck, so I said, 'This sucks, why don't you fix it?' And Bruce was like, 'Why don't you give it a shot? Nothing else is working.'" Van Zandt sorted out the horns by throwing away the charts and singing each part to the players. He soon officially joined the band.

The struggles to make the record remained intense. They worked from the late afternoon until dawn. People sometimes walked out of the studio in anger, and then, after taking a walk around Times Square, returned to the work ahead. Landau helped Bruce understand that he simply had to get the album done. Springsteen would spend hours on one line, Landau lamented. "He'd say, 'Hang on guys, I want to check a line,' and four hours later he'd be sitting there trying to make the most minute changes in one verse." Thirty years later Bruce would recall, "There was a monster working on it. Me, maybe." Bruce appreciated Landau's coaxing and cajoling, and it undoubtedly helped him move forward. But he also refused to compromise on his artistic vision. "The release date is just one day," he would tell Landau. "The record is forever."

Springsteen said time and again, "I had this *horrible* pressure in the studio." Columbia Records was breathing down his back, costs were spiraling, and publicity had him penciled in as the savior of rock 'n' roll. Fans, too, were clamoring for the third album. At one show, Bruce plugged former band member David Sancious's new album. "What about you?" a voice cried from the audience. Springsteen paused and said, "Me? I'm not putting out no records anymore," but then he corrected himself, and said, "No, y'know, pretty soon." But none of that was as intense as the pressure Bruce put on himself. Soon after the release of *Born to Run*, he concluded that "what made the record so hard was *me*."

Iovine recalls that "Bruce would spend eight hours trying to write one line of the lyrics to 'Jungleland' and longer on the guitar part to 'Thunder Road.' He'd try it one way and then tell everybody 'again' and 'again' for days. I fell asleep for four hours one night and the first thing I heard after waking up was Bruce saying, 'Again.'" To stay awake, Iovine would take out a piece of gum, throw it away, and chew on the foil wrapper.

Bruce spent the summer of 1975 in an awful room at the Holiday Inn on the West Side of Manhattan. It had a crooked mirror that drove Bruce nuts. "Every day, before I'd go over to the studio I'd straighten out this crooked mirror," he said. "And every day when I'd come home, that mirror was crooked again. Every time. That crooked mirror . . . it just couldn't stay straight. So I'm there with this crooked mirror and after about a week the room started to look like Nagasaki anyway . . . junk all over the place. And then one day this chick I was with one night in Texas calls up and says she's in Jersey and she doesn't have any place to stay and she's freakin' out! And so finally I say, 'O.K. You can stay here.' So every day I'd go into the studio and there was *that* and then I'd come home and there'd be this crooked mirror." The crooked mirror became a symbol of all that was wrong in his life, and he came to see the recording of *Born to Run* as "the album that mirror became—it was crooked, it just wouldn't hang right."

Every day, Springsteen said, was supposed to be the last day, but days and weeks passed and still there was no end in sight. He was trying to finish the last cut, "She's the One." He was at the piano, and Landau was in the booth, and they had been working nonstop for hours. "I just lean my head down on the piano. It just won't come. And everybody's tryin' to tell me how to do it—they were all there to help me and they were really tryin'—and Landau's sayin' this and that and freakin' out . . . and then, all of a sudden, everybody looks around and Landau has just disappeared, just walked off into the night—night, it was like six A.M.—couldn't take it. He was smart to go home and get some sleep. The whole thing was like that. And when I got home around ten in the morning to the room with the crooked mirror, this chick she says to me—she says it every night when I come home—'Is it finished?' And I say, 'No.' And I could've cried . . . I almost cried . . . Well, maybe I did cry a little."

He told another interviewer, "I bled dry on that thing, groaning, conked out on the floor, half-dead on the street at six in the morning on the corner trying to walk uptown, trying to make it to my hotel room."

Bruce was running out of time. The *Born to Run* tour was set to begin on July 20 in Providence, Rhode Island. Still, the album was being mixed. On July 19, the band rehearsed for the upcoming tour in a room above the studio at the Record Plant in a session that ran from three in the afternoon until ten the following morning. "We mixed the album in nine days straight," recalls Iovine. "Maybe leaving the studio for a few hours to go home. We even slept there. We had to get it finished. Bruce had shows booked. But he had a picture in his head, and as tired as he was, he wouldn't let go of that picture."

Shortly after the release of the album, Bruce recalled at the end spending several days around the clock at the studio: "The last morning. I had a gig in Providence that night; that morning I was singing 'She's the One' at the same time I was mixing 'Jungleland' in another studio downstairs; at the same time I was in another studio, rehearsing the band for the gig that night. That's the truth, I almost died."

There is a photograph that was taken on the morning of the rehearsal. "It's the scariest thing I've ever seen," Bruce said a few months after. "You have to see the band. It should be on the cover of that album. Scariest thing ever. You ain't never seen faces like that in your life . . . we were there for four days, and every single minute is on everybody's face. The light comes through the window, it's like ten in the morning, we've been up for days. We got a gig that night, we're rehearsing, and what's worse is I can't even sing."

And still it wasn't over. He got back to the Holiday Inn, packed, ready to leave, and his girlfriend asks the question she has been asking for weeks: " 'Is it over?' I said no, it isn't over. I could've cried. I could've died when we didn't get it done. We walked out of that studio and I wanted to kill somebody." He said he could never

The band nears the end of a marathon recording and rehearsing session on the final day in the studio, July 20, 1975. (© BARBARA PYLE)

describe the tension making the record: "It was killing, almost; it was inhuman. I hated it. I couldn't stand it. It was the worst, hardest, lousiest thing I ever had to do."

At the end of July, the band was in Washington, D.C., and Virginia. Iovine was creating the mix-down tape, copying from the multitrack down to the two-track, then using a compressor and equalizer to create the official studio production master, from which the album would be pressed. The work is as much art as science. Iovine kept sending Bruce masters and Bruce kept rejecting them as imperfect. One time he threw the test pressings into the pool. He thought about scrapping the album entirely. After so much work and so much pressure to succeed, he felt frightened and paralyzed. The album "scared me off a little bit, maybe. I was puttin' down things I hadn't put down before; that's such a personal thing." "After it was finished? I hated it!" he recalled a year later. "I couldn't stand to listen to it. I thought it was the worst piece of garbage I'd ever heard."

Landau was in San Francisco on vacation when he heard about Bruce's explosion. He told Dave Marsh the essence of what he said to Springsteen over the phone: "Look, you're not supposed to like it. You think Chuck Berry sits around listening to 'Maybellene'? And when he does hear it, don't you think he wishes a few things could be changed? Now c'mon, it's time to put the record out."

Rock critic Paul Williams had been talking to Bruce on and off all through 1975, and he offered a keen insight prior to the album's release. Williams speculated, "There's something he is not saying, though I know he must feel it in his gut: that his third album is all that stands between him and uncontrollable stardom. The record company people can feel it, and they're hot with anticipation. Springsteen can feel it, too, and somewhere deep inside he must be wondering, 'Do I really want to go through that door?'" Bruce told Williams, "You gotta always maintain control over everything. Once it starts to lead you, that's when it starts getting to you."

At long last, Springsteen relinquished control. His prolonged, exhaustive period in the studio was finally over. At the end of August 1975 the record was released. Those three words, *Born to Run*, had evolved into a song and an album that would find its place as a masterpiece of twentieth-century American music and culture. More than thirty years later, even Springsteen admits as much.

THREE

THE SONGS OF *BORN TO RUN*

I wanted it to sound enormous, to grab you by your throat and insist that you take that ride, insist that you pay attention—not just to the music, but to life, to being alive.

—BRUCE SPRINGSTEEN, 2005

IN *SONGS*, Springsteen offers a précis of the album: " 'Thunder Road' opens the album, introducing its characters and its central proposition: Do you want to take a chance? On us? On life? You're then led through the band bio and block party of 'Tenth Avenue Freeze-Out,' the broken friendships of 'Backstreets,' out into the open with 'Born to Run,' and into the dark city and spiritual background of 'Jungleland.' " It is an epic cycle that seems to unfold over the course of an endless summer night, all in less than forty minutes.

SIDE ONE
"Thunder Road"
The album opens quietly, harmonica and piano together. The tune is the deep breath before beginning. In 2005, Springsteen said it was an invitation, something opening up musically. It also builds suspense. The harmonica sounds like a screeching porch door, and sure enough, "the screen door slams." Bruce sings the entire first verse accompanied only by piano. "There is something about the [piano] melody of 'Thunder Road' that suggests a new day—which

64

is why that song ended up first on the record, instead of 'Born to Run,'" Springsteen later recalled.

We are thrust into an action scene. The verbs carry the drama: *slams, waves, dances, plays*. Springsteen pays tribute to Roy Orbison's "Only the Lonely" and establishes immediately a central narrative thrust of the album: loneliness and the search for companionship. Mary is the narrator's answer, but she has already turned him down: "Don't turn me home again/I just can't face myself alone again."

In concert, Bruce often allows just the audience to sing, "Darling you know just what I'm here for," before picking up with the shift that follows. The narrator is there for love, for sex, for excitement. "So you're scared and you're thinking that maybe we ain't that young anymore." Springsteen has written many profound and poetic lines in his career, but none more so than this couplet. He was twenty-four when he wrote it. And yet a generation felt exhausted, as if in the aftermath of the culturally and politically turbulent sixties and early seventies they had all aged prematurely. The only hope is in the darkness of night: "Show a little faith, there's magic in the night." *Born to Run* is a night album, a meditation on the promise of the night as a window of escape, but also a potentially fearful, even deadly place. The narrator is ready to take off with a girl who "ain't a beauty, but hey you're all right." The line works in some fashion as a tribute to women rather than as a demeaning comment. In live performances audiences chuckle, as does Springsteen frequently. The narrator, we assume, is no beauty either. But love and companionship are not only for gorgeous people.

With the next verse, guitar and bass enter. The music has started to build; the song is shifting gears. He offers a litany of delaying tactics, of feeling sorry for yourself: You can hide, you can "study your pain," you can cross yourself, you can "throw roses in the rain," you can "waste your summer praying in vain/For a savior to rise from these streets." The narrator is saying don't bother, don't wait, act now. The influence of Springsteen's Catholic upbringing, and the religious vocabulary that informs his songs throughout his career, is evident here. In "Thunder Road," savior, praying, faith, crosses, redemption, heaven, and promised land are all mentioned. Indeed the song might be read as a religious vision: After all, like a vision, Mary dances across the porch, with "one last chance to make it real"; trading in "these wings on some wheels" suggests angels becoming earthbound; the song closes with references to "ghosts," haunting, and "skeletons." Salvation is to be achieved on the highway with a companion.

Hitting the road to find oneself is so much of a cultural cliché, it is easy to ignore the power that the idea holds. Springsteen certainly didn't invent the dream of escape. America was founded as an escape, and its open geography has provided every generation from the first with an opportunity to experience mobility. Springsteen is working in a long tradition. It is a romantic, runaway dream of taking off and feeling free:

> *Hey what else can we do now*
> *Except roll down the window*
> *And let the wind blow back your hair*
> *Well the night's busting open*
> *These two lanes will take us anywhere*

With those lines the song shifts into its third gear musically: The vocals double, the drums become pronounced, and we hear the glockenspiel for the first time, its tingling flashes like star dust.

"Oh Thunder Road, oh Thunder Road." The vocal energy increases and the song shifts direction yet again with "Well I got this guitar/And I learned how to make it talk." Springsteen said in 2005 that "it was the hokiest line I ever wrote." He added that the guitar was his "instrument of deliverance." Springsteen's guitar, which appears on the cover of the album and which he played for thirty years, cost him $185 at a guitar shop in Belmar. It was a mixture of two guitars: an Esquire neck and a Telecaster body, and it had a sound all its own. The brief lick here of the guitar talking, and another small burst later in the song, are the only times that the instrument comes forward to command our attention. The instrument will be named once more on the final song of the album.

The song builds again toward its close; musically, it sounds like engines revving up. "And I know you're lonely/For words that I ain't spoken." Perhaps those words are "I love you." We don't know. Other suitors have been sent away, but this night Mary is offered freedom and a chance to break certain promises. We know "the ride it ain't free," but we aren't told exactly what the price is that we pay for running away. What we know and feel is that happiness awaits elsewhere. The narrator tells Mary to "Climb in/It's a town full of losers/And I'm pulling out of here to win."

To add emphasis, Springsteen jumps from a minor key with "Mary climb in" to a major key for the screaming finale. Time and again he will use the minor-major shift to set tone and emphasize lyrical tensions and oppositions. What follows is a triumphal minute-long sax and piano duo that has us bounding down the highway. The freedom here is musical as much as lyrical.

Roy Bittan explained that in the song, "there are a lot of ascending and descending piano movements . . . which Garry and I pretty much played together. A lot of the time you really have to put the bass and the piano together on that kind of part. I remember when we were working on 'Thunder Road,' I don't know why, but I had the feeling that these different movements would work much better than just playing all these riffs everywhere. I had this feeling of up and down motion going from one chord change to another."

Of all the songs on *Born to Run*, and indeed across Springsteen's canon, "Thunder Road" may be the most meaningful to listeners. Asked in 1995 why he included it on his *Greatest Hits* CD even though the song was neither a hit nor even a single, he said that "it just felt all-inclusive. It may be something about trying to seize a particular moment in your life and realizing you have to make a very fundamental and basic decision that you know will alter your life and how you live it. It's a funny song because it simultaneously contains both dreaming and disillusionment."

In 2005, for television's *VH1 Storytellers*, he elaborated further: "What I hoped it would be when I wrote the song was what I got out of rock 'n' roll music—a sense of a larger life, greater experiences, hopefully more and better sex, a sense of fun, more fun, a sense of your personal exploration and your possibilities that were in it, the idea that it was all lying somewhere inside of you and just there on the edge of town."

It is a revealing explanation, a combination of the serious and humorous that captures the essence of Springsteen's ongoing faith in the saving grace of rock 'n' roll and the journey of personal growth. Of course the meaning of any song, whether in the performer's or listener's life, does not remain constant. Great art grows and changes as we do and we find new meanings in old songs. "Thunder Road" might best be seen as a celebration of carpe diem—seize the day. In this sense it bears comparison to a poem written nearly 350 years ago by Andrew Marvell, "To His Coy Mistress":

"But at my back I always hear/Time's Winged Chariot hurrying near." Death is at our heels; let's act before it is too late.

"Thunder Road" has elicited its share of personal essays, none better than novelist Nick Hornby's in *Songbook*, a volume in which he writes about various songs that have meaning to him. "I've loved this song for a quarter of a century now, and I've heard it more than anything else, with the possible exception of . . . Who am I kidding? There are no other contenders," Hornby writes. He talks about how the song has survived whereas others have become stale. Hornby says he sees the flaws: the "doomed romanticism," the "overwrought" lyrics. And he points out that "the word *redemption* is to be avoided like the plague when you're writing songs about redemption." And yet the song, "even though I'm not American, no longer young, hate cars, and can recognize why so many people find Springsteen bombastic and histrionic . . . somehow manages to speak for me." For Hornby, the song is about making it, about finding fame, about winning. He personalizes the line about not feeling young anymore and admits to "thinking I wasn't that young anymore for a long, long time—decades, in fact—and even today I choose to interpret it as a wistful observation of middle age, rather than the sharp fear that comes on in late youth."

Hornby expresses his appreciation for a version of the song that Bruce left in the studio, a solo acoustic version that presents "Thunder Road" as "a haunting, exhausted hymn to the past, to lost love and missed opportunities and self-delusion and bad luck and failure." That version works as well, and all Hornby can say is that "an artist who can persuade you of the truth of what he is singing with either version is an artist who is capable of an awful lot."

The novelist goes on to suggest that "Thunder Road," although the first track on the album, sounds as if it refers to what has already taken place and therefore *Born to Run* "begins, in effect, with its own closing credits." Hornby wants the song to provide a final salvation, and we can certainly understand why. But the song lays out hopes and dreams, and the remainder of the album is an investigation into whether, and in what ways, they can be realized.

The meaning of the song in the lives of ordinary Americans was revealed along with so much else after the attacks of September 11, which gave new poignancy to the themes of love and heroism ("I'm no hero/That's understood"). At the time, the *New York Times* ran a series called "Portraits of Grief," thumbnail sketches of the victims. The portrait of Jim Berger, an insurance executive, was titled, simply, "Fan of the Boss." "He knew the words to 'Thunder Road' by heart, and often sang it for his passengers [in his car]," his wife, Suzanne, reported. Springsteen was personally moved by the references to his work, how in memorial after memorial he read of his music being played. At one point he called Suzanne Berger and said, "I want to respect your privacy, but I just want you to know I was very touched, and I want to know more about your husband." After the service for Jim, mourners sang "Thunder Road" and remembered their friend who "taught us all a lesson in unconditional love."

"Tenth Avenue Freeze-Out"

This rhythm-and-blues rocker is probably the most joyous song about being lost and alone ever recorded. It begins with a musical intro and then blasts off, driven by a piano backbeat and horns. Musically, the song pays homage to early rock and soul while blending in more contemporary rhythms.

Place and space are crucial to the geography of *Born to Run*, and Springsteen has moved from road in the first song to avenue here. But if roads, avenues, streets, and lanes provide means of escape, they can also be places of entrapment: "I'm running on the bad side/And I got my back to the wall," the narrator declares in the first verse.

But who is the narrator? The song opens in the third person, mentioning a character named Bad Scooter who is "searching for his groove," looking for his rhythm and a place to fit in. Some have suggested that the initials stand for Springsteen himself. Certainly, the Big Man joining the band in the final verse is Clarence Clemons and, at one level, the song narrates how Bad Scooter and the Big Man came together.

That story, of Clemons joining the band, was for a long time an essential part of the stage show, used by Bruce when introducing "The E Street Shuffle." From the start, Clemons has played Springsteen's foil and sidekick onstage, his sax solos a staple of the sound of the E Street Band. Bruce would confabulate a story of a dark, rainy night on the boardwalk in Asbury Park, after a poorly attended show, and seeing a huge man in a white suit carrying a saxophone coming toward him. He is fearful, and the early telling of the story is honest about the fears of what this big, black man might do to him. Clemons reaches out his hand, the two touch, and sparks fly, which provides the opening to the song.

Clemons tells the story differently. He was playing at one club in Asbury Park and Springsteen was at the Student Prince, a few blocks away. The singer in Clemons's group kept telling him he had to check out Springsteen because she thought the two of them would be great together. In between sets, Clemons walked over to the Prince: "A rainy, windy night it was, and when I opened the door the whole thing flew off its hinges and blew away down the street. The band was onstage, but staring at me framed in the doorway. And maybe that did make Bruce a little nervous because I just said, 'I want to play with your band,' and he said, 'Sure, you do anything you want.' The first song we did was an early version of 'Spirit in the Night.' Bruce and I looked at each other and didn't say anything. We just knew. We knew we were the missing links in each other's lives. He was what I was searching for. In one way he was just a scrawny little kid. But he was a visionary. He wanted to follow his dream. So from then on, I was a part of history."

There are at least two possibilities as to the identity of the "I" who is caught in the freeze-out: the narrator and Bad Scooter are the same person, or the narrator is observing as Bad Scooter and the Big Man join together. I prefer the first reading, which would be clear had Springsteen simply changed the two Bad Scooter references to the first person, but for narrative and dramatic reasons, he didn't. Throughout the album, Springsteen plays with narrative point of view: Only "Jungleland" looks in from the outside. Every other song is about I, we, you, or me.

The narrator is "stranded in the jungle," and discovers on Tenth Avenue that "I'm all alone . . . /And I'm on my own, I'm on my own/And I can't go home." Springsteen's voice here echoes with extra reverb, as if trapped between the walls of buildings and hollering to get out. Even more terrifying, another voice in the background tells the narrator, "Kid you better get the picture."

Loneliness, isolation, disconnection—these are the experiences of the narrator who cannot go home, or who certainly doesn't want to go back there. What is a Tenth Avenue freeze-out? Springsteen said in 2005, "I have no idea what that means to this day, but it's important." Where is Tenth Avenue? Springsteen no doubt had in mind the avenue near David Sancious's house in Belmar. Taking creative license, Daniel Wolff has suggested that, using the geography of Asbury Park as a frame of reference, it is "the barrier to the outside world," the northern lake beyond which lies another world.

Asbury's avenues run north until Eighth, which is followed by Deal Lake Drive. That makes the lake itself figuratively Tenth. Only when Bad Scooter/I connects with another human being, the Big Man/Clarence Clemons, can they "bust this city in half" and break out from the freeze-out, from the experience of exclusion that torments them. Rock 'n' roll will deliver them, and us, too, who can now "sit back right easy and laugh."

Never were those words truer than when Springsteen performed the song live. He used "Tenth Avenue Freeze-Out" to open the Bottom Line shows in August 1975, and once the *Born to Run* tour settled in that fall, it was the first song after the opener, "Thunder Road."

Twenty-five years later, in 2000, it was through this song, more than any other, that Bruce rededicated himself to the E Street Band and the spirit of rock 'n' roll. After reaching stardom in 1975 and megastardom in 1984, he had disbanded the group in 1989. (Steve Van Zandt left in 1984 and Nils Lofgren joined.) He married Patty Scialfa, had two children, and enjoyed some musical successes as well as failures. His father died in 1998, he turned fifty in 1999, and after a decade playing without the musicians with whom he rose to fame (with the exception of Roy Bittan, who played with Springsteen's new band in 1992), he reunited the E Street Band for an exhilarating tour.

"Tenth Avenue Freeze-Out" was the song during which he introduced the band, but introductions were never a simple affair. Early in the tour, in July 1999, he broke into the middle of the song to tell a story: "When I was a young man, I walked as a little child down many avenues. The avenue of love, the avenue of fear, the avenue of hope, the avenue of faith, the avenue of cynicism, the avenue of compassion, the avenue of self-interest, the avenue of sexual pleasure (a popular avenue)—but I was always alone, lost in the darkness. I was always alone, lost in my own bitterness." As he walked, he says, he met the various members of the band, and they each play a few bars as Bruce introduces them, building up, of course, to him pretending he can't remember who he is forgetting and screaming to the crowd, as the music builds, "Say what? Say who?" over and over until finally the sound crescendos and he tears into "the big man joined the band."

By the end of the reunion tour, a year later in Madison Square Garden, Bruce played the role of preacher during the break. He begins to sing "Take Me to the River," and announces that "tonight I want to find that river of life, I want to find that river of love, and the river of faith, and that river of hope. I want to find that river of transformation, where you can go and you can be changed if you work at it. I want to find that river of resurrection where everybody gets a second chance." He goes on to rivers of sanctification, sexual healing, companionship, joy, and happiness and he invites the crowd to join him on the journey "because you can't stumble on it by accident, you've got to seek it out and you can't get there by yourself." He has become the minister of rock 'n' roll throwing a rock 'n' roll baptism, a rock 'n' roll exorcism, and a rock 'n' roll bar mitzvah, he jokes. He moves again toward introducing the band members and builds to "the Minister of Soul, the secretary of the Brotherhood, the emperor of E street," and has the crowd screaming Clarence's name in response to repeated inquiries of "Say who? Say who? Say who?" before picking the song back up.

It was an astonishing performance that simultaneously recapitulated the most hopeful message of *Born to Run* from twenty-five years earlier, symbolized his rededication to the band and the art of rock 'n' roll hysteria, and reveled in the knowledge that can only come from the passage of time: It is the journey together with those with whom you have experienced so much that is the antidote to loneliness and the proof of real love.

"Night"
The song is a sprint, the shortest on the album. Night, of course, is the landscape of freedom, the territory for action. No word in the Springsteen canon has appeared as often, not even *love*. In titles alone there is "Spirit in the Night," "Prove It All Night," "Because the Night," "Something in the Night," "Drive All Night," and "Open All Night." Every song on *Born to Run* includes the word *night*.

The song blasts off with guitar and snare drum. The guitar shifts keys and the piano enters banging eighth notes while the guitar plays drawn-out whole notes over the beat. The tempo is rapid but coherent. Saxophone and piano dominate the intro.

Musically, Springsteen employs a series of minor and major progressions. In this way, musical and lyrical shifts jibe. The minor key condemns the monotonous world of daytime work; the major key offers the possibilities of screeching off into the night. Minor: ". . . you work all day." Major: "To blow 'em away in the night." Minor: ". . . as it changes to green/With your faith in your machine." Major: ". . . off you scream into the night." Minor: "You work nine to five." Major: ". . . and somehow you survive till the night."

At the end, however, just when the listener has been conditioned for another minor-major transition, Bruce stays in a major key, placing extra emphasis on the closing line of the song, "Until all you can see is the night," before the sax solo brings it to a close.

In every musical way, then, the song undergirds the message that is being delivered lyrically—and that message in "Night" marks the foundation of Springsteen's working-class persona.

"You," the narrator opens and repeats again and again. The singer claims to know us. That we go to work every day in jobs that we can barely tolerate, that we are subject to the "boss man" giving us hell. There is nothing to be done but to endure the day and live for the night. It would take time before Springsteen in his songs would develop a critique of an economic system that exploited workers. The title song of *The River*, for example, laments the loss of jobs "on account of the economy." What he first offers in "Night" is an ennobling of the working class by identifying them as having dreams of their own, dreams of escape from the drudgery of work.

Springsteen, as is well-known, is nicknamed the Boss. It is a nickname he despises: "I hate being called 'Boss.' I just do. Always did from the beginning," he said in 1981. It originated when in the early days of the band he would pay them at the end of the week and they would jokingly thank the boss. "I personally would have preferred that it had remained private," he said, but eventually he came to accept the title in self-mocking fashion. The nickname adds resonance to his songs of working-class dreams and realities. Eventually, Bruce would write the line describing himself as "a rich man in a poor man's shirt" as he grappled with the authenticity of his persona, but not here, not on *Born to Run*. Springsteen knows these characters of the night because he is one of them. "I live by night," he has said. "I was never up during the day. People are alive at night."

"You're just a prisoner of your dreams," he declares in "Night." The word *dream* is central to Springsteen's vision, especially here and in the follow-up albums *Darkness on the Edge of Town* and *The River*. On *Born to Run*, in "She's the One," she's "standing in that doorway like a dream"; in "Jungleland," "The rat's own dream guns him down"; and in "Born to Run," we are trapped in "a runaway American dream."

What is the dream that traps us, guns us down, carries us off? As clichéd as it may sound, it is the dream of finding true love, of securing freedom, of escaping the feeling that one's future is predetermined, a routine broken only by whatever excitement the night brings. What makes "Night" so potent is that before Springsteen explores the dark side of the dream of escape—that there may be nowhere to go, that eventually you have to stop running, that there are demons out on the highway at night—he is going to glorify the dream itself.

Work holds no value here; you only work because you have to: "You work all day/To blow 'em away in the night." Deliverance comes from racing your souped-up car, chasing that beauty who is "so pretty that you're lost in the stars." The only faith you can have is in your machine because it is an engine over which you have some control. It's remarkable how many of Bruce's fans, many of them white middle-class kids from cities and suburbs who never raced a car, identified with the romanticism of hot nights on the blacktop.

The experience is physical: "Every muscle in your body sings." The line evokes Walt Whitman in "I Sing the Body Electric." If the daytime work experience is physically exhausting, "busting you up on the outside," the nighttime ride is physically liberating, allowing you to "break on through" to a different state of being, if only for a short time.

Yet even in the darkness there is despair. The song, as triumphant and liberating as it is, reminds us that we run "sad and free." Sadness and despair haunt the album, even at its most triumphal moments. It is testimony to Springsteen's skill as a writer that he never tells why there is so much sadness; he simply shows it. There are no why's explained here: why we are sad, why we have pain ("Thunder Road"), why we are desperate ("Backstreets" and "Jungleland"), why we are scared and lonely ("Born to Run"). Maybe it is because we fear getting older; maybe it is because we are stuck in awful jobs that sap our souls and deaden our spirits; maybe it is because we are still alone; and maybe it is simply our condition, one that we must ultimately accept even as we fight to escape it.

By the time Springsteen released "Racing in the Street" in 1978, the darkness of the road at night obscured whatever freedom it brought. This first-person ballad narrates the story of a drag racer who sounds weary of his life in the streets but knows that there is nothing else to do to continue to feel alive than to "Come home from work and wash up/And go racin' in the street." The narrator wins a race and a girl, but the story turns. She is hopelessly sad, "cries herself to sleep at night," because "all her pretty dreams are torn." It may be that there is no escape and these characters suffer the pain of some version of original sin, trapped in lives that are not of their own making. At the end, they will ride to the sea and try to "wash these sins off our hands," but the stains are indelible.

"Backstreets"

The concluding song of side one of the album carries us away from the freedom of night toward the darkness of fate. The summer is "infested," a foreshadowing of the diseased state of being that is to come. But the lyrics are foreshadowed by the lengthy musical introduction. This is no three-minute rock sprint. It is operatic and theatrical, the piano and organ at first sounding like a church service, then building with themes from the song and exploding into lyricism. The intro lasts more than a minute.

Musically, as Springsteen sings, the environment is hollow, distant: the drums low and echoing, the guitar almost indifferent. The narrator tells of meeting Terry and "trying in vain to breathe the fire we was born in." Note the intentional grammatical error of *was* instead of *were*. Springsteen's characters are working-class, undereducated, and of the streets. Born into fire may lead us to born to run, but here all one can do is run away and hide at night "for our lives," knowing that whatever love we have is "hard and filled with defeat."

"Hiding on the backstreets" is screamed from deep within, primal, angry. The song builds with the second verse. Nothing romantic here—huddled and desperate lovers—except the promise of everlasting love that is not to be ("We swore we'd live forever"). This is a song about betrayal.

The third verse brings a musical turning point as the energy builds and Springsteen shifts the key. People are hurt, "some really dying," with the "whole damn city crying." Breathlessly, the narrator explodes in hatred at Terry, who has lied and left him for someone else. At the end of the verse he drops into a minor key with "when you went away," using the shift to stress his loneliness and hopelessness.

A wailing guitar solo brings us to the conclusion, "laying here in the dark," listening to the confession of "faithlessness." Terry is a "tramp of hearts"—a potent phrase, especially given the "tramps like us" that will follow in "Born to Run." It turns out we are not heroes but commonplace, "We're just like all the rest," and that is the worst reproach of all. The song ends in primal screams and ghostly chants, "Hiding on the backstreets" repeated over and over. It is a where we must be, where we must engage what Ralph Waldo Emerson, in his essay "Self-Reliance," called "the rugged battle of fate."

One reading of the song suggested by fans is that "Backstreets" is about a homosexual relationship. Illicit love can take place only in hidden places, and the characters in the song (Terry is an ambiguous name sexually) struggle not only with one another but with the pressure that comes from "trying in vain" to act like the heroes of the movies—supposedly handsome, manly, heterosexuals. The narrator and Terry must forever hide their love on the backstreets. Interestingly, an early version of the lyrics reads, "Watching the heroes working in the fun house ripping off the fags."

Springsteen has commented on how he was "a misfit in my own town," and therefore did not buy into any of the accepted stereotypes about gay life: "Me and a few other guys were the town freaks—and there were many occasions when we were dodging getting beaten up ourselves. So, no, I didn't feel a part of those homophobic ideas . . . I was open-minded, and I wasn't naturally intolerant."

That does not mean the narrator of the song is gay. The live performances of "Backstreets" in the late 1970s make clear that Terry is a woman, and that the wounds of lost love and hope continue to fester. On the *Darkness* tour, Springsteen would routinely add a long narration at the end of the song. (Some of these lyrics would emerge as part of "Sad Eyes," which would morph into "Drive All Night" on *The River*.) It differed a bit night after night, but the story was the same: Time has passed and he runs into Terry again and he can't forget his love of her, and as he recalls what he swore he would do to show his everlasting devotion, and as the pain of loss returns to him, he denounces her in a primal scream for breaking her promise never to leave him. "Little girl you lied," he cries over and over again. It is the lying that rankles worst of all, a breach of trust and faith that can never be forgotten or forgiven.

SIDE TWO
"Born to Run"
The opening drum beat of Dylan's "Like a Rolling Stone," Springsteen noted, "kicked open the door to your mind"; the opening drum roll of "Born to Run" propelled a generation along their

journey of escape. The song leads off side two. The vocal wail of "Backstreets" fades away. We turn the record over. And we are launched.

One of the song's musical mysteries is how it starts so fast and yet seems continuously to build momentum, a constant crescendo. The fast drum solo from high tom to floor tom sets off the layered sounds of horns, guitar, bass, bells, and drumbeat. Listen to Little Eva's "The Loco-Motion" from 1962 and you have one source for the drum roll. The initial buildup comes from the snare drum. On the first four measures, Ernest "Boom" Carter plays quarter notes on the second beat of every measure. In the second four measures, the snare speed doubles, playing on the second and fourth beat of every measure. The change is subtle, but it transforms the pace of the song.

The song is built around "tight, bare arrangements," Springsteen said, on top of which are layered multiple instruments. There isn't one acoustic guitar in the background, but several compressed guitars that create sonic density. There is even a twelve-string playing single notes. The drums and bass line are equally taut. The result, offered Springsteen, is a "dark tension" in the music.

Bruce starts singing. This time it is not the "I" of "Thunder Road" or "Tenth Avenue Freeze-Out," or the "you" of "Night," or the "me" of "Backstreets." This time it is "we." We are joined with the narrator on this journey; we share the strain of that "runaway American dream." The phrase is a potent one. The American dream of working hard and getting ahead, of making it, of upward mobility, is off-kilter and out of control. The dream has escaped us just as we now seek to run away from it. Listen again to how Springsteen sings the word *dream,* making it sound dreamlike and in the same instant mocking it. That runaway American dream may also be the lost love of "Backstreets"—think of Del Shannon's "Runaway," a hit from 1961 about a girl who breaks a guy's heart and runs off.

Of course, the phrase must also be read in reverse, not the American dream as having run away, but the dream of running away, of getting out. One is born to run because in America the vast landscape has always permitted moving out and on—from crowded churches, congested cities, clattering factories, or claustrophobic homes, roads headed out of town in the direction of new territory to be explored.

Musically, although the horns drop out and Carter plays more on the cymbals, the guitar begins creating anticipation by playing twangy low eighth notes. It foreshadows a change that comes as Bruce sings, "Sprung from cages out on Highway 9." The guitar and glockenspiel play up and down a triad chord, providing an uplifting musical feel. These first guitar licks echo Duane Eddy's 1960 song "Because They're Young."

After he sings "steppin' out over the line," there is a dramatic instant of silence: A quick run down the toms, and then the instruments cut out. Springsteen cries, "Wooooaah," and the instruments jump back in. It's easy to miss, and the moment is subtle, but it rebuilds the energy level and creates anticipation. What, after all, is going to happen when we step out over the line?

The concluding lyrics of the first verse tell us what we are running from in vivid imagery: "This town rips the bones from your back." We are trapped. Death awaits us, probably at our own hand. It is shocking to realize that the word *suicide* appears twice before the first chorus.

"We gotta get out while we're young." Think back to "Thunder Road." (Bruce also recorded "A Love So Fine" during the *Born to Run* sessions, a song that would become "So Young and in Love," recorded during the *Darkness* sessions.) Getting out, of course, is a rock convention. Indeed, Springsteen often covered the Animals' 1965 hit "We Gotta Get Out of This Place." (The song includes the lines "so young and pretty" and "you'll be dead before your time is due.")

Springsteen then chooses the perfect word to describe us: *tramps*. It suggests homelessness and rootlessness. It also compels us to think about sexual license, the "tramp of hearts" in "Backstreets." Tramping further evokes a musical tradition—Woody Guthrie and *Bound for Glory*. A tramp is created by the society in crisis: The Depression spawned thousands of tramps. But it is also a choice to reject conformity for self-sufficiency. Chaplin embodied individual humanity and morality in his character of the Little Tramp, who time and again defeated more-powerful forces and found love. The final scene of *Modern Times* has the tramp and his girl walking down the road into the sunset, running away from the American dream of work and upward mobility to find their own special place. Several critics seeing Springsteen perform live would describe him as "Chaplinesque."

With those three words—*born to run*—Springsteen encapsulated his vision of American culture. There were other blues and rock songs with *born* in the title: "Born Under a Bad Sign" and "Born to Be Wild," for example. If the first speaks of American innate depravity and the second of American violence, then "Born to Run" speaks to the essential identity of America as a nation of citizens always on the move, seeking the better chance, looking to belong but also yearning to escape. On his guitar, Springsteen bends up to the major chord, and we are gone.

There is a good chance Bruce also knew the country song "Born to Lose," covered by both Johnny Cash and Ray Charles.

Rock critic Greil Marcus points out that "Born to Lose" is an old punk tattoo and that the songs on the album "take place in the space between 'Born to Run' and 'Born to Lose,' as if to say the only run worth making is the one that forces you to risk losing everything you have."

The second verse and chorus are musically similar to the first, but Springsteen adds elements to keep up the energy. Vocally, the sensuality intensifies. An organ plays over "just wrap your legs 'round these velvet rims." The layers all come together and the lyrics build to their inevitable conclusion, the articulation of the theme of the song, the album, the body of Springsteen's work: "I want to know if love is wild/girl I want to know if love is real." Listen to the voice on *real*, how at the end it rises, cracking high.

The sax solo following the second verse pushes us along, accompanied by a fast jazz drum rhythm. Excitement builds with the addition of a bell-guitar-piano combination. With "the amusement park rises bold and stark," a violin section, playing in the higher registers, enters. The song keeps building, sounding operatic and full. Bruce ends "I wanna die with you Wendy on the streets tonight/In an everlasting kiss" with a defiant *Huuhh*.

In time, Springsteen's work would move away from the romance of death, but not here. The narrator and Wendy are in a love/ suicide pact, the only way in which they can have each other forever and find escape, ironically, from the "death trap, suicide rap." They will get out before the machine grinds them up, even if "getting out" means "dying young."

Following Bruce's *Huuhh*, the instruments join together, moving somewhere, but the direction is musically murky. Anticipation builds in the listener. How will this be resolved? Where are we going? Bruce then provides one of the great count-offs in musical history to break the tension, and every instrument joins together for the symphonic final verse.

"Broken heroes," "sadness," "madness." Only a true and lasting love can make one whole, happy, and sane. "We're gonna get to that place," the narrator sings, but do we believe him? Is there really such a place? Isn't this really about the journey, not the destination? "We'll walk in the sun," but what then? Springsteen would not seek to answer that question for his characters and himself until years later. The musical pinnacle of the song comes with the third and final "Baby we were born to run." Penetrating, echoing vocal instrumentation slows the song and brings it to a close, the final notes not so much ending as fading in the distance.

Starting in 1976, Bruce played "Born to Run" toward the end of sets or as an encore, and he has done so every time he has played with the band since. The lights come on, everyone sings in unison, and the arena elevates.

Only on the *River* tour did he sometimes open with the song. On October 3, 1980, he came onstage in Ann Arbor, Michigan, and began with "Born to Run." Remarkably, he forgot the words: "I knew it was gonna happen. I listened to the song ten times just before the show, but when I walked up to the microphone my mind was blank. I went back to the drums and all of a sudden I heard the words faintly in the back of my mind and I realized the audience was singing. That was a real thrill. It was like a special bond. They weren't just sitting out there. They were involved."

The song took on special poignancy on December 9, 1980, the day after John Lennon was assassinated. Playing at the Spectrum in Philadelphia, Bruce came onstage and said, "It's a hard night to come out and play tonight when so much's been lost . . . The first record . . . the first record that I ever learned was a record called

'Twist and Shout,' and if it wasn't . . . if it wasn't for John Lennon, we'd all be in some place very different tonight . . . It's . . . it's an unreasonable . . . world and you have to live with a lot of things that are just unlivable . . . and . . . it's a hard thing to come out and play but there's just nothing else you can do . . ." With that, the band broke into "Born to Run."

Springsteen commented on how the song's meaning grew over time. In 1984 he said, "Now 'Born to Run,' the song means a lot more to me than it did then. I can sing it tonight and feel like it breathes in all those extra years . . . It still feels really real. Very real, for me. It's one of the most emotional moments of the night. I can see all those people and that song to them is like—that's their song. It's almost as much the audience's as it is mine."

In 1988, Springsteen first performed the song acoustically, and doing so transformed it. On April 27, 1988, in a show in Los Angeles, here is how he introduced it:

This is a song, it's changed a lot over the years as I've sung it, it seemed to be able to open up and sort of let the time in. When I wrote it, I was twenty-four years old and I was sitting in my bedroom in Long Branch, New Jersey. When I think back it surprises me about how, how much I knew about what I wanted because the questions that I asked myself in this song, it seems like I've been trying to find the answers to them ever since. And I guess when I wrote this song, I thought I was writing about a guy and a girl that wanted to run and keep on running, never come back. And that was a nice romantic idea, but I realized that after I put all those people in all those cars, I was gonna have to figure out some place for them to go. And I realized that, in the end, that individual freedom when it's not connected to some sort of community or friends or the world outside, ends up feeling pretty meaningless. So I guess that guy and that girl, they were out there looking for a connection, and I guess that's what I'm doing here tonight. So this is a song about two people trying to find their way home, and I'd like to do it for you, dedicate it to you—just saying that this song's kept me good company on my search, and I hope it's kept you good company on yours.

And so as he and his fans aged, and married, and had children, the song took on new meanings. Acoustically it slows down, and without the musical pyrotechnics it breathes and becomes a song about arriving rather than leaving—finding and making that place. Realizing one cannot run forever is not defeat. Rather, it pays tribute to the runaway dream and suggests that we can indeed succeed, live on in a love that is forever wild and real.

"She's the One"
After the four-and-a-half-minute jolt of "Born to Run," "She's the One" starts quietly, a twelve-string played on upstrokes. Piano and guitar carry the song through its first verse. Springsteen's voice echoes. The song is about total heart-pounding obsession for a girl: "killer graces" and a smile that "kills me." Love and death remain metaphorically intertwined. And the girl's eyes "shine like a midnight sun." (Recall that "Thunder Road" lies "like a killer in the sun," and "Born to Run" ends with the dream of walking in the sun.)

After Bruce sings "she's the one," the percussion explodes and vocal harmony enters, making the song sound like what is being sung: "thunder in your heart at night." What emerges clearly is the famous Bo Diddley beat of three-pause-two, a potent fusion of blues and rock riffs to which Springsteen is paying tribute. (Listen to Diddley's "Who Do You Love." Or think "Not Fade Away," the Buddy Holly song famously covered by the Rolling Stones and played by Springsteen in concert in 1978 followed by "She's the One.")

The language of the second verse makes clear that this obsession is almost religious: "kneeling in the dark." We're told, "There's this angel in her eyes/That tells such desperate lies," and we are returned to "Backstreets," where Terry lies like an angel on his chest and confesses all the lies. "No matter . . . how far you run" suggests a limitation to the dream of escape: There are feelings and memories that can't be left behind and that will chase you down in the end.

At the bridge, Springsteen switches to a minor key and his voice intensifies, becoming louder, more passionate. This adds emphasis to the lines, "Just one kiss/She'd fill them long summer nights/With her tenderness." The sax solo fills the space between the incantations of "She's the One." The song builds to an end, Bruce's vocalizations expressing what words alone can't: desire, desperation, longing.

In concert in the late 1970s, Springsteen offered increasingly fanciful introductions to the song. This is from a show in Oxford, Ohio, in October 1976:

"Scientists were excavating over in Egypt . . . They were excavating at the site of a proposed Holiday Inn and as they dug down into the heart of the earth they came upon a tomb so they rolled away the stone and all they heard was this beat. They found out that, through experiments, that whenever this beat was played, men would take women and women would take their men into a deep dark corner, and they'd get real close and they'd dance. They found traces of this beat in the soil on Mars. They traced it back to the beginning of the universe when all the sounds exploded and they found that it originated on earth in the deepest, darkest part of the world somewhere off Route 18 in New Jersey. When this beat gets played, girls throw off their clothes and jump into the aisle, grown men fall to their knees and cry, good girls go bad, and the bad girls get worse. So if all this stuff don't happen tonight, it's your own fault."

Lest anyone not understand the source of the song, in concert Springsteen started playing Bo Diddley's "Mona" or "I Need You Baby" (famously covered by the Rolling Stones on their first album), and then would proceed straight into "She's the One," often generating twelve or thirteen minutes of musical bedlam that sought to bring to pass what he predicted in his presong rap.

"Meeting Across the River"

This piano-and-trumpet ballad (Randy Brecker playing) provides a musical and narrative break from the buildup of the previous songs. In every way, musically and vocally, the song exudes an atmosphere of despair, hopelessness, and false optimism on the part of the narrator looking for his one last chance to make a score. (The working title of the song was "The Heist.")

While there is a complex chord progression to the song, Springsteen again uses the minor-major changes to draw attention at certain places: for example, "She'll see this time I wasn't just talking/Then I'm gonna go out walking."

The previous songs of the album express a desire to leave, to run, to escape the trap; here the narrator is actually going someplace else, across the river, a natural boundary that can be crossed only through a tunnel. "The other side" can be many places besides

New York from New Jersey. It is the underworld, a landscape of illicit, illegal, dangerous transactions. It is also death.

There is a romantic subtext in the narrator's relationship with Cherry, but this song is not about love but manhood: "Here stuff this in your pocket/It'll look like you're carrying a friend." Not an actual weapon, but the appearance of one. The lines that follow remind us of the class consciousness of these characters: "Change your shirt, 'cause tonight we got style."

"And the word's been passed this is our last chance." Who passed it, and a last chance for what: to pay off a debt, to prove oneself, to walk freely away. In "Thunder Road" there was also a "last chance." And "Born to Run" is a "last chance power drive." Whatever the answers, the song ends quietly, the piano fading, and we are left hoping the narrator and Eddie make it, but somehow knowing they will not.

So evocative is the song that, in 2005, a number of fiction writers offered their own imaginings of it in a collection of "stories inspired by the haunting Bruce Springsteen song." Novelist Martin Smith explains, "It's what's *not* in the lyric, rather than what is, that makes the song so intriguing." Calling "Meeting Across the River" "an epic character story that Springsteen tells with the spare precision of haiku," Smith invites readers to imagine backstories and endings for Eddie, Cherry, and the narrator.

The song marks, as do several others on the album, a critical shift in Springsteen's writing. No longer did he feel the need to unload the dictionary. No longer did he write elliptically or circularly. He had learned how to show not tell, in the truism of what makes for good writing. He had learned how to paint a scene lyrically and musically and situate the listener at the heart of it. Roy Bittan put it best: "In the past, when he would try to say something, it took him the equivalent of the Great American Novel to say it. Since then, he's learned how to be a great short-story writer."

"Jungleland"
It took Springsteen some sixteen months to write, refine, and record "Jungleland." He went through take after take, saying "again," "again," "again," as he sought something he found only by experimenting with various musical styles. It marks a culmination of narrative tendencies evident on his first two albums, it marks a transition to a deeper, fully produced sound, and it marks a farewell: He will never again write a song this long, this character-laden, or this operatic.

Bruce later explained that early in his career, "I wrote several wild, long pieces—'Thundercrack,' 'Kitty's Back,' 'Rosalita'—that were arranged to leave the band and the audience gasping for breath. Just when you thought the song was over, you'd be surprised by another section, taking the music higher. It was, in spirit, what I'd taken from the finales of the great soul revues."

The epic song begins with violin (played by Suki Lahav) and piano. The violin sets the elegiac tone for the song. Then a tinkling piano carries us to the narrative. The mood is weightless, even hopeful as the story opens. A character named the Magic Rat drives into town, a "homecoming" of sorts. He meets a barefoot girl "drinking warm beer in the soft summer rain"; this is one of the most evocative images in the Springsteen canon, summarizing almost in haiku the essence of his early work.

In the second verse, the organ joins in at "churches to the jails." Potent dualisms puncture the song: hungry and hunted; what's flesh and what's fantasy. The characters are trapped between extremes, neither of which provides solace. This is a song where physicality dominates intellect ("And the poets down here/ Don't write nothing at all"). The verbs carry the song: *pulls, rolls, rips, shuts, flash, explode, struggle.*

"Jungleland" is a dangerous place, where gangs assemble at midnight. But in the third verse, Springsteen reimagines the scene as a rock 'n' roll *West Side Story*: "An opera out on the Turnpike/ There's a ballet being fought out in the alley." "Jungleland" is a "death waltz." The song is a turnpike opera where street characters, rather than fighting with knives, battle each other with flashing guitars. Musically, this is where there is a shift in the song as Springsteen shouts rather than sings "The hungry and the hunted explode into rock'n'roll bands." The key shifts for these two lines.

The change in key foreshadows the start of the next section, where we arrive after a stinging guitar solo. The astonishing sax solo that follows the line "Just a look and a whisper, and they're gone" carries us away. It lasts more than two minutes. It allows us to imagine the action that is taking place, telling its own story of the evening, leading us to the return of the violin and then a somber solo piano banging out chords.

A new verse begins, and it seems that we are headed to resolution. Springsteen keeps changing chords and keys, jumping on the line "Outside the street's on fire" but then switching up to a piano-and-violin chord that fades into silence as he reaches the end: "And in the quick of the night they reach for their moment/And try to make an honest stand." We are told they "Wind up wounded, not even dead." Death would be romantic. Being wounded, crippled, forced to survive nine-to-five days of drudgery and long nights of unfulfilled, indeed unfulfillable, desires is not. With cries of the heart, accompanied by piano and violin, "Jungleland" comes to a close. Here is one of those places where the stress and strain of making the album bled into the music itself. The howls were improvised, but Landau recalls that when he heard them he knew that had to be how the record ended.

It is "the Rat's own dream" that guns him down and that is the most terrifying acknowledgment of all—that the runaway American dream will kill us in the end, and the dream of escape is just another version that entraps us. Springsteen would continue to probe dreams on his next album, *Darkness on the Edge of Town*. By then, following several tortuous years of legal wrangling that would lead to separation from his manager Mike Appel, and having experienced the underside of stardom, he was no longer the carefree punk out on the streets. Indeed, the cover photograph is a stark comparison to the shot on *Born to Run*. Springsteen is clean shaven, his hair trimmed, his look stern. He still wears a white T-shirt and black leather, but he is caught indoors, framed against window and wall. He would say that "on *Born to Run* there was the hope of a free ride. On *Darkness*, there ain't no free ride—you wanna ride, you gotta pay."

"Badlands" opens *Darkness* with the warning:

Talk about a dream
Try to make it real
you wake up in the night
With a fear so real
Spend your life waiting
for a moment that just don't come

"Adam Raised a Cain" emanates from "the dark heart of a dream." In "Racing in the Street," "all her pretty dreams are torn."

In the title song, characters live "on the line where dreams are found and lost." In "Prove It All Night," "if dreams came true, oh, wouldn't that be nice." In "The Promise," recorded but left off the album, "when the promise was broken, I cashed in a few of my dreams."

And in "The Promised Land," Springsteen advises:

> *Blow away the dreams that tear you apart*
> *Blow away the dreams that break your heart*
> *Blow away the lies that leave you nothing but lost and*
> *   brokenhearted*

Springsteen followed *Darkness* two years later with a double album, *The River*, that was dual themed, dividing the exhilaration and despair that he often yoked together musically and lyrically in a single song into separate songs of love and loss, passion and longing. The love songs are pop-rock and party songs, usually under four minutes long: "The Ties That Bind," "Crush on You," "Cadillac Ranch," "Sherry Darling," "You Can Look (But You Better Not Touch)," "Ramrod." Of course, there is still tension at times between sound and lyrics, as in "Hungry Heart," a happy-sounding song about a guy who leaves his wife and kids.

The other side is a continuation of the themes of darkness and dreams, offered as somber, melancholy ballads. In "Independence Day," a son takes leave of his father "cause the darkness of this house has got the best of us." In "Drive All Night," a couple whose love is at its end is "lying in the heat of the night like prisoners all our lives." With the mention of fallen angels "crying in defeat," the song evokes "Backstreets."

On *The River*, the dream unravels: "Someday these childish

dreams must end" ("Two Hearts"); "To say I'll make your dreams come true would be wrong" ("I Wanna Marry You"); "Just to end up caught in a dream where everything goes wrong ("The Price You Pay"); "Baby there's nights when I dream of a better world" ("Jackson Cage"); "Once I dreamed we were together again" ("Point Blank").

The title song is one of the most poignant in Springsteen's catalog. He wrote it after singing a Hank Williams tune in his hotel room. "I used a narrative folk voice—just a guy on a bar stool telling his story to a stranger on the next stool," he said. "I based the song on the crash of the construction industry in the late 1970s and the hard times that fell on my sister and her family." With a haunting harmonica-and-guitar opening, it tells in the first person the story of man remembering the romance of his young life, when he met Mary at age seventeen. But he got her pregnant, and the narrator has to marry and work construction to support his young family. But jobs are scarce. What has happened? Where has life gone? He tries not to remember the romance of hot summer nights holding his teenage love close:

> *Now those memories come back to haunt me*
> *they haunt me like a curse*
> *Is a dream a lie if it don't come true*
> *Or is it something worse*

The American dream is worse than a lie. It is a setup to keep us in line and to make us believe that we can fashion our own lives. In the end we can't. Springsteen, of course, is not alone in his assessment. Writers from Herman Melville and Richard Wright to Arthur Miller and Toni Morrison have all probed the underside of the

American dream. "You can't just be a dreamer," he has said. "That can become an illusion, which turns into a *delusion*. Having dreams is probably the most important thing in your life. But letting them mutate into delusions—that's poison."

The final song on *The River* can be taken as one ending to a story that began when the narrator and Mary in "Thunder Road" pulled out of town to win: "Wreck on the Highway" (the title taken from a Roy Acuff song) is a first-person tale of a guy who sees, driving home from work, an awful accident on the side of the road, blood and glass everywhere, the victim calling for help. The narrator gets home, but in the middle of the night he tells us, "I sit up in the darkness" and think about that wreck on the highway. The song, Springsteen has said, "is about confronting one's own death and stepping into the adult world where time is finite."

Born to Run, *Darkness on the Edge of Town*, and *The River* are best treated as a trilogy that offers an ongoing meditation on dreams and darkness, escape and entrapment, freedom versus fate. *Born to Run* launched Springsteen's exploration of those dreams. We may die chasing them. Or perhaps they chase us and track us down. In the end they are all we have, the dream of love, the dream of escape, the dream of redemption, the dream of blowing away the dream, and while the story almost always ends badly, every so often we manage to connect with a love that is not at all a dream. Rather, we know it is wild and fully real.

FOUR

THE GEOGRAPHY OF *BORN TO RUN*

The primary questions I'd be writing about for the rest of my work life first took form in the songs on Born to Run *("I want to know if love is real"). It was the album where I left behind my adolescent definitions of love and freedom.* Born to Run *was the dividing line.*

—BRUCE SPRINGSTEEN, 1998

CRAWDADDY'S PETER KNOBLER asked Springsteen in 1975 if there was a concept behind the album. "The only concept that was around *Born to Run*," he answered, "was that I wanted to make a *big* record, you know, that sounds like these words. Just like a car, *zoom*, straight ahead, that when the sucker comes on it's the *wide open*. No holds barred."

To achieve the sound he desired, he relied on the band in ways he hadn't previously. It was on *Born to Run* that Springsteen defined his role as bandleader more than guitar player. On the album, "I really went towards the band," he said in September 1975. "It's not acoustic at all—there's no acoustic guitar, I don't think. A little more in the band direction."

Early in his career, Springsteen realized there was any number of virtuoso guitar players. He came of age, after all, in what he called "the day of the guitarist. Alvin Lee and Jeff Beck and Clapton and Hendrix." He was the fastest local gun, but he knew already that there would be more to his music than blazing electric

97

guitar: "There's a lot of guys who play really well. There's not a lot of guys who *write* that well." He explained: "If I was going to create my own point of view, my own vision, it wasn't going to be instrumentally—it was going to be more through songwriting . . . I became more arrangement oriented, I got more interested in how the thing was going to function as an ensemble."

In an interview weeks after the release of the album, he elaborated on his influences and his perception of himself as a bandleader: "Whatever I hear, I digest very quickly, and it comes back out the way I want it to. All the Stax stuff and Atlantic stuff, I'm very into that. Wilson Pickett, Sam Cooke, Sam and Dave, Eddie Floyd, the MGs, Steve Cropper . . . The best band leaders of the last ten, twenty years have been your soul band leaders. They whip them bands into shape. I tend to use my band that way. I'm doing different things, but in that tradition." He especially admired the control James Brown had over his band: "He spits and those guys do somersaults. It's incredible."

On *Born to Run*, Springsteen said, "I really started to develop a musical personality of my own." That meant leaving behind the obvious musical influences that informed the first two albums and finding a voice and a sound that, in fusing and transcending the work of scores of other artists, became uniquely his own.

The album, he said at the time, was deeply personal. In a keen insight into the work, he suggested that "the strain of the whole album comes through on the album." Lyrically, "most of the songs are about being, like, nowhere. Just being out there in the void. Every song on the album is about that, I think. About being, like, nowhere and trying to make heads and tails out of it, trying to figure it out?"

If Springsteen felt lost while writing and recording *Born to*

Run, he also created a cast of characters who struggled to be found and to find an escape from loneliness and a place for love. There is narrative coherence to the album. Part of that unity is a remnant of Springsteen's original concept, which was for the songs to represent the passing of a full day in the characters' lives. Springsteen abandoned that idea. But he embraced the characters on the album by making them "less eccentric and less local . . . They could have been anybody and everybody . . . These were the beginnings of the characters whose lives I would trace in my work for the next two decades."

The importance of place in Springsteen's music is no secret. Long ago Dave Marsh, in his biography *Born to Run*, discussed Springsteen's "remarkably specific sense of place." Bob Crane, in *A Place to Stand*, has gone further, probing in depth the way Springsteen "allows [place] to take shape as a character, and, at its best, as a force that influences the choices and decisions of his protagonists." Springsteen says that from early on, "I began to write about the importance of place in your life, the way you carry the texture of a place forever. There's not a lot of rock music about that. My first record, *Greetings from Asbury Park, N.J.*, they wanted me to say I was from New York. New Jersey was just no place to be from, like saying, 'Hi, I'm from Nowhere,' but for some reason, I liked the idea that you're dealt a certain hand of cards and you have to make something of it. Didn't change my name either."

If his "early albums were about being someplace and what it was like there," then, Springsteen thought, "*Born to Run* is about being nowhere at all." Springsteen commented on this when *Born to Run* was released. In an interview, Peter Knobler mentions that the album seems far from Asbury Park, and Bruce responds, "I was going to have a song about back home on it, but I didn't get to it.

There's a few oblique references. But most of the songs are about being nowhere. Just being out there in the void. Every song on the album is about that, I think. About being nowhere and trying to make heads and tails out of it, trying to figure it out? It's such a personal album." What he meant was that the specific settings themselves matter far less than "the idea behind the settings." Springsteen's comment speaks to the journey of escape and search for love that is at the heart of the album. But there is also the geography of being lost, the geography of being nowhere at all. The contours of *Born to Run* build on an exploration of spatial, temporal, and moral geography.

An understanding of that geography begins with the album cover, which is pure dynamic movement. The cover is a classic, beautifully designed by John Berg and Andy Engel and with a cover photograph taken by Eric Meola that is one of the iconic images in rock history. Meola, only a year older than Bruce, has gone on to a distinguished career as a professional commercial and artistic photographer. At the time, he was a fan as much as a photographer: He had seen Bruce perform several times in the few years since opening his studio in 1971 and had spent time at the Record Plant while the album was being recorded. But getting Bruce into the studio in the late summer of 1975 was not easy. Springsteen kept canceling appointments to work on the album. Finally, Meola couldn't stand it anymore and he told Mike Appel that either Springsteen makes the next appointment or there wouldn't be another one.

When Springsteen and Clemons arrived on June 20, 1975, for the photo session that would last only two hours (yet yield more than seven hundred images), Meola had a firm sense of where Springsteen came from and what his early music represented. He

Born to Run album cover. (COURTESY BRUCE SPRINGSTEEN, ERIC MEOLA, AND SONY BMG)

had discussed beforehand shooting in black and white, and Bruce and Clarence brought with them a variety of black and white props—a radio, sneakers, hats. Meola was seeking a certain look: "I wanted something that was nearly impossible to print, but beautiful to look at if printed perfectly—somehow innocent yet street-smart." They discussed nothing as far as setup or look. "I would just shoot," Meola recalls. "He wanted Clarence on the cover from the beginning, and the whole thing of isolating them against a white background just worked."

Meola took some stunning shots that day: a portrait of Bruce beneath a fire escape; a shot of Bruce with Clarence's disembodied arm pushing him; an intimate portrait of Bruce smiling that appears in the liner notes along with the words to the songs. And he took multiple exposures of the scene that would become the iconic cover. It is clear why almost all of these were rejected. Leaning back-to-back, Bruce and Clarence seem less joined together and more in dynamic tension to each other. And Bruce looks grim—no joy here. Bruce's arm on Clarence's shoulder and smile is much better. But only in one image is his hand on the neck of the guitar, and that makes a significant difference in the balance of the composition. The outtakes would be used by Columbia in advertisements.

The final cover photograph still rivets our attention. "The cover said it all," Springsteen later explained. Clemons recalled, "I set the pose up. I stood up and struck a pose and Bruce leaned in on me. And it was perfect." Springsteen leans on his bandmate. He is wearing a leather jacket, and the dangling belt buckle and long flowing hair create a sense of motion. Bruce is dressed casually, even sloppily: His T-shirt is ripped; his necklace slightly twisted. The shadows and play of black and white that Meola recorded add to the depth and dimensionality of the shot. Look at Bruce's hand holding

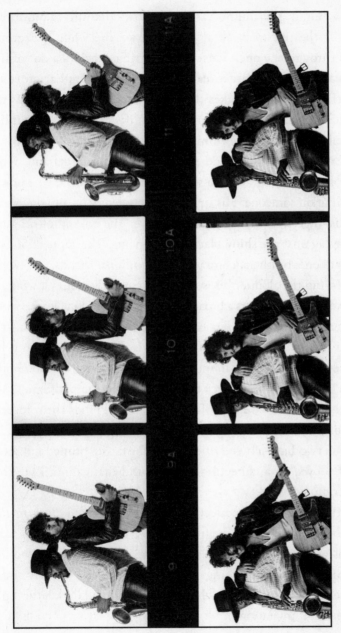

Born to Run cover shoot contact sheet. (© ERIC MEOLA 2006)

up his guitar. The thumb casts a shadow. His fingers move from white at the tips to black at the knuckle. The white background pours through the open spaces. His earring provides a dot of light in a sea of darkness. Bruce leans one way and the guitar provides a powerful horizon that takes the eye in another direction. His profile is cherubic. His eyes gleam; his grin lifts his face. It is as if he is remembering something funny and is going to share it with us.

Bruce is not alone, and this is the central drama and significance of the photograph. To see only the album cover, we know he is leaning on someone. His right arm rests gently on a higher shoulder, his fingertips just scraping the sleeve. The bottom of his guitar touches against the shiny black leather pants. The connection is an intimate one: brothers, comrades, companions, friends.

To flip the album over is to see Clarence Clemons blowing into his saxophone. He wears a broad-brimmed black fedora, leather pants, a white shirt lined with sets of black stripes. The whites of his eyes glance toward Bruce and half his face is illuminated, the other in darkness. Clemons too is in motion, playing, leaning, even bumping.

Opening the fold gives the full force of the photograph and design. These men are happy, and rock 'n' roll binds them together on a journey. The print type is so unassuming and underplayed it is as if the two have left the titles in the dust. The printed names are like shadows, an architectural background that cannot keep these men confined.

The cover works perfectly for an album titled *Born to Run*. Even before we listen to the first song, we know that this is a narrative of action: moving, going, running, hiding, riding, looking, searching, meeting, reaching. The two men are on a journey and we receive the album, with its white background and dark lettering, as we would an invitation.

® "COLUMBIA," ® MARCAS REG. © 1975 CBS INC.

Prisoners of
Rock and Roll.

A labor of Love.
Bruce Springsteen's
long-awaited
release,
"Born to Run."

On Columbia Records ®
and Tapes.

Bruce Springsteen
Born To Run
including:
Night/Jungleland
Backstreets/Thunder Road/She's The One

Advertisement for *Born to Run*.

That Springsteen chose to be represented with Clemons deepens the resonance of the album by connecting it to a long-standing cultural tradition of pairs on journeys of self-discovery. Race is an important factor here. In literature and film, there are numerous biracial pairs on journeys of various kinds: Ishmael and Queequeg in *Moby Dick*; Huck and Jim in *The Adventures of Huckleberry Finn*; Tony Curtis and Sidney Poitier in *The Defiant Ones*. But these pairs are seldom equals. They are all outsiders—orphans or criminals—who are escaping something.

Bruce and Clarence, too, may be running away, because what is rock 'n' roll if not escape from complacency and convention into exuberance and rebellion? But if their dream is one of escape, they dream it as equals and partners. The message of racial egalitarianism is extraordinary by the standards of the day, when so few rock bands were integrated. This is a curious phenomenon that has not been explored thoroughly enough. It is well-known, of course, that rock's roots run deep in the tradition of black rhythm-and-blues artists. And audiences for rock shows in the fifties were often desegregated. But when it came to playing rock music, there were white artists and black artists and little crossover. Few bands from the 1960s and 1970s were integrated. Booker T. and the MGs, the Jimi Hendrix Experience, Sly & the Family Stone, and Love each had album covers that showed black and white musicians together. And that is about it until *Born to Run*.

Springsteen is not trying to make any kind of statement. David Sancious and Ernest Carter are also black, making the first incarnation of the E Street Band one of the most integrated rock 'n' roll bands in history. Over the years, Clarence has also played sidekick and foil to Springsteen's onstage antics, never more so than during "Tenth Avenue Freeze-Out." Commentators have made much of Bruce kissing Clarence on the lips, and dancing and bumping with him, and proclaiming him king of the world and master of the universe. However one chooses to read the theatricality of their onstage relationship, they are bound together in a common journey of liberation that is all the more achievable because they are not alone.

There is another presence on the cover of *Born to Run*. Attached to Springsteen's guitar strap is an Elvis Presley Fan Club Pin. Only the gleaming white edge of the pin and a silhouetted figure are visible. The badge reads, at the top, ELVIS THE KING and, below, FAN CLUB OF N.Y.C. On the sides of the Elvis portrait, it says KING'S COURT and ELVIS PRESLEY. Only members of a New York fan club received the pin, and what membership lists exist do not include Bruce, so it is unclear how he got the pin. What is clear is that he wore it to the *Born to Run* photo sessions and, in doing so, he intended to pay homage to the one figure whom he has time and again credited with changing his life and transforming society.

"Elvis is my religion," says Bruce. "But for him, I'd be selling encyclopedias right now." Watching Elvis on *The Ed Sullivan Show* led to his first guitar, but at age seven his hands had been too small to play it, so he put it aside for a few years. Still, he couldn't imagine "anyone *not* wanting to be Elvis Presley." Time and again Springsteen has talked about how rock 'n' roll saved his life, and the list of influences always begins with Elvis. In 1998, Bruce told Will Percy that "you could make an argument that one of the most socially conscious artists of the second half of this century was Elvis Presley, even if he didn't start out with any set of political ideas that he wanted to accomplish. He said, 'I'm all shook up and I want to shake you up,' and that's what happened. He had an enormous impact on the way that people lived, how they responded to themselves, to their own physicality, to the integration of their own nature."

Elvis saved Bruce twice over. He not only gave him a dream to pursue, but through Elvis's life Springsteen also learned how to survive the dream coming true. In 1976, in the midst of a hastily put-together tour of the South, Bruce found himself in Memphis. He, Van Zandt, and a publicist decided to take a taxi to Graceland. When Bruce got there at around three A.M, he saw lights on and thought, I gotta see if he's home. Springsteen climbed over the gate and started walking up the driveway. A guard stopped him near the house. Bruce asked if Elvis was home and the guard said he was in Lake Tahoe. He tried talking his way in, saying what a big rock star he had become. The guard gently ushered him toward the gate.

Years later, when Springsteen's own fame approached that of Elvis's, he came to a deeper understanding of the meaning of the episode. He admitted to a concert audience that he "used to wonder what I would have said if I had knocked on the door and if Elvis had come to the door. Because it really wasn't Elvis I was goin' to see, but it was like he came along and whispered some dream in everybody's ear and somehow we all dreamed it." In 1987 Springsteen told *Rolling Stone*, "I do not believe that the essence of the rock 'n' roll idea was to exalt the cult of personality. That is a sidetrack, a dead-end street. That is not the thing to do. And I've been as guilty of it as anybody in my life. When I jumped over that wall to meet Elvis that night, I didn't know who I was gonna meet. And the guard who stopped me at the door did me the biggest favor of my life. I had misunderstood. It was innocent, and I was havin' a ball, but it wasn't right. In the end, you cannot live inside that dream."

Springsteen's mature reflections on the price and meaning of fame would allow him to continue to do his work and escape a lonely or tragic end. This was all in the future. The twenty-four-year-old kid who wore an Elvis fan club button believed in the saving power of rock 'n' roll and marveled at how Presley's music "came in and took away so many people's loneliness and gave so many people a reason and a sense of all the possibilities of living." Maybe *Born to Run* could do something similar.

On the album cover, Bruce and Clarence are not lost. They are headed somewhere, dreaming of somewhere, a runaway dream. They may not know the precise destination, but they are searching, and we are invited along on the journey. That journey on the album's eight songs covers a spatial geography of roads, streets, avenues, highways, and lanes to which the songs refer. It is also the city, the beach, the park, the river, and the jungle. There are specific locations named—Highway 9, Harlem, Stockton's Wing, to cite a few—but the specific seem to carry less freight than they did on his previous album where E Street, Asbury Park, 57th Street, and New York City figured prominently in the titles.

Born to Run is less particularistic, and therefore more accessible and inclusive. For us to feel that we are partaking in the journey, not just hearing about it, it helps that the geography is largely generic. "When the screen door slams on 'Thunder Road,'" Springsteen explained later, "you're not necessarily on the Jersey Shore anymore. You could be anywhere in America."

Springsteen says he took the title for "Thunder Road" from a poster for the Robert Mitchum movie. Only after imagining the place did he find it. He was in the desert one summer, driving to Nevada. He came across a house with a picture of Geronimo with the word *landlord* on it and a sign that said, THIS IS THE LAND OF PEACE, LOVE, JUSTICE AND NO MERCY. It pointed down a little dirt lane that said Thunder Road.

The physical space of "Thunder Road" positions outside against inside, and that screen door slamming in the opening line is the boundary. "Don't run back inside," the narrator says after Mary appears on the porch. "These two lanes will take us anywhere," he swears. The narrator offers his hand to bring her from the porch to the front seat and implores her to climb in. The word *climb* does its work perfectly: It has the connotation of rising, of conquering the limitations of space for movement upward.

Together Mary and the narrator will leave "a town full of losers." In the geography of *Born to Run*, towns and cities are noxious places. "This town rips the bones from your back/It's a death trap, it's a suicide rap," warns the title song. The city is a jungle, where one is "stranded," as in "Tenth Avenue Freeze-Out," or where one hears "the whole damn city crying," as in "Backstreets," or where, in "Jungleland," the Rat is gunned down "in the tunnels uptown."

The characters in *Born to Run* are trapped by the space they inhabit: They have their "back to the wall," ("Tenth Avenue Freeze-Out") or they are "stranded in the park" ("Backstreets"), or they "struggle in dark corners" ("Jungleland"). Roads, avenues, highways, and streets offer the way out, but they are not themselves benign or ideal places. "Thunder Road" is "lying out there like a killer in the sun," "Tenth Avenue" is on the wrong side of town and greets you all alone in a freeze-out, the highway is "jammed with broken heroes," and "the street's on fire in a real death waltz."

And so in the geography of *Born to Run*, place is not the location for finding salvation and love. Instead, a different geography offers the possibility of escape—the geography of time. In *Born to Run*, time of life (youth), time of day (night), and time of year (summer) are paramount.

One line in "Thunder Road" encapsulates the sense of time

that runs through the album: "So you're scared and you're thinking/ That maybe we ain't that young anymore/Show a little faith, there's magic in the night." It is remarkable to think that Springsteen wrote the line about not feeling young anymore when he was twenty-four, and that it resonated as profoundly as it did among a generation of late teens for whom *Born to Run* was the defining album of their lives. The song "Born to Run" repeats the message: "We gotta get out while we're young." (It is worth noting that in *Wings for Wheels*, he sings, "I wish I could take you to some sandy beach where we'd never grow old.")

Of course youth culture has always been central to American history. This was the new world, free of the corruptions of the old. From the American Revolution onward, rebellions political, social, and cultural were spearheaded by youth. The countercultural revolution of the 1950s and 1960s, of which rock 'n' roll was a crucial component, was no different. Whether it was Beats or hippies, teenagers and young adults came to shape the dominant culture not only with music but also films, literature, art, and television both about and for them. "Born to Run" became the anthem of the next generation, and no song captures more completely, in words and music, the euphoric hopes and romantic dreams of the young.

The fear of not being young anymore, even among those in their teens and early twenties, was a specific fear tied to a generational moment that helps explain the power and success of *Born to Run*. In the summer of 1975 those in their late teens felt especially lost. They had missed out on the Beat rebellion of the 1950s and the civil rights and antiwar movements of the 1960s, but those impulses to challenge authority were part of their makeup. Yet it felt like the conflict of us versus them was quickly morphing into the world of "me." In the mid-seventies, a sense of national and personal malaise reigned. Nixon resigned, the Vietnam War ended ignominiously, and even rock 'n' roll itself seemed stagnant: It had been ten years since Dylan sent shock waves with "Like a Rolling Stone" and his performance at the Newport Folk Festival.

When the album was released, Springsteen spoke to the cultural shift from the 1960s to the 1970s: "What's happened in the '70s is that people are starting to worry about themselves . . . Looking out for number one. People have gotten very cynical, and have lost that sense of unity and community—which may have been superficial in the '60s, but it was there. People have gotten a little too jaded and cynical to go for that too much, and they don't trust anybody and they don't believe anything they hear. That's the climate of the country right now."

Thirty years later, Springsteen offered an equally cogent analysis of the impact of *Born to Run*. Interviewed on public radio's *Morning Edition* in April 2005, he was asked specifically about "thinking we're not that young anymore." His answer deserves to be quoted at length:

> The thing people tend to forget about *Born to Run* is that it was post-Watergate, post-Vietnam. People just didn't feel that young anymore, and that is part of what made that record present, because I was dealing with a lot of classic rock imagery and classic rock sounds but I was writing in a particular moment when people had sort of their legs cut out from underneath them. People weren't sure where to stand or where the country was going or what we were going to be about, and a lot of that searching for home and searching for place—that's what all the characters are doing. They're leaving something—they're leaving something and they're going somewhere they don't know where

they're going. They're trying to find some people to accompany them. Somebody they love or care about. But they're in the middle, they're in the no-man's-land between here and there. I think that's what it felt like in those days. It managed to combine a certain youthful optimism with a certain amount of weariness and a spiritual searching, people moving through a pretty dark world. So that was its currency, and that's why it lasted.

"Searching for a place" speaks to the geography that is the essence of the album. That place is not spatial but temporal, and if the chronological geography of the album is peopled by youth, the essence of time is the night. It is under cover of night and into the night that one makes one's getaway, that one finds freedom or meets fate.

"Night" is the anthem of this temporal geography, and it permeates *Born to Run*. The day is marked by working nine to five in a joyless job trying to "survive till the night," which is the only time you feel alive. "Out on a midnight run," in search of love, "off you scream into the night."

The album opens with the declaration on "Thunder Road" that "there's magic in the night." The narrator and Mary will be "riding out tonight to case the promised land." In "Tenth Avenue Freeze-Out," "the night is dark." In "Backstreets," doomed lovers are "slow dancing in the dark," where "in the deep heart of the night" they could be set "loose from everything." But "laying here in the dark," the narrator absorbs those "tears of faithlessness."

The title song is also a night song. The dramatic opening juxtaposes the sweat of day with the glory of night. Perhaps one day the narrator and Wendy will "walk in the sun," but just as likely they will die "on the streets tonight/In an everlasting kiss." In "She's the One," the sun is a midnight sun and desire hits hardest "at night when you're kneeling in the dark." Finally, the dramas of "Meeting Across the River" and "Jungleland" take place at night. The night is "holy" and lovers become "desperate as the night moves on."

The night doesn't guarantee love, but it is the landscape in which one might find it. The profundity of *Born to Run* is that it is no simple paean to happiness. Springsteen knows that freedom and fate, optimism and pessimism, light and darkness, joy and sadness, are all bound together. "We'll live with the sadness," he states in "Born to Run." "Her love could save you from the bitterness," he declares in "She's the One." In "Night," "You run sad and free." There are no clean breaks from the past, and not even the night, where, as in "Jungleland," you can "wind up wounded, not even dead," assures victory. But it is the starting point for any journey of escape and discovery.

Born to Run is not an album about any night, but a summer night. Springsteen and summer go together, of course, like pick and guitar. Springsteen's music is the music of the streets and the shore and sweaty nights. No doubt one reason for the references to summer in the songs is that Bruce was in the studio all summer in 1975 furiously trying to finish the album. In narrating the birth pangs of the album, Dave Marsh describes the endless sessions in the studio and how neither Bruce nor Landau nor Appel "had any vestige of a tan; their skins were ivory white, like rock and roll ghosts."

Springsteen transferred what he didn't get to experience outdoors in the summer of 1975 and earlier into the lyrics he wrote indoors. Given the pressure on Springsteen to succeed with this album, and considering the turmoil of the recording sessions, the line in "Thunder Road" about wasting "your summer praying in vain/ For a savior to rise from these streets" takes on added meaning. For many, Springsteen himself would be that savior, but both he and the narrator of "Thunder Road" reject that role for the summer simplicity of rolling down the window and letting the wind blow back your hair.

In "Tenth Avenue Freeze-Out," the narrator is "taking all the heat they was giving." "Backstreets" takes place during a "soft infested summer," and the characters are "getting wasted in the heat." "Born to Run" begins with sweat, and the "kids are huddled on the beach." The title character in "She's the One" (originally titled "Virgin Summer Nights") will "fill them long summer nights." And in "Jungleland," a barefoot girl is "drinking warm beer in the soft summer rain." Just as the night can both liberate and destroy, so too is summer both a dreamland and a wasteland.

Finally, *Born to Run* is imbued not only with a geography of space and a geography of time, but also a moral geography that runs from love and faith to hatred and loss. From "Thunder Road" to "Backstreets" and again from "Born to Run" to "Jungleland," the album moves from the hope of salvation to the despair of defeat.

Faith, praying, savior, redemption, promised land: The vocabulary of "Thunder Road" is a religious lexicon of salvation. *Born to Run* is where Springsteen's spiritual interests, rooted deep in his Catholic upbringing, first take shape. "I guess in *Born to Run*," Springsteen said in 1984, "there's that searchin' thing; that record to me is like religiously based, in a funny kind of way. Not like orthodox religion, but it's about basic things, you know? That searchin', and faith, and the idea of hope."

Morality is not achieved by slavishly adhering to conformity, but by having the courage to break free of conventions. "Darling you know just what I'm here for," the narrator declares. What is he there for? Love? Sex? Companionship? He tells her she's not a beauty, but that's okay, there is still magic to be made. He invites her to find redemption "beneath this dirty hood," which refers to his car but is also sexually suggestive. "All the promises'll be broken," he offers. What promises? The promise to be good? The promise not to become entangled with the boys Mary has time and again "sent away"? The promise not to run off? We want Mary in the end to go along for the ride, to choose victory over defeat, and perhaps even to find love along that "dusty beach road."

In the morality tale of "Backstreets," infidelity destroys friends who had become lovers and takes with it the dream of breaking free. The love that exists from the start is no romantic ideal. Rather it is "hard and filled with defeat." Other lovers are "desperate." Terry's infidelity breeds breakdown and hatred. But perhaps the worst part of it all is the realization that the everyday and commonplace is their fate. "And after all this time to find we're just like all the rest" is perhaps the most painful lesson of the affair. There is no escape possible; heroes exist only in the movies, and we can't be like them. In "Thunder Road," the narrator proclaims, "I'm no hero." And in "Born to Run," the "highway's jammed with broken heroes." Escape will come, if at all, from being who you are and not from who "we thought we had to be."

When the dream and promise of escape and love on the road and the backstreets is destroyed, it leaves scars that seem never to heal. In "The Promise," a song written the year after *Born to Run* appeared—and unreleased until *18 Tracks* in 1999—the narrator declares, "When the promise was broken, I cashed in a few of my dreams." The song ends, "Thunder Road, for the lost lovers and all the fixed games . . . /Thunder Road, we were gonna take it all and throw it all away."

The dialectic of freedom and fate, love and hatred, is repeated on side two of *Born to Run*. In the title song, the narrator and Wendy will break free, even if the only way to do so is by dying out on the streets. By contrast, in "Jungleland" the protagonists "reach for their moment," but they do not reach their destination. "Jungleland" is a world of shadows and violence, where rock bands become gangs and desperate struggle is all one can hope for. Religious imagery permeates this song: The action occurs on a "holy night," and an organ plays behind the phrase "from the churches to the jails." There are "visionaries" in the parking lot, but the night envelops them.

For an album that is so full of life and desire, death haunts the record much as those ghosts that haunt the dusty beach roads of "Thunder Road," where "heaven's waiting." The "light of the living" in "Tenth Avenue Freeze-Out" suggests the darkness of the dead. In "Night," "somehow you survive." In "Backstreets," people are "hurt bad some really dying." "She's the One" has "killer graces," a smile that kills. "Meeting Across the River" is a "last chance," and "Jungleland" is a "death waltz."

Young lovers dying tragically is a romantic strain that goes back centuries, and Springsteen is playing with the clichés while imbuing them with narrative and musical vitality and originality, much as *West Side Story* reimagined *Romeo and Juliet*. The trope was a staple of the pop rock of Springsteen's youth: "Teen Angel" and "Tell Laura I Love Her," both from 1960, and "Leader of the Pack," from 1965. And the link between rock 'n' roll and tragic death became enshrined when Buddy Holly perished in a plane crash in 1959. The year before, Danny and the Juniors sang, "Rock 'n' roll is here to stay/It will never die." Only the music, which so often was about tragedy and death, would live on.

In the moral universe of *Born to Run*, dying is not to be feared if with it one finds everlasting love. All of us are scared; all of us are lonely. And all we seek in this hard-working, soul-trying, dream-breaking life of ours is the knowledge that love is wild, love is real. "We're gonna get to that place/Where we really want to go/and we'll walk in the sun," the narrator bravely predicts. In the geography of *Born to Run*, that "place" may be an actual location, or it may be a particular time, or it may be a place in our hearts that gives us the faith to carry on.

FIVE

THE RECEPTION OF *BORN TO RUN*

After it was finished? I hated it! I couldn't stand to listen to it. I thought it was the worst piece of garbage I'd ever heard

—BRUCE SPRINGSTEEN, 1976

WITH THE RELEASE of *Born to Run* in August 1975, Springsteen became a national sensation. But as John Rockwell pointed out in the *New York Times* on August 15, 1975, if stardom was to come, it was a well-deserved fame years in the making. Rockwell attended the August shows at the Bottom Line and deemed them "among the great rock experiences of those lucky enough to get in." He went on to praise Springsteen as "a great lyricist and songwriter, he is a wonderful singer, guitarist and piano player, and he has one of the best rock bands anybody has ever heard, and he is as charismatic a stage figure as rock has produced."

The dilemma, Rockwell pointed out, was that the first two albums did not sell, and the record company seemed to be losing interest. One reason was that Clive Davis, president at Columbia when Bruce signed, was forced out. With a change in the executive offices came a change in the company's enthusiasm. Another reason was that Springsteen's manager, Mike Appel, struck people as arrogant and aggressive. Executives simply did not want to deal with his demands. Perhaps most noteworthy of all, Bruce's wide-ranging talents made it difficult for him to decide what he should be doing musically. "The indecision," Landau later said, "comes from fear. If you do one thing that means you can't do another. Bruce wants it all. He always wants it all."

Paul Nelson made similar points in a piece published in the *Village Voice*, titled "Is Bruce Springsteen Worth the Hype?" Nelson was in a good position to answer. He was one of the few critics to applaud Dylan's jump from folk to rock, and he wrote for a number of publications, including *Rolling Stone*. About the Bottom Line shows, Nelson observed that "when you can achieve just about anything you want onstage, it's hard not to stay there until you've rung all the bells, and one often gets the feeling that Bruce is having so much fun he'd gladly pay the crowd to let him do just that."

The problem was capturing the live experience on record. With the album finally done, Nelson reported that "in the studio, Bruce was astigmatic and shortsighted, a perfectionist who frequently took the long way around simply because he didn't know the short one. That depression had set in would be an understatement." The result, however, was well worth the wait. "For me," Nelson reported, *Born to Run* is "his best record, curbing most of the excess but none of the force of the only artist I know who could combine the sound of Phil Spector with the singing of Roy Orbison (the names come from Bruce)."

John Rockwell was already listening to *Born to Run* at the time of his initial article, and two weeks later he published the first major review: "Springsteen's Rock Poetry at Its Best." The album, Rockwell asserted, "should be all [Springsteen] needs to push him over the top."

Rockwell gushed: "Mr. Springsteen's gifts are so powerful and so diverse that it's difficult even to try to describe them in a short space. Sometimes his lyrics still lapse too close to self-conscious mythmaking but generally they epitomize urban folk poetry at its best . . . And Mr. Springsteen's themes perfectly summarize the rock experience, full of cars and love, street macho and desperate aspiration. Hearing these songs is like hearing your own life in music, even if you never lived in New Jersey."

Rockwell also commented on the music, which "stays true to its essential simplicity and directness, even if the textures can approach almost orchestral richness." He concluded that *Born to Run* "seems one of the great records in recent years . . . you owe it to yourself to buy this record."

On September 1, *Newsweek* published an assessment under the title "Bruce Is Loose." Simultaneously reporting the hype and adding to it, the piece said that Springsteen "inspires the sort of pandemonium that recalls the glory days of Mick Jagger, the Beatles and Elvis Presley." *Born to Run*, claimed the authors, "reveals Bruce Springsteen to be perhaps the most adept high priest of rock's most dominant pitch these days—eclecticism . . . he is also an immensely assured vocalist and guitarist. Backed by his terrifically tight band . . . Springsteen rocks passionately with a throaty, virile, roomy baritone. But it is also a voice filled with other voices, a sensibility saturated with other sensibilities."

It was a good review, read by a national audience, but Bruce had earned good reviews before. Heading into the fall it remained to be seen whether *Born to Run* would sell. Certainly, Robert Hilburn's assessment in the *Los Angeles Times*, at the end of September, helped build excitement, especially since Bruce and the band were readying to leave for a string of shows at the Roxy in Los Angeles.

Hilburn began his review by talking about Elvis and the fragmentation of rock into various subcategories—country, jazz, pop. He introduced Springsteen by declaring, "Now we have someone with the ambition, instincts and vision to put some of the pieces back together. That's where Bruce Springsteen comes in. He is the purest glimpse of the passion and power of rock 'n' roll in nearly a decade. His *Born to Run* album comes to grips with the emotional essence of rock 'n' roll so well that I think it could give even Elvis chills. If Elvis ever heard 'Thunder Road' from the album, it might make him phone Sam Phillips, get back into the studio in Memphis and get serious about his music once more."

As much as Hilburn loved the album, he had some criticisms. He thought the sources of his ideas—whether Orbison or Spector— were too evident, that some of the lyrics were not up to the music (he pointed to the rhyming of *bell* and *hell* in "Night"), and that some of the production was uneven (he called the trumpet in "Meeting Across the River" a "Broadway skyline cliché"). Still, he thought, the album belonged alongside the best ever made. Ten years later, Hilburn offered this assessment: "*Born to Run* breathed with the same kind of discovery that made Elvis Presley's *Sun Sessions* and Bob Dylan's *Highway 61 Revisited* the two most important rock albums before it. Listening to all three works, you feel present at the forging of a major artistic vision. You sense the artist's excitement at finding something within himself that he hadn't known was there until it burst forth in the studio."

In October, *Rolling Stone* published a follow-up by John Rockwell and a review of the album, written by Greil Marcus. Rockwell continued to wax eloquent about the Bottom Line shows and contemplate the nature of stardom. What he appreciated especially about Springsteen was that he took the history of all musical styles seriously, recycling and reinterpreting "bits and pieces from so many rock, pop, R&B and even Broadway artists of the past twenty years—from Elvis to Dylan to the Drifters to Van Morrison to

Leonard Bernstein and his *West Side Story*." Springsteen, Rockwell observed, "has gone on to make an original statement that owes its depth to that very past."

Such was the genius of *Born to Run*. Springsteen may have felt like a postheroic figure, lamenting the lost musical world of early rock, soul, and R&B. He was playing at a historical moment when rock had lost its way, and by singing about a vanished world and characters trapped in lives of meaninglessness he reenergized that world and, with a fusion of musical styles old and new, gave it urgency. "*Born to Run*," Rockwell reported, "seems to be catching on nationwide with a vengeance."

Greil Marcus's review showed why he was the premier rock critic of his generation. Reviewer and columnist for *Rolling Stone*, Marcus had just published *Mystery Train*, a book of essays that brought rock criticism to the level of the best literary criticism. He began the review by saying that rumors of the live performances had reached him in California, and he felt deprived about not having seen the band live because the first two albums gave him little reason to believe the hype: "Both seemed at once flat and more than a little hysterical, full of sound and fury, and signifying, if not nothing, not much."

Marcus delivered his verdict about the third album early on: "It is a magnificent album that pays off on every bet ever placed on him—a '57 Chevy running on melted-down Crystals records that shuts down every claim that has been made. And it should crack his future wide open."

"The stories Springsteen is telling," Marcus noted, "are nothing new, though no one has ever told them better or made them matter more. Their familiar romance is half the power . . . We know the story: one thousand and one American nights, one long night of fear and love." The lyrics were glorious, but the music made the album special: "What is new is the majesty Springsteen and his band have brought to the story. Springsteen's singing, his words and the band's music have turned the dreams and failures two generations have dropped along the road into an epic—an epic that began when that car went over the cliff in *Rebel without a Cause*."

Marcus called the guitar lines in "Born to Run" "the finest compression of the rock & roll thrill since the opening riffs of 'Layla,'" and the opening of "Backstreets" "so stately, so heartbreaking, that it might be the prelude to a rock & roll version of the *Iliad*." Marcus makes a central point about the relationship between the lyrics, which are largely indistinct on the first few hearings (Springsteen was urged to have them printed on the album and did so), and exhilarating music that tells the story wordlessly: "To hear Springsteen sing the line 'Hiding on the backstreets' is to be captured by an image; the details can come later. Who needed to figure out all the words to 'Like a Rolling Stone' to understand it?"

Marcus put the theme and meaning of the album this way: "You take what you find, but you never give up your demand for something better because you know, in your heart, that you deserve it."

Lester Bangs, who had been fired from *Rolling Stone* in 1973 and now edited *Creem*, a monthly rock magazine published out of Detroit, also offered a glowing assessment. Bangs, like Marcus, began by locating himself geographically, in his case in the Midwest, where he had not seen Springsteen but where already there was skepticism about all the hype from the "extravagant claims" that had been made about the rock performer. "You can smell the backlash crisp as burnt rubber in the air," Bangs reckoned, but none of it was forthcoming from him. Instead, he expressed little doubt that *Born to Run* would be the "finest record released this year."

Like other commentators before him, Bangs noted that Springsteen was rooted in 1950s rebellion movies "filtered through Sixties songs." What made him extraordinary was that "he reminds us what it's like to love rock 'n' roll like you just discovered it, and then seize it and make it your own with certainty and precision." Bangs especially appreciated that lyrically Springsteen had tightened up his style, "no longer cramming as many syllables as possible into every line." Commenting on life in the 1970s as "a time of squalor and belittled desire," Bangs praised Springsteen's music as "majestic and passionate with no apologies."

In one of the first reviews of his career, Jon Pareles, who would go on to *Crawdaddy, Rolling Stone,* and a position as chief music critic at the *New York Times,* predicted that "*Born to Run* will be the album that brings Springsteen stardom." He offered an insightful take on the change from the first two albums: Calling Springsteen a "thinking man's delinquent," Pareles noted that "he's lonelier on *Born to Run.* Exuberance has turned to paranoia. Less biographical now, closer to the allegory, Springsteen is forced toward one more American Dream—escape."

Pareles was not only tuned to the lyrical shifts but the musical as well, and with the latter he was not necessarily persuaded that more was better: "Someone convinced Springsteen to suspend his pure funk sense of dynamics and timing it seems. Most of the songs just roar flat out, accelerator to the floor, volume control at ten." Of course, that was the point, but in the process Pareles thought that songs such as "Backstreets" suffered from too much reverb and that "She's the One" pounded too hard too quickly. Springsteen might be "excessive in every direction at once . . . but he gets away with it."

At the *Village Voice*, Robert Christgau, who began writing rock criticism in 1967 for *Esquire* and would serve as music editor for the *Voice* for several decades, asked, "Just how much American myth can be crammed into one song, or a dozen, about asking your girl to come take a ride? A lot, but not as much as romanticists of the doomed outsider believe. Springsteen needs to learn that operatic pomposity insults the Ronettes and that pseudotragic beautiful loser fatalism insults us all. And around now I'd better add that the man avoids these quibbles at his best and simply runs them over the rest of the time. If 'She's the One' fails the memory of Phil Spector's innocent grandeur, well, the title cut is the fulfillment of everything 'Be My Baby' was about and lots more. Springsteen may well turn out to be one of those rare self-conscious primitives who gets away with it."

Pareles and Christgau both identified the elements in Springsteen's work that might have brought older listeners to despair: It was as much derivative of the pop sounds and themes of the early 1960s as a complement to them. But no one else understood how to revitalize past chords into present conditions. Springsteen did more than get away with it; he simultaneously made the past relevant while updating it, and he triumphed through sheer exuberance.

Writing in *Record World*, an industry publication, David McGee said that Springsteen was too smart and seasoned to allow stardom to affect him, "to become a victim of a runaway American dream." With *Born to Run*, McGee placed Springsteen in the pantheon of greats: Presley, Berry, Beatles, Stones, Dylan. His genius was to echo the past while hearkening to the future. "The music," McGee gushed, "is urgent, full of abrupt stops and startling changes of tempo; the lyrics tell powerful stories of characters on the edge, living out rock and roll dreams," dreams that in 1975 "are bleaker than those of the past." "If Brecht and Weill had written rock music," declared one critic, "they would have been reincarnated as Bruce Springsteen." Another writer offered that *Born to Run* just may be the most important album since the Beatles' *Sgt. Pepper's Lonely Hearts Club Band.*"

In *Circus Raves,* thirty-four year old Stephen Holden, who would go on to serve as music and film critic for the *New York Times,* also compared *Born to Run* to other great albums. In a piece titled "Springsteen Paints His Masterpiece," he placed it alongside *Exile on Main Street, Who's Next,* and *Layla* as one of the decade's great albums. The challenge of making *Born to Run* succeed "would not have been won were not the songs of such extraordinary caliber and Springsteen's singing so uninhibited. Both 'Backstreets' and 'Jungleland,'" Holden observed, "conclude with some remarkable singing— feral howls and moans of agonized despair whose intensity is bone-chilling." The sound here was "harsher and more sophisticated," moving beyond Dylan and Van Morrison. The result "is a cacophonous, near-monophonic density, best heard very loud." Holden praised the piano arpeggios of "Thunder Road," the "Shakespearian" curtain raiser of "Tenth Avenue Freeze-Out," the "tour-de-force" of "Jungleland," and, about "Born to Run," wrote: "I can't remember a more thrilling song of the road." In one of the most incisive cultural readings yet offered, Holden explained that "Springsteen embodies the myth of rock & roll as an urban, proletarian outburst. By personifying the poet-hood, boy-man, rebel-hero so central to the iconography of American mass culture from Brando, Dean, and Presley through Dylan, Springsteen reminds us that rock & roll came from the streets as a cultural necessity, an instinctual urge toward self-transcendence and self-definition. I've no doubt that rock & roll has literally saved Bruce Springsteen . . . Just as certainly, Bruce

Springsteen has arrived at the right time to help save rock music from its present state of enervation with his seemingly limitless energy and talent."

If Holden focused on the male myth of rock 'n' roll, another reviewer, Frank Rose, emphasized Springsteen's debt to girl-group rock: the Crystals, the Chiffons, the Ronettes, the Shangri-las, and the Shirelles. These "Doo-Wop Queens" offered "virtually the only type of rock which treated teenage daydreams, frustrations, triumphs, and heartbreaks like facts of life instead of subjects of unwitting parody." For Springsteen, those themes and the doo-wop sound, much of it produced by Phil Spector, marked a time that he wanted to revive as an alternative to the hard-rock drug culture that followed it. Springsteen himself says he never partook in drugs. "Rock has always been escape from reality," Rose wrote, but "the fog of drugs and revolution" had proven a dead end by 1975 and conformity once again was in force. Springsteen's characters are "cornered and looking desperately for a physical or emotional getaway." That is precisely what the girl groups sought as well: "They weren't seeking a higher state of consciousness in songs like 'Leader of the Pack'; they were waiting for deliverance . . . It's more than a little ironic that a decade after the Crystals' last hit, the agent of their deliverance should be so widely touted as ours—Maximum Punk come roaring down the boulevard in flesh and blood, faded denim and black leather, still on the lam, still looking for that never-never land where teen dreams come true."

Behind these initial reviews, as well as Springsteen's touring, the album climbed up the charts in the fall. Curiously, the only pan of the album came from a regional newspaper that covered the local music scene in New Jersey, New York, and Eastern Pennsylvania, Springsteen's backyard. Writing in the *Aquarian*, Joe Edwards called the album a "one-dimensional disappointment." Although he praised "Born to Run" as the best song of the decade, a song "which should be played if anyone ever asks for a clear, concise description of rock and roll," and he also raved about "Thunder Road" and "Backstreets," he concluded that the songs on the album were "formulaic, derivative, clumsily written, and produced in a heavy-handed way." He made no mention of "Jungleland." The review carries the hurt of a jilted lover. The *Aquarian* was there when Bruce started, and it didn't want to lose the poet of the streets and the shore. But he was no longer the secret of local journalists, and Edwards took some parting shots as Springsteen moved out onto the national scene.

Within weeks, the *Aquarian*'s worst fears came to pass when, in what surely was one of the great publicity coups of all time, Springsteen appeared simultaneously on the covers of *Time* and *Newsweek* on October 27. *Time*'s cover read ROCK'S NEW SENSATION above a day-glow portrait of Bruce in T-shirt and tam-o'-shanter, grinning widely with guitar pointed upward. Jay Cocks, who had written about Bruce for *Time* more than a year earlier, begins the piece on a somewhat cynical note, wondering how much of Springsteen is cultivated image and how much is authentic: "He nurtures the look of a lowlife romantic even though he does not smoke, scarcely drinks and disdains every kind of drug."

But by the second paragraph Cocks turns his attention to the music, which he describes as "primal, directly in touch with all the impulses of wild humor and glancing melancholy, street tragedy and punk anarchy that have made the distinctive voice of a generation." Cocks praised *Born to Run* as signifying a "regeneration, a renewal of rock." He attended the October shows at the Roxy in Los Angeles and wondered how the laid-back West Coast crowd

Time magazine, October 27, 1975. (REPRINTED THROUGH THE COURTESY OF THE EDITORS OF *TIME* MAGAZINE © 2008 TIME INC.)

would react to the energetic Eastern rocker. They loved it, responding with enthusiasm to the rock poet. Cocks, having followed Springsteen for a while, understood what others could not possibly know: After ten years of playing every gym and club that would have him, Springsteen, at the age of twenty-six, had "mastered the true stage secret of the rock pro: he seems to be letting go totally and fearlessly, yet the performance remains perfectly orchestrated." But that is not to say it is a sham. "The music is forever for me," Springsteen told Cocks. "It's the stage thing, that rush moment that you live for. It never lasts, but that's what you live for."

Letters to *Time* from readers following the cover story ran the gamut. One wrote that "Springsteen's verse is one with my soul. His switchblade songs are finite anthems to my state, and the infinite emotions of my friends." Another predicted that "a year from now we'll be wondering whatever happened to Bruce Springsteen." A third accused him of selling out on the new album, whereas a fourth proclaimed Bruce "a musical messiah whose time has come. I only hope he is not crucified by renown."

Newsweek's cover, titled "Making of a Rock Star," had a photograph of Springsteen that makes him look almost Christlike: neat hair and beard, white blousy shirt, and a beaming smile while playing guitar. But the accompanying article, by Maureen Orth, was far more cynical and critical than *Time*'s. She reported that the album had "rocketed to million-dollar gold album in six weeks," and that Bruce was a "genuine pop-music phenomenon," but she thought there was so much hype that "the publicity about his publicity is now a dominant issue." And this was without knowing that *Time* had simultaneously put him on the cover. Orth reported that Springsteen had already been damaged once before by the publicity machine that dubbed him the next Dylan even before his first album. According to

New York DJ Dave Herman, as far as he was concerned, "He was already a dead artist who bombed out on his first album."

Orth's piece said almost nothing about the album and expressed skepticism as to whether Springsteen would endure as a rock star. Most of the backlash against Springsteen came in the form of disgust with the hype, not the music, even though writing about the hype only fed the publicity machine. One writer, however, went further. Henry Edwards asked in the *New York Times*, "Is Springsteen really the Rock Messiah he is cracked up to be?" Edwards found the songs on *Born to Run* "an effusive jumble, his melodies either second-hand or undistinguished, and his performance tedious." He called "Thunder Road" "repetitious," "Born to Run" an overly "familiar theme," and "Jungleland" a "glossy species of fake poetry." Edwards attributed it all to nostalgia for a rock moment that had passed and the needs of record companies facing dwindling sales. Critics not intent on inventing a new superstar, Edwards concluded, "may be forgiven if after the first ten minutes of hearing Springsteen sing, they find the hoopla tiresome and the performer vacuous."

Several readers of the *Times* expressed their displeasure with Edwards's "irritating review." One pointed out that the comparison to other great musical artists "indicates not the derivative nature of his music but its power to synthesize and reshape styles for his own purpose." Another called Edwards ignorant for labeling Springsteen's performances tedious: "His rhythms and arrangements are a breath of fresh air to music fans tired of breathing the stagnant fumes of rock music." As for Springsteen's lyrics being "fake poetry," one reader suggested that Edwards apply his test to the words of any great artist including Bob Dylan, or William Shakespeare for that matter.

Five years later, Springsteen would say how much he was troubled by the title of Edwards's piece, "If There Hadn't Been a Bruce Springsteen, Then the Critics Would Have Made Him Up." "That bothered me a lot," he said, "being perceived as an invention, a ship passing by. I'd been playing for ten years. I knew where I came from, every inch of the way. I knew what I believed and what I wanted."

Discussions of hype continued through the fall, and they threatened to diminish the larger success of *Born to Run*. Even *BusinessWeek*, which did not typically cover rock, got in the act with a piece on "The Merchandising of a Superstar." Recounting Columbia's strategy for building an audience for *Born to Run*, the article ultimately made the point that if publicity is all a performer has, the act quickly disappears. A piece on "The Selling of Springsteen" in London's *Melody Maker* made a similar point: "The word 'hype' in the music business has come to mean the conning of the public/media into waxing poetic over something that hardly deserves such attention. This, therefore, is no hype because [Springsteen] is really good."

Rockwell of the *Times* also fired back at his colleague Edwards. He resented the implication that the enthusiasm for Springsteen was disingenuous. "The fact remains," he reminded readers, "that nearly all the people who have written enthusiastically about Mr. Springsteen have done so simply because they love his music . . . Ultimately, Mr. Springsteen's future depends on what it has always depended on: his own ability to keep on writing songs of the same quality he's written so far. If he can do that, he'll stop being a 'hype' and start being a legend instead."

Now we take for granted the "hustling for the record machine" that Springsteen sang about in "Jungleland." It is a reminder of innocence about marketing and advertising in the mid-1970s that the efforts to promote *Born to Run* would be seen as scandalous. Elvis had Colonel Tom Parker, Dylan had Albert Grossman, and, for now, Springsteen had Mike Appel pushing hard to get as much hype going as possible. (One writer described the showy, pushy Appel as a cross between Ed Sullivan and Joseph Goebbels.) Columbia, eager to recoup its investment, was more than happy to comply. "If he survives all the publicity," claimed a writer in the *Guardian*, "he deserves to become as influential a figure for this decade as Dylan was for the sixties or Presley for the fifties."

As for Springsteen, he found the entire experience distasteful; long-desired success had arrived, but the hoopla made him feel angry and empty. He only wished he could feel as bandmate Steve Van Zandt did, buying multiple copies of the weekly magazines and spreading them out over the hotel bed. The only reason he agreed to the interviews with *Time* and *Newsweek* was "for one of the things I did want. I wanted 'Born to Run' to be a hit single. Not for the bucks but because I really believed in the song a whole lot and I just wanted to hear it on the radio, you know. On AM. Across the country. For me, that's where a song should be." Other than that he wondered, "What am I doing on the cover of *Time* and *Newsweek*? I'm not the President. I'm really just a simple guy. I got my band and my music and I love them both. That's my world. My life. It always has been."

But the success of *Born to Run*, so desired and dreamed of by the ambitious Springsteen, cost him his innocence: "There was a point when I felt very low after *Born to Run*. I felt bad for two, three, maybe four months. Before that, it had been me and the band and we'd go out and play. We'd sleep where we could and drive to the next show. All of a sudden I became a person who could make money for other people, and that brings new forces and distractions into your life."

Before leaving for London in November, Springsteen told a reporter that the campaign labeling him as the future of rock 'n' roll "was a very big mistake and I would like to strangle the guy who thought that up." When he arrived for his show on November 18 at London's Hammersmith Odeon, he discovered that Columbia had put up posters that proclaimed, FINALLY LONDON IS READY FOR BRUCE SPRINGSTEEN. Springsteen tore them off the wall. How dare the record company promote him in this way, no less in the backyard of the Beatles, the Stones, the Who, and the Animals? "People keep telling me I ought to be enjoying all this but it's sort of depressing to me," he confessed. In 1998, he recalled the incident: "I felt that—that it was insulting to the audience, you know. And so, you know, I got nuts and—and—and I was right . . . If I wasn't going to be good, I didn't want somebody telling people what to think."

The London music scene was eagerly anticipating Springsteen's first visit. However much the publicity had turned fans off, they had been reading enthusiastic reviews since the first album. In 1973, *New Musical Express* titled an article "Was Bob Dylan the Previous Springsteen?" *Melody Maker* reported in 1974, "If you're lucky he'll finish his set with a rendition of 'Twist and Shout' complete with the ascending build-up between verses that sounds just like John Lennon was standing beside crouched over a Rickenbacker and yelling his loudest to drown out the screams." By 1975, a writer in *Melody Maker* proclaimed, "I listen to Springsteen like I used to listen to Dylan, John Lennon and Chuck Berry—as though a life depended on it."

It is conceivable that some British fans first heard not Springsteen's version of "Born to Run" but the cover version released by former Hollies lead singer Allan Clarke. Clarke, who had numerous hits in the 1960s, began a solo career in 1971. Whatever good judgment he showed in being attracted to Springsteen's music, the idea of covering "Born to Run" could not have been a bigger mistake. Among the many songs Springsteen's "Born to Run" blew away in fall 1975 was a cover of his own work. (A more successful cover by Liverpool pop band Frankie Goes to Hollywood was released in 1984.)

Not everyone was swept away by Springsteen onstage. Simon Frith, a rock critic and sociologist, reported from London that there was an "odd buzz" because "everyone was expecting something but no-one knew what." The band came onstage and Frith was immediately shocked by Springsteen's size: "I mean, he's so bloody small! . . . On the cover of *Born to Run* Springsteen is leaning *down* on this big black man so it was kind of a shock to see that he actually came up to his nipples." Frith then mocked Springsteen's big wooly cap and dirty pants and facial hair: "My God, he's Dustin Hoffman being Ratso Rizzo in *Midnight Cowboy*! This is the future of rock and roll???"

Frith admits that "later on I thought maybe and then yes . . . I had seen why you have to see him. The Springsteen stage show is a jumpy, nervous, desperately dramatic affair . . . It took me a while to figure out his persona, his eagerness to please, his love of his band and violent vision." Frith went on to provide a psychological analysis: "Springsteen was the kid on the block whose parents didn't give a shit, who *lived* on the street, raggedy and surviving. He is not the laid back hero that rock stars like to pretend to be, but neither is he the fearful observer most rock stars are . . . Springsteen's secret is his absolute belief in what he's doing." What Frith did not think highly of was the band, which "was pretty crummy in its technical range and subtlety." They also lacked style, which British critics in particular (see Bowie/Roxy/Queen) welcomed—because "Englishmen are so embarrassed by their emotions that they even play rock behind layers of make-up and silken underwear." Springsteen, Frith concluded, was an American product through and through.

A reviewer of the November 18 show in an English journal disagreed with Frith: "Springsteen mesmerized the audience with numbers from all three of his albums, proving that the raw power of the records is even stronger live." The reviewer's only disappointment was with the encores, old rock numbers such as "Good Golly Miss Molly." "This just isn't what he is best at," but by this point "he could have played the National Anthem and the audience would have gone wild." Calling Springsteen a "street poet and musician turned method actor," the reviewer in the *Guardian* suspected that it was a "sub-standard" night for Springsteen, but thought it was "still an impressive performance." Another review, in the *Record Mirror,* stated that what Springsteen "turns out to be is the leader of a sharply defined rock band that at times hits heights of crisp cutting power that can be equaled by very few others. He doesn't need the hype."

Melody Maker also asserted that "Springsteen Delivers the Goods," but offered a more subtle analysis of the strengths and weaknesses of the show. Part of the problem was the elevated expectations that came from reports of the searing shows at the Bottom Line in New York and the Roxy in Los Angeles. Part of it was also a cultural difference in audience reaction—the English tended to reserve applause for the end. Because Springsteen and the band "feed directly off their audience," explained Michael Watts, "they require the kind of intimacy and spontaneity that American fans seem more prepared to give." By the time the band returned to

London for a second and final show on the twenty-fourth, all inhibitions on both sides had dissolved. Springsteen played forty-five minutes overtime and returned to the stage five times. About the second show, the *Guardian* reported that it "matched up to all the torrent of publicity." "I'd pay just to hear him talk and dance all night," Watts proclaimed.

Watts also identified a crucial element in the Springsteen persona that others missed: "In his comic movement and baggy, unfashionable trousers, he is truly Chaplinesque." Another writer noted that Springsteen "uses his guitar like Charlie Chaplin uses his cane." A third also pointed out his "Chaplinesque sense of humour." Watts also observed how the woolen hat made him look something like a longshoreman. Just as Ben Franklin adorned a beaver cap when he went to Europe, Springsteen came with a prop that signaled he was from the American streets.

Most of the English reviews of Springsteen's show and album were gushing. Dave Seal, in the journal *Arnold Bocklin*, said the album demonstrated that Springsteen is "one of the few '70s performers to hit you hard in the guts consistently and when he wields his street-punk flick knife the old shiver down the spine reaffirms that rock music can be genuinely emotional." Seal thought not since *Highway 61 Revisited* had anyone produced such stunning lyrics and music. But Bruce "is a rock and souler like Bobby never was," Seal stated, and he goes on briefly to mention an issue most reviewers in the States never brought up: race. "The lynchpin of the band is Clarence Clemons . . . Clarence is black in the bargain and lends that influence to Bruce's rock background." Seal ended by expressing fear that the stardom might rob Springsteen of some urgency and vitality, but then predicted that "Bruce is probably sufficiently his own man to keep guard of his genius."

The UK's *Sounds* magazine offered a measured review of the album. Jerry Gilbert admitted that he had "grown to love it," but feared new fans might not understand the uncontrollable genius that is contained here more than on the first two albums. It is Clemons's saxophone that provides the truly magical moments on the album, Gilbert claimed, especially on "Jungleland," a song, he said, that harks back to Springsteen's writing style of eighteen months earlier. Elsewhere, however, Gilbert did not find enough "variation of mood." The review, like most of the English reviews, struggles against the strong undertow of advanced expectations and hype. Still, Gilbert concluded, "Bruce Brilliance Still There."

Melody Maker's issue of November 15, 1975, in anticipation of Bruce's first visit, screamed the headline, SMASH HIT SPRINGSTEEN: BORN TO ROCK 'N' ROLL. In a lengthy interview, Springsteen explained his attitude about all the hype: "You can't jive the kid in the street, no matter what everybody says. He don't care what's on the radio, don't care what somebody is saying. The kid on the street, I think, sees what's jive." The interviewer then asked how much of *Born to Run* is autobiographical. "I don't know," Springsteen answered. "It's hard to say. I don't really write like that. I write overall feelings of things . . . mixed in with lots of different shades of the same reality."

One of the few entirely negative reviews came from Roy Carr in *New Musical Express*, claiming that Springsteen's "skillful portrayal of the stereotype guitar-slinging street corner pug (just outside the law but not so he'll get trashed) is so well-defined that Hollywood couldn't have cast the role more accurately." *Born to Run* may be "aimed right. It just doesn't go off . . . many of the tracks amount to an attempt to evolve an impression of artificial *verité* as Springsteen sweats through his urban rock-renewal programme." In one of the more humorous lines in any review, Carr opines that "the desperation with which Springsteen has attempted to leap off Dylan's bike seems to have involved him in a head-on collision with Roy Orbison." With this, Springsteen himself might have agreed.

Charles Murray's piece in *New Musical Express*, however, separated recorded Springsteen from live Springsteen. He disdained the "ponderous mock-Spector arrangements" on *Born to Run* and Springsteen's inability to leave out anything from a song: "good idea, bad idea, no damn idea at all, sling it in man, it'll fit." The records, Murray thought, "are dumb and irrelevant; forget 'em, they're trash, they're a shadow show in a distorting mirror, and he's not really there at all. It's possible to hear his records and hardly dig him at all; it ain't possible to see his show and walk out quite the same. Only 'Tenth Avenue Freeze-Out' on the new album does justice to Springsteen's stage vibe." That stage presence, honed "with every bar trick in the book," is soaring, rollicking, quivering, and quaking.

Murray also discussed race. Focusing on Clemons, he pointed out that he "looks like the living incarnation of R&B . . . the cat whose musical contributions invariably kick the numbers into overdrive." Murray thought that Springsteen "presents a perfect white interpretation of black music for white people . . . the purest assimilation and distillation of the styles and ambience of timeless uptown Saturday night classic R&B." This is why he thought the records didn't make it: "On the records the focus is on Bruce the soulful poet rather than on Springsteen the whompin' stompin' R&B man." But live, his "R&B Punk Ballet Company is one of the best things I've ever seen on a rock 'n' roll stage."

Yet a third writer in *New Musical Express* said that "friends tell me this grows on them, but so far it sounds like a classic case of the record company 'getting' behind the wrong record. Bruce's previous *Wild, Innocent and E Street Shuffle* was spontaneous combustion, but *Born to Run* is about as exciting as a night storage heater."

New Musical Express notwithstanding, most writers on either side of the Atlantic praised *Born to Run*. In France, one critic gushed, "This album is fantastic in every sense of the word," and called it "one of the greatest rock albums ever." In Germany, a reviewer called it "a lively and convincing work . . . a final and logical move out of a musical past into a future without confining categories where his music stops demanding comparison." And a reviewer in Japan said, "In America he is poised to join the ranks of heroes." Even James Wolcott, who would go on to a distinguished career as a cultural critic for *Vanity Fair* and the *New Yorker*, in his critical assessment for *Circus Raves*, called it Springsteen's finest album and the fulfillment of early promise: "It marks the transition from Critic's Favorite (and Cult Hero) to On-the-Charts-with-a-Bullet."

Having said that, Wolcott went on to disparage the album. He called the writing "pale-colored poetry" that does not stand out and the vocals "cardboard." Springsteen's voice, Wolcott claimed, is "inadequately expressive, uncommanding and monotonous." He offered a different critique as well: a feminist one. He accused Springsteen of sexism and took particular offense at the line in "Thunder Road," "You ain't a beauty, but hey you're all right." Same with the "wrap your legs 'round these velvet rims" of "Born to Run." Wolcott suggested that the "dirty t-shirt machismo" could lead to "a reactionary impulse of phallic sovereignty." He concluded that despite Springsteen's enormous talent and charisma, his was not the "sort of force which changes the lives of a generation . . . So far I haven't been blinded by the light."

Ten years later, after the release of *Born in the U.S.A.*, when Springsteen had risen to a nearly inconceivable level of stardom,

Wolcott in *Vanity Fair* condemned "The Hagiography of Bruce Springsteen." His piece was directed not so much at Springsteen as the rock critics who all fell in line and "shuffled behind the Boss bearing gold, frankincense, and myrrh." Wolcott was sickened by "the elephant caravan of blather that now attends his every move. Piety has begun to collect around Springsteen's curly head like mist around a mountaintop." But Wolcott conceded that it was a credit to Springsteen's power as a musician that he had demonstrated staying power and proved wrong the cynics who said he was largely a media invention.

The earliest and most incisive analysis of the relationship between the reviews of *Born to Run* and rock-critic publicity came from Robert Christgau in January 1976. In a piece titled, "Yes, There Is a Rock Establishment," he probed the role of that fraternity in making Springsteen a star and further analyzed the appeal of Springsteen's persona, which predated the hippie and psychedelic turn of the late sixties and thus flooded some critics with teen nostalgia.

Put simply, Christgau was amazed to discover that reviews could lead to sales. He had always thought of rock criticism as more of a guidebook for those who had already heard the music or were looking for insights into new music. But he didn't think of rock critics as rock fans who ballyhooed their favorites and generated success. Christgau observed that "both the relative unanimity and the geographical spread of Springsteen's critical support were unusual but not unparalleled (cf. Randy Newman). What was new was the rapidity with which sales followed raves."

The story that had been missed, Christgau thought, was that Springsteen's success also marked the "first victory of a brand-new grouping of five journalists who for want of a more felicitous term I have to label the rock-critic establishment." These were journalists who had moved the center of gravity for rock criticism to New York from places such as Detroit and Boston. They knew each other and socialized with one another. And at least two of them had moved well beyond their roles merely as critics toward becoming fans and supporters. Christgau identified the five as John Rockwell of the *New York Times*; Paul Nelson, then writing for the *Village Voice* and *Rolling Stone*; Dave Marsh, who had founded *Creem* in Detroit in 1969 and moved to New York in 1973 and at the time was the review editor at *Rolling Stone*; Jon Landau, who had been review editor at *Rolling Stone* and of course wrote for the *Real Paper* and had moved from byline to producer line; and Christgau himself, self-declared "Dean of American Rock Critics."

Christgau put Marsh, "Springsteen's most fervent and effective critic-fan," at the center of it. Already Marsh was writing a book on Springsteen; he was friends with Springsteen's supporters at Columbia; it was Marsh who first took Landau to see Springsteen. Marsh, Christgau said, "is the complete rock and roller" and "a protégé and good friend," but unlike him or the other "co-establishmentarians, I find it hard to think of [Springsteen] as rock and roll future. For both Marsh and myself, that is a serious (although certainly not decisive) doctrinal disagreement."

Christgau's analysis of Springsteen's appeal went beyond what others had already noted about Springsteen's appeal to the past. Christgau thought it was more than just respecting musical roots generally; rather, it was a return to the specific sound of the early sixties, "a rich if somewhat silly period that nurtured both the soul style . . . and a wealth of not-so-ephemeral pop rock and roll, consummated in the enlightened hedonism of the Beach Boys and the great production machines of Motown and Phil Spector. This is

Springsteen's era—he may talk Berry and Presley, but his encore is Gary U.S. Bonds."

Half of Springsteen's critics and fans, Christgau speculated, are "delighted by his music because they weren't lucky enough to have been glued to their radios in 1963." And the other half, he thought, Marsh and Greil Marcus among them, "are delighted to experience the most unequivocal pleasures of their adolescence all over again." Springsteen had arrived at the right moment. The mid-seventies lacked "hope and innocence"; the rock hero of the times was the "visionless" Elton John. It took nothing away from *Born to Run* to say that it "may go down as the great album Phil Spector never made."

But Springsteen, Christgau thought, needed to go beyond an "aesthetic strategy" that recovers the high-octane energy of early 1960s rock and add to it "a patina of tragedy, just to remind us that things aren't so expansive anymore." This was not the future of rock 'n' roll: It was too sentimental and it wasn't nearly new. Yet despite the "false step" that *Born to Run* may represent (it "sacrifices breadth for focus, spontaneity for power, humanistic narrative for expressionistic statement"), and despite the cabal of critics who tirelessly promoted and befriended the Boss, there was still a chance that Springsteen could avoid becoming "yet another maudlin trials-of-a-rock-star opus." He might indeed break through and combine perspective and talent to prove the rock critics right after all.

Only a year after Springsteen exploded into stardom, the *Born to Run* ride was over. The album would still find new converts, but Springsteen was engaged in a lawsuit against his manager Mike Appel to regain the rights to his music. Springsteen's suit, filed on July 27, 1976, alleged that Appel "wholly failed and neglected to administer the financial affairs of Bruce Springsteen." Appel countersued, alleging breach of contract. The dispute kept Springsteen out of the recording studio, which meant his follow-up album didn't appear until three years after *Born to Run*, an eternity in the music business, where hits are built upon hits and artists staying in the public eye. After the suit was settled in May 1977, Springsteen explained why not having copyright control over his songs was insufferable: "I'd written 'Born to Run' and the money from that song, well maybe that belongs to someone else, maybe someone else is responsible for the money that song made, or something. Maybe that's true. But the song, that song is mine. That belongs to me."

"It got so where, if I wrote a book, I couldn't even quote my own lyrics," he said in 1978. "I couldn't quote 'Born to Run'! That whole period of my life just seemed to be out of my hands. That's why I started playing music and writing in the first place—to control my life. No way I was gonna let that get away."

Tony Parsons of *New Musical Express* thought it was a good time, a year later, to reassess the album, to make judgments based on listening to the music and not what one was reading or hearing about it. Maybe the editors at *New Musical Express* had some regrets over how harshly they had treated Springsteen in 1975. In "Blinded by the Hype," Parsons confesses that "I loved the album the first time I heard it, and knew that at last Springsteen was going to get the recognition he deserved." He praised "Thunder Road" for Springsteen's vocals; he loved the way "Tenth Avenue Freeze-Out" brought back the Stax soul sound; "Night," he said, was a "frantic outpouring of rage, frustration, love and hope." Parsons argued that "Backstreets" was the best song on the album: "It gets inside you and reminds you of things you'd rather forget. It has that kind of power—the power of a love song written out of the actual experience of an artist capable of expressing his deepest emotions in words and music." About "Born to Run" all he could say was if there was any justice in the world, it should have been a number-one single. He loved the contrast between the Fender ripping on "She's the One" and the distant sax and soft piano on "Meeting Across the River." And then the finale, "Jungleland," "a worthy ending to one of the best rock albums of last year . . . dare I say it, a *great* album."

And so *Born to Run* took wing, hype and backlash, praise, criticism, and reconsideration, at its heels. It ripped through the cultural malaise of 1975 by fusing the past to the present to ignite what felt like a limitless future. It didn't matter whether you were fifteen or thirty-five in 1975, whether you grew up on the sounds of the fifties or sixties or not. The album spoke to the moment. And it still does. Not even in 2005, on the occasion of its thirtieth anniversary, had it become a nostalgia act—new generations coming of age hear it for the first time and are transfixed. The romantic dreams of escape have not faded. The bleak realities of life have not dissipated. The hope for redemption and salvation still drives us forward. Time passes, but the making of identity never ceases.

SIX

BORN TO RUN THIRTY YEARS ON

Here's a song I wrote about fifteen years ago . . . I was just twenty-four, I was living in Long Branch . . . oh, man, I felt, I felt pretty ready, I guess . . . it was in the afternoon, and it took me a long time to write this song . . . I always say that this song is kind of like my birthday song, you know . . . I spent quite a few months thinking about what I wanted to say . . . and how I wanted to say it and the stuff that I asked myself in this song fifteen years ago, the questions . . . they're the questions that I've been chasing down the answers to ever since.

—BRUCE SPRINGSTEEN, 1988

BORN TO RUN rose to number three on the Billboard charts in 1975. It sold well over a million copies that year. As Robert Christgau noted in January 1976, "Neither Bette Midler nor David Bowie has ever made a platinum album, and not counting two greatest-hits collections, Bob Dylan has earned only one, *Nashville Skyline*." The single of "Born to Run" reached number twenty-three on the Billboard chart. Considered too long for AM radio, it found regular play on the FM dial. By 2003, the album had sold more than six million copies.

Survey after survey includes *Born to Run* on lists of all-time classic albums: In 2000, National Public Radio included it among the one hundred most important musical works of the twentieth century. In 2003 *Rolling Stone* ranked the album number eighteen

147

of all time; the Zagat Music survey guide for 2003 listed it first; the Library of Congress added it to the National Recording Registry in 2003; in 2006 *Time* included it in its list of the top one hundred. On *Rolling Stone*'s 2004 list of greatest songs, "Born to Run" is number twenty-one and "Thunder Road" number eighty-six. It can be found on countless listener polls for local radio stations. WFUV in New York, for example, had an Essential Albums listener poll, and *Born to Run* came in second; for their Essential Songs listener poll, "Thunder Road" was first and "Born to Run" third.

"Born to Run" quickly entered the culture at large. In 1979, Chris Cerf wrote "Born to Add" for *Sesame Street*, the breakthrough Jim Henson puppet show on public television. It was performed by Muppets calling themselves Bruce Stringbean and the S Street Band. "Born to Add" opens, "When we are all in the streets and we see one car/We always add one and make it two . . . Kids like you and me/ Baby we were born to add." In 1983, Eric Meola's cover photo got the same treatment when the Sesame Street *Born to Add* album cover showed a guitar-playing Bert leaning on a saxophone-playing Cookie Monster. By then, many of Springsteen's twenty-something fans from 1975 were now thirty-somethings with children.

The year after Cerf's parody, what might have seemed like a joke but wasn't took place in the New Jersey State Assembly as legislators considered a bill to make "Born to Run" the state's unofficial anthem. Apparently, the idea began when a New York disc jockey introduced the song by saying, "Everyone please rise for the New Jersey state anthem." Assemblyman Richard Visotcky, Democrat from Garfield, introduced the bill.

Opinions on the matter varied. Writing in the *New York Times*, Richard Lee, an editor at the *Montclair Times*, supported the proposal. While acknowledging that Springsteen "is obviously not a

Sesame Street *Born to Add* album cover.

Francis Scott Key," he was born in New Jersey and "New Jersey is the very essence of his music . . . With songs like 'Born to Run,' he has suddenly made it fashionable to be from New Jersey." One reader from New Jersey agreed: "I think it is only fit that 'Born to Run' be our state anthem, since it is the sound of New Jersey."

The sound of "Born to Run" was one thing, the lyrics another. Some wondered whether a song that mentions suicide and death and plots escape from a town that "rips the bones from your back" should be celebrated as the state anthem. One assemblyman declared that "the message of this song is to avoid responsibility, and escape. We have a responsibility not to put a stamp of approval on this philosophy." The comedian Robert Wuhl took a more humorous approach. He created a routine in which he went through the lyrics and invited the audience to imagine what a state flag based on the song might look like. The bill would not be acted upon; "Born to Run" would have no standing as official or even unofficial state anthem as far as the legislature was concerned. (A bill proposed in 2006 to create a special "Born to Run" license plate, with the proceeds going to the New Jersey food bank, also expired without action being taken.)

At the precise moment "Born to Run" received cultural approval and legislative disavowal, Springsteen suffered a spiritual crisis. He had just completed a five-year burst of creative energy, a period that saw in succession three remarkable albums: *Born to Run*, *Darkness on the Edge of Town*, and the double-album *The River*. Only Dylan, who successively recorded *Bringing It All Back Home*, *Highway 61 Revisited*, and *Blonde on Blonde* (also a double album) can be said to have had an equally fertile period. And after *Blonde on Blonde*, Dylan withdrew for a while from the public scene.

In fall 1982, Springsteen released *Nebraska*, a stark, haunting solo acoustic album. Leaving behind the band at a time when his star was still in the ascendency ("Hungry Heart," off *The River*, had reached number five on Billboard's Hot 100) may have been a risky career move, but Springsteen was following his muse. The album allowed him to lower expectations and return to his identity as a solo acoustic artist, which was how he had been signed to begin with. He would revisit that role time and again across his career.

Evoking Woody Guthrie and Hank Williams, with guitar and harmonica, Springsteen sings about outcasts and criminals, but also honest men stranded on a desolate American landscape.

David Michael Kennedy's cover photo of a bleak, empty horizon shot from the front seat of the car looking down the highway is an iconic image that pays silent tribute to Robert Frank's *The Americans*, a book of photographs taken on a cross-country trip between 1955 and 1957. Springsteen knew the book—Eric Meola had given it to him as a gift around the time of the photo shoot for *Born to Run*.

A central line of the album is "Deliver me from nowhere," which appears in two songs. Gloom and darkness cover this land where "luck may have died and our love may be cold," where a father's house is "shining 'cross this dark highway where our sins lie unatoned." But there is also hope for renewal and redemption: "Maybe everything that dies someday comes back." People are on the move, from the law and from debt. Terrible things happen to people: Love is broken, children are lost. On the road, the "turnpike sure is spooky at night when you're all alone." And yet the album ends, "At the end of every hard earned day people find some reason to believe." That statement, however, may be more about the power of self-delusion and blind faith than hope.

"*Nebraska* comes as a shock," wrote Steve Pond in *Rolling Stone*, "a violent, acid-etched portrait of a wounded America that fuels its machinery by consuming its people's dreams." At the moment he recorded it, Springsteen felt dislocated and depressed. He took a cross-country trip with a friend in a car he had bought for a few thousand dollars. "I was 32, and I wasn't a kid anymore," he recalled in 1992. "At the same time I wasn't attached and didn't have a home life." Springsteen was flooded with despair when they stopped in the South and heard a band playing by a riverbank: "I walked around the crowd and felt very detached and far away.

I had the sinking feeling that something had gone fundamentally wrong . . . it was an empty feeling, floating feeling, like I had gotten lost." He returned to New Jersey and began seeing a psychiatrist ("200 freaking bucks an hour"), closing in on some truths about himself and then running away from them again.

Springsteen had been thinking a lot about his father, the forces that trapped Douglas but allowed his son to escape. Throughout the *River* tour he played "Independence Day," a song about his teen years, during which "there was just no way this house could hold the two of us." It is a mournful ballad in which independence carries little freedom and much pain. Introducing the song on tour in 1981, Springsteen grew more aware that there was a deep connection between the personal and the historical, the individual and the political. If the American dream had failed Douglas Springsteen, the problem wasn't the dream itself, or his father. The problem was that people were kept in ignorance. Schools did not teach students what they needed to know, settling for facts where truths were required. Springsteen's trip to Europe opened his eyes about America, and he foreshadowed in his comments onstage themes that would become increasingly pronounced in his work. A quarter of a century later, opening a tour overseas, he would say, "You're very conscious of your American-ness when you're in Europe."

In Paris, on April 19, 1981, he opened the show with a song he hadn't performed before, a rearranged version of Elvis Presley's "Follow That Dream." The midtempo tune, which anticipates many of his later ballads, movingly recapitulates the theme of the search for love ("Follow that dream wherever it may lead/To find the love you need") while adding a potent social critique:

Now every man has the right to live
The right to a chance, to give what he has to give
The right to fight for the things he believes
For the things that come to him in dreams

Bruce announced in Paris that he was reading a book that was having a profound effect on him: "I just started to read *The History of the United States* [*A Pocket History of the United States*, by Henry Steele Commager and Allan Nevins], and the thing about it is that I started to learn about how things got to be the way they are today, how you end up a victim without even knowing it, and how people get old and just die after not having hardly a day's satisfaction or peace of mind in their lives." A week later, in Brussels, he further developed his thoughts: "I was reading this book, it was called *The History of the United States*, and in it you find out, I found out how I ended up where I was and how the chances of me breaking out of that kind of life, or anybody breaking out of that kind of life, get slimmer and slimmer every day." And then, in Rotterdam, "I read this book *The History of the United States*, and in it I found out where I came from and how I ended up, where I was and how easy it is to be a victim of things that you don't even know exist and you don't even know are there, 'cause I go back and I see my friends at home and there's a lot of people there that had strong hearts and force and power inside them that just got crushed."

What crushed them was an America that promised a good life, and encouraged people to work hard to obtain it, and then never delivered on the promise. What crushed them was, for want of greater specificity, "the forces of history"—capitalist greed, the class system, empire building. The book helped Springsteen to understand that one had to fight continually: for freedom, for equality, for justice, for the dignity of work and the comforts of a home. Springsteen's next album would explore what happens to people who become victims of historic forces beyond their control, and it would thrust him into the center of a musical and cultural whirlwind.

In 1984, nearly ten years after its release, *Born to Run* took a backseat to the explosion that made Springsteen into a megastar: *Born in the U.S.A.* The album, like *Born to Run*, provided an image and a sound that rhymed with the times. Springsteen reinvented himself physically—appearing muscle-bound in workingman's shirt and jeans, a bandanna around his head. And he experimented musically, adding synthesizers to his sound for the first time. Photographed by Annie Leibovitz for the cover, Bruce is shown from his shoulders down facing an American flag, a red baseball cap in his back pocket. If the title and cover screamed patriotism, the songs themselves offered a continuation and embellishment of some long-standing themes as well as the development of some new ones.

Politicians might try to associate the anthemic title song, which leads off the album, with a glorious resurgence of American patriotism among a younger generation (Springsteen was only thirty-five), but anyone who paid attention to the first line, "Born down in a dead man's town," and understood Springsteen's earlier work realized this was a continuation of the dual theme of entrapment and escape. "I'm ten years burning down the road/Nowhere to run ain't got nowhere to go," cries the narrator. Indeed, it had been ten years since "Born to Run." And now, unemployed, with loved ones lost, on the edge of the penitentiary, the narrator awaits an American birthright that will not be delivered. Springsteen first conceived the song as an acoustic number in which one can feel the despair. But the tension between the words and the sounds in the rock version adds a potent dimension. Fists are pumped at the chorus, and the song becomes not only an affirmation but also a protestation. It is also the device of the tension between verse and chorus, a device Springsteen first started using on songs such as "Badlands." The verses, Springsteen says, were the blues, the chorus the gospel.

In "Cover Me," the outside natural world has turned toxic (rain, snow, wind). Times are difficult, but still there is the fantasy of survival with a love that blinds us. These are songs of workers looking for employment or fun, but they find little opportunity and their enjoyment lands them in trouble. "Downbound Train" is one of the most plaintive songs in the Springsteen canon, a song that sounds as if we are chugging down through the valley. The narrator works menial jobs and has lost his love without knowing why—one day she says, "Joe I gotta go." Joe is left broken in a dark room with an empty bed, and he hangs his head and cries.

Side two opens with a declaration of "No Surrender," a momentary resurgence of spirit from being "tired and you just want to close your eyes and follow your dreams down." Ten years down the line, there is the feeling of having aged. If in "Thunder Road" you were scared and thought that maybe you weren't that young anymore, now "I'm ready to grow young again." There is war outside, and the narrator, who speaks more simply and directly than he might have years earlier, seeks only to make real "these romantic dreams in my head." But no sooner is the hope of love proclaimed than it is lost in "Bobby Jean," a sad, wistful song about two people who were once close ("We went walking in the rain talking about the pain from the world we hid"), but she has gone away and all the singer can hope for is that she'll one day hear on the radio this good-bye song about a lost love. The poignancy of the song is deepened by its subtext: Steve Van Zandt had decided, after ten years, to leave the band.

Even "Dancing in the Dark," Springsteen's proof that he could write a pop hit if he wanted, repeats the themes of the dream of escape from aging and work and a town where "they'll be carving you up alright." To get through the boredom and restlessness one can only dance in the dark. The album ends in uncertainty—times have gotten worse in the narrator's hometown. He's married, has a kid. He's thinking of "getting out." But this is no longer the dream of liberation. It is being caught between the place that once was and now is. The father repeats for his son what his father said to him: This is your hometown. What to do about it would become a question to which Springsteen would return. But no matter how far you run, Springsteen told audiences in introducing "My Hometown" in concert, "You always, you always carry where you come from with you for the rest of your life."

Born in the U.S.A. sold more than fifteen million copies and sat at number one on the charts in the summer of 1984. It is the second-best selling recording of the decade next to Michael Jackson's *Thriller*. It also generated seven top-ten singles. The tour that followed played to packed stadiums, the first time Springsteen moved outside of arenas. In the presidential campaign that fall, Ronald Reagan, at a campaign stop in New Jersey, declared, "America's future rests in a thousand dreams inside your hearts; it rests in the message of hope in songs so many young Americans admire: New Jersey's own Bruce Springsteen. And helping you make those dreams come true is what this job of mine is all about." Walter Mondale, the Democratic nominee, furious that Reagan would try to enlist the rock star, said, "Springsteen may have been born to run, but he wasn't born yesterday."

Of course Reagan and other conservative Republicans couldn't have gotten it more wrong. "Born in the U.S.A." was no hymnal to the glory of the nation. Rather, it is a song about the broken American promise. Bruce, who abjured politics, felt he had no choice but to respond. In concert in Pittsburgh on September 21, Springsteen said, "Well, the president was mentioning my name in his speech the other day . . . and I kind of got to wondering what his favorite album of mine must've been . . . I don't think it was the *Nebraska* album, I don't think he's been listening to this one." He then launched into "Johnny 99," a song about an unemployed worker "with debts no honest man can pay," who requests the electric chair.

The *Born in the U. S.A.* tour lasted from June 1984 to October 1985. Before playing "Born to Run," he would often offer a version of the following remarks: "I lived in a little town where there was nothing going on and . . . you didn't seem to get the information you needed to get out, and rock 'n' roll came jumping out of my radio and said one thing to me, it said, 'Let freedom ring' . . . and that's what this is all about, so . . . but remember, we gotta fight for it."

Springsteen represented the working-class fighter not only in his lyrics and appearance but also in his performances—his shows ran for well over three hours with an intermission. He was there to do a job and to do it well. And he refused to sell out. Lee Iacocca might have offered millions for the rights to use "Born in the U.S.A." in a car commercial, but Springsteen wouldn't allow it, not for that song or any other. More than one critic noted how "offstage, Mr. Springsteen apparently practices what he preaches. He doesn't seem to want or need to be a star, to be different from the middle Americans he sings about." That analysis came in August

1985, three months *after* Springsteen married actress Julianne Phillips. Whatever Springsteen's flirtation with the Hollywood lifestyle did to besmirch his image, his divorce less than two years later and his relationship with Patty Scialfa, a New Jersey musician who had joined the *Born in the U.S.A.* tour and sang backup vocals, seemed to more than correct it. Even if fans puzzled over the purchase of a fourteen-million-dollar estate in Beverly Hills, they relished Bruce's finding true love with Patty.

Assessments of Springsteen's album and tour discussed his evolving American vision. Stephen Holden, writing in the *New York Times*, explained that "for all the exhilaration and energy in the album's songs about joy rides, high school memories and friendship, *Born in the U.S.A.* is a sad and serious album about the end of the American dream—of economic hope and security, and of community—for a dwindling segment of our society." Robert Palmer, Holden's colleague, declared that "after a decade of rock stardom, Mr. Springsteen has become something more than a rock icon, more than an entertainer. The lyrics to his songs are studied intensively . . . He is a kind of latter-day Woody Guthrie singing about America—not the major enclaves of the rich, but small-town, working-class America, where young people frustrated by dead-end jobs, factory shutdowns and the sound of shattering hopes and dreams are as much a part of the picture as the more traditional rock-and-roll imagery of fast cars and summertime romances."

Jon Pareles, also in the *New York Times*, analyzed Springsteen's mass appeal and identified him as taking "an old-fashioned populist approach—he speaks, and sings, for the inarticulate and disenfranchised. But unlike a politician, he offers no program for new glory days. Character study by character study, he simply maps an all-American despair. Meanwhile, the vitality of his performances and the E Street Band's music—*Born in the U.S.A.* includes some of the most exuberant noises ever captured in a recording studio—lends his music an unspoken optimism, hope despite the odds."

Not everyone agreed. In the *Washington Post*, Richard Harrington wrote that Springsteen "has become a brooding, boorish visionary, with no respite of working class advocacy or the resilient spirit of youth." The pessimism of the songs troubled Harrington as much as anything, as if "rock 'n' roll is just another American dream turning sour." Of course, that was the point. More fans than ever made the journey with Springsteen into the darkness that was now not only on the edge of town but also at the center of the country.

Other critics noted that despite the hardships of "a place where crumbling towns and rusting factories crush the spirits of good people, but hope never dies . . . In the best tradition of rock and roll, defiance almost always wins . . . The key to it all may be one line from 'Thunder Road'; Springsteen barely whispers it in concert, and the audience sings a ghostly harmony: 'Show a little faith, there's magic in the night.'"

After two years of magical nights, the tour came to an end and the E Street Band did as well. The *Born in the U.S.A.* superstardom had taken its toll: "I went through a very confusing time, a depression, really. I began to reassess everything I'd gone through. Like the success I'd had with *Born in the U.S.A.* Did I like it? Did I want to do something like it again? Was I misunderstood? I also thought a lot about the iconic status that my music had attained. Sure, my music had always had a mythic edge to it, but, well, I just felt overwhelmed by the whole thing. I felt dehumanized."

A live boxed set came out in 1986 and debuted at number one (it included live versions of "Thunder Road," "Tenth Avenue Freeze-Out," "Backstreets," and "Born to Run"), and then in 1987 the band separated. A few members played on several tracks of Springsteen's 1987 *Tunnel of Love*, an album filled with melodic songs of sadness, loneliness, and loss where, in the closing song, "Valentine's Day," one confronts the "bitterness of a dream that didn't come true." The band did a brief tour in 1988, but changing where members stood onstage did not shake things up. In 1989, Springsteen officially disbanded the group. He did it because he needed to explode the image that he had helped create, the macho star. "I just kind of felt 'Bruced' out," he said. He didn't want to be trapped in the past, "where you start to replay the ritual, and nostalgia creeps in."

It was on the *Tunnel of Love* tour that Bruce premiered the acoustic "Born to Run"—guitar and harmonica, often prefaced with comments about the importance of finding community and connection, of finding one's way home. On June 25, 1988, in London, he introduced it by looking back:

Here's a song I played the first time I ever came to London. I was a young lad—twenty-five. I wrote this song just the summer before. I was living in this little house a block or so in off the beach, and I guess I sang this song at the Hammersmith Odeon in 1975 and I've been singing it every night ever since. And I guess as I've sang it through the years, its meaning has changed quite a bit for me. When I first wrote it, I figured I was writing about this guy and this girl that wanted to get in the car, drive, keep on driving and never come back. It's kind of a nice romantic idea. But as I got older, I realized I'd put all these people in all these cars and I was gonna have to figure someplace for them to go. I was gonna be able to figure someplace where I belonged, so as I sang this song through the years, I realized that that guy and that girl were out there looking for some connection, trying to find some sense of community, some sense of meaning beyond their own individual freedom and someplace maybe that they could call home. And I realized that home wasn't out there over the next hill or around the corner but that it was buried deep down inside of me, and that if I had the guts I might be able to get a little piece of it. Anyway, this song has taken me many places. I hope it's kept you good company on your search for whatever you're looking for, as good as it's kept me company on mine. So I'd like to do this for you tonight, wishing you all love, home, and happiness.

And so Springsteen continued on his personal, musical, and lyrical journey. He became a father, he recorded with other musicians, and he recorded alone. He also went into therapy and has called it "the best thing I did." "That was really valuable," he explains. "I crashed into myself and saw a lot of myself as I really was. And I questioned all my motivations. Why am I writing what I'm writing? Why am I saying what I'm saying? Do I mean it? Am I bullshitting? Am I just trying to be the most popular guy in town? Do I need to be liked that much? . . . So I went through an intense period of self examination. I knew that I had to sit in my room for eight hours a day with a guitar to learn how to play it, and now I had to put in that kind of time just to find my place again."

In 1992 he released *Lucky Town*, an album of songs he wrote and recorded in three weeks in his home studio, playing almost all the instruments himself. He simultaneously released *Human Touch*. Springsteen may have always been something of a critics' darling, but *Human Touch* received some very negative reviews, leading *Entertainment Weekly* to ask, "Whatever Happened to Bruce?" *Lucky*

Town, it seems, suffered guilt by association, though the reviews at the time often praised it: *USA Today* called it "pensive and emotionally absorbing." *Rolling Stone* called some of the songs "rousing" and "elegant." A Canadian journalist reported that the album "is a delight, a stripped down solo outing full of grit, humour, and life that finds Springsteen laughing at both his good fortune and his own self pity."

Lucky Town is particularly relevant to the story of *Born to Run* because Springsteen viewed it in 1992 as marking the next step on the journey for those characters he put in motion in 1975. He told Stephen Holden, in an article titled "When the Boss Fell to Earth, He Hit Paradise," that "in 1974, I was a 24-year-old sitting on my bed in Long Branch, N.J., saying, 'Hey, I want to know if love is real.' If you listen to 'Born to Run,' that's the question the song asks. If you've followed my characters over the years, you could see them struggling and failing and losing each other and finding each other again, and losing themselves and finding themselves in pursuit of some sort of answer to that question. I felt that if you had followed my characters all the way back to *Born to Run, Lucky Town* was the place where they were going."

The album is a paean to family and home building, to finding love and sticking with it, to confronting one's identity honestly and finding refuge from the muck of a world that sullies your soul. There is no nostalgia here for the past or pining for the future; these are the "better days with a girl like you." And there's honesty about the posture of being "a rich man in a poor man's shirt." In the title song, the narrator "had a coat of fine leather and snakeskin boots/ But that coat always had a thread hangin' loose." Time to trade all that in for the joys of "building me a new home." "If I Should Fall Behind" is a secular hymn to love and eternity ("Now everyone dreams of a love lasting and true/But you and I know what this world can do"), and "Living Proof" a testament to the meaning of a child's birth in a "world so hard and dirty so fouled and confused." The narrator recalls:

> *Just tryin' so hard to shed my skin*
> *I crawled deep into some kind of darkness*
> *Lookin' to burn out every trace of who I'd been*
> *You do some sad sad things baby*
> *When it's you you're tryin' to lose*

But the birth of his child gives him renewed faith, a respite from life's drought. In the baby, the narrator has found living proof. Springsteen declared that "the guy in 'Living Proof' is the same guy as the one in 'Born to Run,' except he's covered a lot of miles in between."

If the darkness of *Lucky Town* is muted, it is still here in songs such as "The Big Muddy," where we're trapped "waist deep in the big muddy," and "Souls of the Departed," where the narrator laments the deaths of young soldiers and expresses the intention to save his own son if he can "build me a wall so high nothing can burn it down/Right here on my own piece of dirty ground."

Lucky Town is a deeply spiritual and personal album, with layered guitars and steady beats. It is influenced by country musicians such as Hank Williams and Merle Haggard, in whose work Springsteen found an answer to the question, "After *Born to Run*, it was, O.K., now what?" First country musicians, and then Woody Guthrie, who had "a bigger, broader canvas" than the country stars, were all addressing the question of "the consequences of the choices you make." Several songs, including the closing "My Beautiful Reward," are nearly hymns, with roots in bluegrass and folk. Pareles noted that "the twang of hand-picked guitars and the kick of real drums represent a fortress for a family man, a defense against a post-modern world of rootlessness and moral ambiguity." In 1995, Springsteen explained the connective tissue of his work: "I wanted to write about things that people always have to go through at some point in their lives. My music wasn't going to be about fashion or style. It was going to be about family and struggle and identity questions, spiritual questions: Who am I? Where am I going? How do you live an honest life, and is it possible? How do you make the kinds of connections that keep you from the worst of yourself and bring out the best of yourself? And then there's fun and good times—how do you find them?"

The same year *Lucky Town* came out, Los Angeles punk band Social Distortion issued *Somewhere Between Heaven and Hell*. The coincidence is worth noting: If Springsteen's rockers were seeking a landing place from being "Born to Run," Social Distortion's punkers were screaming about being "Born to Lose," one of the signature songs on the album. The chorus goes, "Born to lose, was what they said/You know I was better off dead/Born to lose, you're just bad news/You don't get a second chance." If the song didn't become an anthem for another generation seeking its place, it certainly captured the brutal reality of working-class life. Springsteen thought *Somewhere Between Heaven and Hell* was "a great rock & roll album," and "Born to Lose" "great stuff."

In 1995, twenty years after *Born to Run*, Springsteen discovered in Tom Joad, the heroic figure of Steinbeck's *Grapes of Wrath*, an essential part of the American impulse toward seeking justice for wounded, everyday people. Springsteen recalls that at age twenty-six he first saw John Ford's film version: "I remember thinking that's what I wanted my work to be. I wanted it to have something to do with people's lives, to be about how people fall back upon love, and faith, and hope, and ultimately each other, even after the world reveals itself." The title song, "The Ghost of Tom Joad," includes the lines, "The highway is alive tonight/But nobody's kiddin' nobody about where it goes." Twenty years after "pulling out of here to win," Springsteen refocused on how the journey goes awry and how people end up dislocated and dispossessed.

A revealing interview given on the *Tom Joad* tour made the personal connection between his music and his childhood: "I believe that your politics are emotionally and psychologically determined by your early experiences. My family didn't have a political house. We didn't have a cultural house. There was a lot of struggle in my parents' life. In Jersey, when I was 19, they traveled West to start a new life. They didn't know anybody. They had $3,000 to make it across the country with my little sister. My mother worked the same job her whole life, every day, never sick, never stayed home, never cried. My dad had a very difficult life, a hard struggle all the time at work. I've always felt like I'm seeking his revenge. My memory is of my father trying to find work, what that does to you, and how that affects your image of your manhood, as a provider. The loss of that role is devastating. I write coming from that spot—the spot of disaffection, of loners, outsiders. But not outlaws."

One of the outcasts he had written about before Tom Joad was a Philadelphia lawyer dying of AIDS. "Streets of Philadelphia," which he wrote for the film *Philadelphia*, received the Academy Award for Best Song of 1994. In 1995 he also reunited in the studio with the E Street Band for the purposes of recording a few new songs for his *Greatest Hits* album, which soared to number one on the charts. For that album he recorded "Blood Brothers," a song about lifetime companions carried forever in one's heart, if not by one's side. The song starts with acoustic guitar and builds. "Now the hardness of this world slowly grinds your dreams away/Makin' a fool's joke out of the promises we make," Springsteen sings. There is melancholy here about "time and memory" fading away, but Springsteen is turning back from the despair that comes with knowing that dreams do not end the way you hope, and that behind every promise is a lie. "I'll keep movin' through the dark with you in my heart," he sings, and a lengthy harmonica solo carries him further on down the road.

In writing about death and blood connections, Springsteen may also have been thinking about his father, who died from cancer in 1998. That year, Springsteen dedicated *Songs* to Douglas and included the photograph that his aunt had showed him of a proud, defiant young man in uniform. Asked in 2005 about ways in which he had imitated his father, with whom he had bitter conflict growing up, Springsteen answered with a question: "Well, what is my costume? My costume is a work shirt. I'm a guy who's played music my whole life. I've never held a daily job, outside of gardening and housepainting and roof tarring when I was fifteen or sixteen years old. I've been a musician my whole life, but when I went to work, I put on that work shirt. What was that about? I could have put on the paisley shirt or the sequined jacket or something else, but I chose the work shirt. That's what I continue to write about, those kinds of characters and the people whose lives are under a great deal of stress."

Thinking back on his youth following his father's death—and turning fifty—perhaps encouraged Springsteen to make plans for an E Street reunion tour in 1999. Recording with the band had reminded him how much he needed to stay connected to friends from his teen years, a time before he became an international commodity. He had figured out that he could go off in solo directions yet also work with the band whenever it felt right. Camaraderie with the band, he said, kept him from falling "into the abyss of self-destructiveness."

In preparation for that tour, Springsteen finished a song he had in his notebooks. Drawing from an old folk spiritual, "The Train," as well as Curtis Mayfield's classic "People Get Ready," he rededicated himself and the band to a new song, "Land of Hope and Dreams," riding not in a car but on a train, riding together, everyone included. Thematically it is a return is some ways to *Born to Run* ("You don't know where you're goin'/But you know you won't be back"), but the darkness has yielded to light on this heavenly trip.

On March 15, 1999, Springsteen was inducted into the Rock and Roll Hall of Fame. U2's Bono gave a speech at the induction ceremony worth quoting at some length. After talking about how many rock stars burned out or acted bizarrely or became too full of themselves, Bono said:

> Bruce Springsteen, you always knew, was not gonna die stupid.
> He didn't buy the mythology that screwed so many people.
> Instead he created an alternative mythology, one where ordinary
> lives became extraordinary and heroic . . . He's America's writer,
> and critic . . . In 1974, I was fourteen. Even I knew the sixties
> were over. It was the era of soft rock and fusion. The Beatles
> were gone. Elvis was in Vegas. What was going on? Nothin' was
> going on. Bruce Springsteen was coming on, saving music from
> the phonies, saving lyrics from the folkies, saving leather jackets

from the Fonz . . . In Dublin, Ireland, I knew what he was talking about. Here was a dude who carried himself like Brando, and Dylan, and Elvis. If John Steinbeck could sing, if Van Morrison could ride a Harley-Davidson . . . It was something new, too. He was the first whiff of Scorcese, the first hint of Patti Smith, Elvis Costello, and the Clash . . . America was staggering when Springsteen appeared. The president just resigned in disgrace, the U.S. had lost its first war. There was going to be no more oil in the ground. The days of cruising and big cars were supposed to be over. But Bruce Springsteen's vision was bigger than a Honda, it was bigger than a Subaru. Bruce made you believe that dreams were still out there, but after loss and defeat they had to be braver, not just bigger. He was singing, 'Now you're scared and you're thinking that maybe we ain't that young anymore,' because it took guts to be romantic now. Knowing you could lose didn't mean you still didn't take the ride. In fact, it made taking the ride all the more important.

It took guts to be romantic; it took guts to be populist; it took guts to be domestic; and in the next turn of Springsteen's career, it took guts to be political. In 1985, Jon Pareles pointed out that "unlike a politician, [Springsteen] offers no program for new glory days . . . he simply maps an all-American despair." But Springsteen's social concerns and platform led Jack Newfield of the *Village Voice* to wonder, "Can Springsteen Ignite Political Passion?" Newfield observed that "Springsteen is singing against a whole national drift toward Reaganism, materialism, narcissism, union-baiting, rat-race careerism." A piece in the *Christian Science Monitor* pointed out that with fund-raising and consciousness-raising events such as Live Aid and Farm Aid, rock stars had become a political force, "none more so than Springsteen who may qualify as the first popular singer to be recruited by a president of the United States as a character reference."

It was one endeavor to write and sing about social issues; it was quite another to exercise any sort of political leadership, and Springsteen had no intentions of doing so. Even as the "Born in the U.S.A." flap in 1984 drew Springsteen to offer political comments, he admitted to not being registered to vote and not knowing "that much about politics. I guess my politics are in my songs." From early in his career, he didn't feel he should say what he was trying to accomplish: "I want people to find out for themselves. They should search out the songs. That's what I'm doing. I'm searching it out."

In 1992, Springsteen said simply, "I don't come out and promote politicians." He had always believed that rock 'n' roll itself was inherently political and transformative, that Elvis did not need overt politics to shake things up—all he had to do was move his hips. He said in early 1996, "I heard a political message in rock music. A liberation message. A message of freedom. I heard it in Elvis's voice. That voice had its implications. You weren't supposed to hear Elvis Presley. You weren't supposed to hear Jerry Lee Lewis. You weren't supposed to hear Robert Johnson. You weren't supposed to hear Hank Williams. And they told the story of the secret America."

Springsteen had performed on behalf of political and social-justice causes (No Nukes in 1979, We Are the World in 1985, and Amnesty International in 1988, for example), but it was not until 1996 that his public stance about politics began to change. That fall he appeared before a crowd in California to encourage them to vote against Proposition 209, which would have reduced funding for affirmative-action programs, and he performed "The Promised

Land." That same month, Bob Dole, the Republican candidate, blasted "Born in the U.S.A" from his campaign bus as he toured central New Jersey. The *Asbury Park Press* received the following letter from Springsteen: "I read in the *Press* this morning that my music was appropriated for the Republican rally for Bob Dole in Red Bank yesterday. Just for the record, I'd like to make it clear that it was used without my permission and I am not a supporter of the Republican ticket."

Then came September 11, 2001. The catastrophe did not make Springsteen any more politically aware, but it certainly advanced his understanding of his role not only as a rock star but also as a public figure to whom fans looked for guidance. Pulling out of a beach parking lot a few days after the tragedy, Springsteen encountered a fan who shouted from his car, "We need you." "That's part of my job," Springsteen told a reporter. "It's an honor to find that place in the audience's life."

Springsteen was moved deeply by how frequently his name and work came up in "Portraits of Grief," published in the *New York Times*, and at memorial services. Time and again, obituaries mentioned "Thunder Road"; time and again comments such as this one appeared: to Steven Lillianthal, a victim of 9/11, "Springsteen concerts were like balloons. You wanted to hang on to them. And one was never enough." Springsteen said about the portraits, "I found those to be very, very meaningful—incredibly powerful."

The tragedy of 9/11 led him to attend church with family: "It's something we do once in a while, a small and intimate church. I like the people and I like the pastor and I liked his approach with the kids [his three children]. It gives the kids a little sense of place. It gives them a place to meditate on the experience of the Eleventh, and to have that experience in a congregation of people all trying to grapple with the spiritual significance of what had occurred."

Springsteen responded musically with *The Rising,* his first album of new material with the E Street Band since 1984. In these songs of love and loss, of redemption and resurrection, of everyday people performing heroic acts, Springsteen was one of the first to offer a durable artistic response to 9/11. Working with a new producer, Brendan O'Brien, he also premiered a rich new sound that had some trademark characteristics of the old (the major-minor shifts that gave *Born to Run* such drive) but also the new: Writing in *Rolling Stone,* Kurt Loder observed that O'Brien "brought guitars forward instead of keyboards, found ways for Mr. Springsteen to sing without shouting and slipped a country fiddle or a gospel choir into some arrangements." "Like *Born in the U.S.A.* before it," Loder continues, "*The Rising* sounds unlike any other record of its time; in an era of rock murk and heavy synthetics, it flaunts its hard, bright guitars and positively walloping beats . . . Every song on the album is unified, to an extent, by a mood of romantic longing and a yearning for human connection. In the end, they all flow together."

Calling Springsteen "The Poet Laureate of 9/11," A. O. Scott offered an astute assessment of Springsteen's creative trajectory: "Since *Born to Run*, the album in which he first discovered his prophetic vocation, Springsteen's lyrics have often given a religious inflection to the durable rock 'n' roll themes of desire, frustration, and the longing for liberation, fusing Berry's vocabulary of cars, guitars, and pretty girls with the language of apocalypse and salvation, purgation and redemption. And these are more than just themes: The dialectic of despair and triumph is built into the musical structure and aural texture of the songs themselves, which enact, and induce in their listeners, the very emotions their words describe."

On *The Rising,* strength, faith, hope, and love are the nouns of "Into the Fire." And "Waiting on a Sunny Day," "Let's Be Friends," and "Mary's Place" are each in their way reminders and renewals of the dream of love and the promise of rock 'n' roll. "All people have is hope . . . a hope grounded in the real world of living, friendship, work, family, Saturday night," Springsteen said at the time. "And that's where it resides. That's where I always found faith and spirit. I found them down in those things, not some place intangible or some place abstract. And I've really tried to write about that basic idea my whole life."

The success of *The Rising* only increased the calls for Springsteen to enter politics. One group in fall 2002 circulated a petition to nominate Springsteen as a third-party candidate to run for senator from New Jersey. Springsteen responded, "If nominated, I will not run. If elected, I will not serve." But within two years, he decided that the time had come, if not to run for office, to use his platform to campaign for political change.

In August 2004, Springsteen published an editorial in the *New York Times.* Titled "Chords for Change," he announced that he would be part of a broad constituency of musicians touring under the umbrella name Vote for Change. "Our goal," he explained, "is to change the direction of the government and change the current administration come November." He explained that "personally, for the last 25 years I have always stayed one step away from partisan politics," but he felt given the performance of the Bush administration, "the stakes have risen too high to sit this election out." Over his entire career, "I've tried to think long and hard about what it means to be an American," and now it was time to fight for "the country we carry in our hearts."

That stirring phrase displayed a deep understanding of what

Americans want to feel about their nation. Springsteen would again mention the history book that influenced him so powerfully when he first read it in 1981, but this time he took its lessons a step further. It had helped him to understand the forces that trapped his father, and now it helped him understand what could be done about it. Having exposed through his work the ways in which the American dream was a lie, he now sought to reclaim it. He told a British interviewer that Commager and Nevins's book "had an enormous effect on me . . . a very powerful history of the U.S.A. It went back to that core set of democratic values that the country guided itself by sometimes and sometimes not. It was the first thing I read that made me feel part of a historic continuum—feel our daily participation and collusion in the chain of events. As if this was my historical moment. In the course of your lifetime how your country steers itself is under your stewardship."

In Philadelphia on October 1, 2004, before launching into "Born to Run," Springsteen, in what he laughingly called his "public-service announcement," offered his most impassioned and explicit speech about the country:

> We remain a land of great promise but it's time we need to move America towards the fulfillment of its promises that she's made to her citizens—economic justice, civil rights, protection of the environment, respect for others, and humility in exercising our power at home and around the world, these core issues of American identity . . . America is not always right—that's a fairy tale that you tell your children at night before they go to sleep—but America is always true, and it's in seeking these truths that we find a deeper patriotism: Don't settle for anything less.

Not a few of his fans resented his overt march into political endorsement. Many of them were themselves conservative working-class followers who leaned Republican. A chat room on Springsteen's Web site was titled "Bruce Stay Out of Politics." One contributor wrote, "As a Springsteen fan of over 25 years, I am appalled by his campaigning for one of the candidates." Another resented Springsteen using his cultural position "against me politically," a position earned in part by conservative fans having bought his records and concert tickets. Others felt less troubled and attended the concerts for the music, not the message. "We support Bruce and we support Bush," said one police officer who wore a shirt emblazoned with the American flag that read, BRUCE FAN. BUSH FAN.

Springsteen made four appearances with Democratic nominee John Kerry, who used "No Surrender" as his campaign song. In Cleveland on November 1, Springsteen performed "The Promised Land" and "No Surrender" and dedicated a third song to a woman "who is actually a neighbor of mine, just a few minutes away from me in New Jersey. And she was one of the 9/11 widows known as the Jersey Girls, who, when the administration was stonewalling the 9/11 Commission, held their feet to the fire and got the truth out. So I want to do this tonight for her." He then played "Thunder Road."

Whatever his disappointment at the election results, Springsteen did what he always did: He found solace in his music and his writing. He performed at several benefits, put the finishing touches on a new solo album, and prepared to issue a multidisc set to commemorate the thirtieth anniversary of *Born to Run*.

Devils & Dust, a solo album Springsteen released in April 2005, continued to explore the questions first formulated thirty years earlier. Springsteen explained the connections: "On *Born to*

Run, there's that sense of longing to break free—but to what? Longing to move forward and ahead—but to where? Through *Devils and Dust* I've been trying to answer those questions. *Born to Run* was very pivotal in that it expressed my most hopeful feelings and some of my desires . . . All backed with an enormous dose of fear, of course."

Most of the songs on *Devils & Dust* had been written and recorded more than ten years earlier. It didn't matter, just as it didn't matter in 2001 that "City of Ruins" was a song Springsteen had written a year or two before 9/11. Artistic work sometimes rhymes with the moment (as with *Born to Run* and *Born in the U.S.A.*), sometimes trails it, and sometimes is ahead of it. Springsteen began to use the metaphor of the canary in the coal mine as artistic model—canaries were used to warn coal miners of leaking methane gas. Of course, in those cases the canary issued its warning by dying. Springsteen issued his by singing. "There's a part of the singer going way back in American history that is, of course, the canary in the coal mine," Springsteen observed. "When it gets dark, you're supposed to be singing. It's dark right now. The American idea is beautiful idea. It needs to be preserved, served, protected and sung out."

The title song, written for the album, expresses the fears of a soldier who is "a long, long way from home" and wonders "What if what you do to survive/Kills the things you love." The album goes on to narrate the struggles of a variety of characters: cowboys, a boxer, immigrants, "ne'er-do-wells and desperadoes struggling on the margins of America." "It's personal and political," Springsteen said at the time. "I'm singing about the same ideals: fairness and justice and creating some place you feel proud to call home." And it is about love.

The ideas of home and love appear repeatedly: "I could walk you all the way home," "I knew the fight was my home," "It's your love here that keeps my soul alive," "I wanna find me a world, where love's the only sound," "Love leaves nothin' but shadows and vapor," "I walked the valley of love and tears and mystery," "For your love I give God thanks." And in "Jesus Was an Only Son," those words did not have to appear, because the hymn is a testament to the theme of ultimate love and homecoming.

> *A mother prays, "Sleep tight, my child, sleep well*
> *For I'll be at your side*
> *That no shadow, no darkness, no tolling bell,*
> *Shall pierce your dreams this night."*

But there is a deep sadness, knowing that, in the end, a mother cannot protect her child. There's a "destination that can never be reached," the narrator sings. During the *Devils & Dust* tour, Springsteen offered a lengthy introduction to the song that went into the influence of the church and Catholic school on his upbringing. In a monologue that brought tears to many fans, he explained that he tried to imagine Jesus just as a mother's son, and he concluded this way as he began singing the song:

> The first thing that strikes you when you have your kids is that there isn't anything you wouldn't do to keep them safe, and the second thing that strikes you is that you can't. If you figure that the choices we make in our life are given their weight by the things we sacrifice for them, parts of life we choose, and you give up some other part. I always figured that Jesus had to be thinking about the part of life he was giving up, that it was

beautiful this time of the year down in the Galilee, that there was that little bar just across from the beach and they needed a manager, and Mary Magdalene could tend bar and he could save the preaching for the weekends, and they could've had a bunch of kids and got to watch the sun fall on their face, their lungs fill with air at night when they're sleeping, and see the next day, and the day after that, and the day after that, and the day after that.

The explicit turn to religious themes was unusual, though the language of faith and salvation and spirituality had filled Springsteen's work from the beginning. "*Born to Run*," Springsteen once said, "was a spiritual record in dealing with values . . . [It] really dealt with faith and a searching for answers." But now reviewers seized on the religious. HAVING LOST HIS BET ON JOHN KERRY, THE BOSS TURNS TO A HIGHER AUTHORITY, read a headline in the *New York Times*. (Another headline read, BORN AGAIN IN THE U.S.A.) Springsteen, who says he is not a regular churchgoer, has admitted that as time passed he "got a lot less defensive" about the Catholic imagery in his work. "It's not a negative thing," he said. "There was a powerful world of potent imagery that became alive and vital and vibrant, and was both very threatening and held out the promise of ecstasies and paradise. There was this incredible internal landscape that they created in you."

Springsteen ended shows on the tour with a hypnotic performance of a song by Suicide called "Dream, Baby, Dream" for which he added several verses. Sitting at a pump organ with synthesizer playing behind him, the song was part lullaby, part hymn, totally musical, and going on for more than eight minutes, repeating again and again the words, "Dream, baby, dream." "Keep the fire burning," he sings. "Dry your eyes/I just wanna see you smile," he repeats over and over. "Come on, open up your heart"—a request that is both romantic and spiritual. He gets up from the organ but the synthesizer keeps playing. If the song sounds like a lament at the beginning, someone telling you to have hope where there is none, by the end it lifts heavenward, picking up the pace. He walks offstage having delivered a message of faith in the power of dreams. Thirty years after the "runaway American dream" of "Born to Run," Springsteen had returned to a belief in "dreams and visions."

Combined with such themes as escape, justice, and home, Springsteen's spiritual vision deepened the contours of an American identity that he had been mapping for thirty years. In 2005, *Born to Run* was also born again with the issue of a multidisc set including a remastered compact disc, a documentary on the making of *Born to Run* titled *Wings for Wheels*, and a concert DVD of the November 18, 1975, show at the Hammersmith Odeon, a performance that received a range of responses from the English press. The collection provided an opportunity to reconsider the masterpiece thirty years down the road.

To promote the anniversary, Springsteen spoke about the album: "Everything I knew and dreamed about was packed in those songs. I had the desire to be great, to do something passionate, to capture something about living that I was yearning for myself." He explained to Terry Gross that on *Born to Run*, the characters are running from something but they are also running to something. And that "'to' was always, Where do I live? Who am I? What's my place? And my characters weren't really rebellious. I always felt they were outsiders trying to figure out how to get in." And once they find a place, they try to shape where they live and work and ultimately bring up their children. All his music, he said, was about that—and also, he joked, the question that rock music had posed from the beginning: "Will you pull your pants down?"

In another interview, Nick Hornby asked Springsteen why songs like "Thunder Road" and "Born to Run" still resonated thirty years on: "People took that music," Springsteen said, "and they really made it theirs. I think I worked hard for that to happen. I am providing a service and it's one that I like to think is needed. It's at the core of trying to do it right, from year to year. It's the motive when you go out there. You want that reaction: 'Hey, I know that kid. That's me!' Because I still remember that my needs were very great, and they were addressed by things that people at the time thought were trash, popular music and B movies . . . But I found a real self in them that helped me make sense of the self that I grew up with—the person I actually was."

In reconsidering the album thirty years later, Jon Pareles reminded readers that it transformed Springsteen from "a local sensation into an American rock archetype." "Wired with poetic precision and operatic intensity," is how Ashley Kahn put it in the *Wall Street Journal*. Robert Christgau, writing for *Blender*, said, "The biggest problem with Bruce Springsteen's 1975 breakthrough album was always how unabashedly it proclaimed its own greatness . . . Yet it sounds greater today than it ever did."

Writers such as Pareles and Christgau had reviewed the album when it first came out. The anniversary proved an occasion for a much younger generation of writers to consider *Born to Run* for the first time. Clayton Purdom, a reviewer for the music Web site Coke Machine Glow, looked back and located the album's significance:

What Springsteen represents is no less than a bridge between the classic rock of our parents and the punk rock that birthed all relevant contemporary music (excepting hip hop, of course). The worn story goes that the Ramones and their ilk were reacting against the tired dinosaurs of rock by reducing it to its simplest forms, shredding the prog rock posturing and conceptual wankery of the bloated '70s. This story is true, but it doesn't mention that Springsteen did it first, and he did it without sacrificing the inherent beauty of rock and roll as a massive cultural force, and he did it in a manner relevant to the everyday people that rock and roll music is supposed to be relevant to, not some skinny leather-clad hipsters in a New York basement. He did it first, and he did it biggest, and he did it best. And he did it on *Born to Run*.

Similarly conscious of generational issues, the online magazine *Stylus* offered a call to reclaim the greatness of the single: "If ever a song desperately needed a second chance after decades of baby boomers beating it into submission from their weak car stereos, it's 'Born to Run.' Four minutes that manage to encapsulate everything Springsteen represents." The album "endures because of its honesty in the face of cynicism, its commitment to hope in the face of inevitable misfortune. All this should have made *Born to Run* the most uncool record of all time. Instead it was one of the greatest. Still is."

It is not surprising that the thirtieth anniversary of *Born to Run* led some reviewers to locate themselves by how old they were when the album came out. In "Tramps Like Us," Eric Alterman, of the *Nation,* tells us he was fifteen at what he is certain was "the worst time to go through adolescence ever invented." Alterman's essay recaptures the social and cultural context out of which the album emerged and into which it was received. "The American

Century," Alterman explains, "was melting like cheap plastic left out in the sun . . . Inside post-Watergate, post-Vietnam, post-idealist America, the economic foundations of prosperity were eroding . . . From a pop culture standpoint, pretty much everything that had given 1960s culture its passion, energy and creativity had disappeared and been replaced by exhaustion and exploitation." Into this context erupted *Born to Run*, a product of its time and place and yet timeless in its themes.

Not everyone was willing to honor Springsteen's achievement. Although the New Jersey Senate passed by voice vote a pro forma resolution paying tribute to the thirtieth anniversary, the United States Senate did not. The resolution was sponsored by Senators Jon Corzine and Frank Lautenberg of New Jersey. Resolutions congratulating and honoring are passed routinely, but Senator Bill Frist, the Republican majority leader, refused to allow it to come up for consideration. The spiteful action was seen as political payback for Springsteen having supported John Kerry so publicly. Writing in the *New York Times*, novelist Harlan Coben pointed out the irony that "many of Mr. Springsteen's characters—the factory worker, the soldier, the working stiff seeking release, the Friday-night racer looking for escape—would vote Republican."

Of course, *Born to Run* is neither Democrat nor Republican, young nor old, East Coast nor West. It is American. Lester Bangs spotted this in 1975 when he reviewed the album: "Bruce Springsteen is an American archetype," he declared. Springsteen has said he writes American music, that he is interested "in what it means to live in America . . . to chart the distance between American ideals and American reality." Unpacking that is no simple matter. It means he is traveling musical paths that run from gospel, rhythm and blues, soul, and rockabilly through folk, early pop, and rock 'n' roll.

It means he is traveling lyrical roads that run from Ralph Emerson, Herman Melville, and Walt Whitman through Mark Twain, John Steinbeck, Ralph Ellison, Flannery O'Connor, Jack Kerouac, Raymond Carver, and Cormac McCarthy. It means that he is traveling scenic highways that run from John Ford and Martin Scorcese to Dorothea Lange and Robert Frank.

It means, mostly, that he is working on the problem of what it means to be an American—the big questions of identity and location, of values and morality, of individualism and community, of love and home. These, of course, are not strictly American questions but human ones. In the American context, however, they take on particular resonance. Essential to the endeavor of American identity is liberation. That is the point, he has said time and again:

The greatest pop music was music of liberation. Bob Marley, Bob Dylan, Elvis Presley, James Brown, Public Enemy, the Clash, the Sex Pistols. Those were pop groups that liberated an enormous amount of people to be who they are, to suss through their identity. To begin to find a way of looking at the world and to find a way to move through the world. And perhaps a way to impact upon the world. The best pop music reaches all the different parts of your life . . . And that was why, the subjects I wrote about, that's what I was concerned with. I wanted to address your family. I wanted to address your country. I wanted to address your Saturday night in the bar when you're dancing and having a good time. Your relationships with the person you love and the people that love you. These were things that, to me, I found all of this inside of pop music. In the beauty of the singers' voices, in the way that the music made me feel. And also, in what it made me feel that I could do.

Springsteen, of course, did not invent the runaway dream. That dream runs deep in American culture and traces back to the nation's very origins, in which explorers and dissidents, inventors and visionaries, saw in the New World an opportunity to reinvent themselves, or perfect themselves, or empower themselves. For many more, who arrived here not by choice but by force, the dream of escape began the moment they landed. Generation after generation, immigrants especially, came searching for something, escaping what they left behind and then escaping what they found upon arrival.

Springsteen provided a specific generation at a specific historical moment with a soundtrack that exploded from speakers and stage. That the album was about the search for meaning and the probable hopelessness of the pursuit made it all the more romantic and powerful. In 1975, I listened to *Born to Run* again and again and again. I absorbed it, contemplated it, internalized it, and reacted to it—I took total ownership of it. The album fed my fantasies, expressed my fears, and encouraged my own dream of escape and search for connection. More than thirty years later, it still does.

ENCORE: "WHAT ELSE CAN WE DO NOW?"

It's embarrassing to want so much, and to expect so much from music, except sometimes it happens—The Sun Sessions, Highway 61, Sgt. Pepper, *the Band, Robert Johnson,* Exile on Main Street, Born to Run—*whoops, I meant to leave that one out.*

—BRUCE SPRINGSTEEN, 2005

PREPARING FOR a worldwide tour in October 2007 in support of *Magic*, a new album, Roy Bittan and Steve Van Zandt spoke with Scott Pelley of *60 Minutes*. Pelley asked them if, after more than thirty years, they hated playing "Born to Run" over and over again.

Bittan responded by saying how he once heard Tony Bennett asked by an interviewer whether he was sick of singing "I Left My Heart in San Francisco." His answer was, "It gave me the keys to the world." "Well, there it is, that's it," Bittan said.

Van Zandt had a different answer. He chortled, "I figure if we do a few more tours I might actually learn it. So, you know, I mean, we live in hope."

By 2007, Springsteen, too, was trying to live in hope for a country he saw spiraling in the wrong direction. More than ever, he believed that his music might have a meaningful impact. In 2006, he issued *We Shall Overcome: The Seeger Sessions*, and toured with a remarkable eighteen-piece backup band that provided an education in

American musical history: folk, country, blues, swing, gospel, zydeco, rock. Springsteen performed classic American folk songs such as "John Henry," "Old Dan Tucker," and "Jacob's Ladder." He also did "Eyes on the Prize" and "We Shall Overcome," spirituals central to the civil rights movement. And he premiered a new song that he had written: "American Land," a celebration of America as a nation of nations, in Whitman's apt phrase. The song opens with the immigrant's question, "What is this land America so many travel there?" The answer is a land where "there's treasure for the taking, for any hard working man/Who will make his home in the American Land."

In fall 2007, when Springsteen released *Magic*, his fifteenth studio album and the first with the E Street Band since *The Rising*, he discussed his vision: "My songs, they're all about the American identity and your own identity and the masks behind the masks behind the masks, both for the country and for yourself," he told *Rolling Stone*. "I'm interested in what it means to be an American, he explained to *60 Minutes*. "I'm interested in what it means to live in America. I'm interested in the kind of country that we live in and leave to our kids. I'm interested in trying to define what that country is. I've got the chutzpah or whatever you want to say to believe that if I write a really good song about it, it's going to make a difference."

In a way, Springsteen had come to embrace what Bob Dylan had fled from: the protest song. He understood, of course, that for the song to succeed it had to have a life outside of its political content and context. It must stand on its own and have multiple meanings for the listener or else it would fail; it would only be a headline, not a work of art.

Consider the opening line of "Livin' in the Future," a song Springsteen said onstage and in interviews was about what was happening at the time: "A letter come blowin' in on an ill wind."

Dylan's "Blowin' in the Wind," from 1963, became an anthem for the civil rights and antiwar movements of the 1960s. It did not refer to specific events but posed a series of questions, the answer to which was "blowin' in the wind"—an ambiguous enough phrase to be read as optimistic or pessimistic or both.

Springsteen is more overt in "Livin' in the Future," which repeats his long-standing conceit of blues verse and gospel chorus. Election day has led to authoritarianism; liberty "has sailed away on a bloody red horizon"; the seas are rising. Springsteen told *60 Minutes*, "when people think of the American identity, they don't think of torture, they don't think of illegal wiretapping, they don't think of voter suppression, they don't think of no habeas corpus . . . those are things that are anti-American."

If lyrically certain songs on *Magic* sounded overtly political (in "Last to Die," he paraphrases John Kerry's line delivered in 1971 to the Senate Foreign Relations Committee: "How do you ask a man to be the last man to die for a mistake?"), musically and thematically much of the album addresses ideas Springsteen first developed on *Born to Run*. Until 2005, when he spent time listening again to his signature album, he says, "I forgot how good that record was." The fusion of romanticism and darkness so indicative of his work on *Born to Run* would reemerge on *Magic*.

The album title brings to mind the "magic in the night" of "Thunder Road," though now the "long night" is "as dark as a grave" ("Devil's Arcade"), "on the road the sun is sinkin' low" ("Magic"), "you can't sleep at night" ("Your Own Worst Enemy"), "we took the highway till the road went black" ("Last to Die"), and this is "the last lone American night" ("Radio Nowhere").

As for romance, lyrically there is none on *Magic*: In "Girls in Their Summer Clothes," Springsteen sings, "She went away, she cut me like a knife" (to a jaunty Beach Boys riff). The narrator now is past the point where girls in their summer clothes stop for him. And in "I'll Work for Your Love," overflowing with religious imagery, "Your tears, they fill the rosary/At your feet, my temple of bones/Here in this perdition we go on and on."

And yet musically, the album is as accessible and hard-rocking as anything Springsteen had attempted in a long time. It evokes the chords and rhythms of *Born To Run* ("I want a thousand guitars/I want pounding drums," he sings on "Radio Nowhere"). There are blasts of power guitar along with the distinct sounds of Clemons's sax, Bittan's piano, Federici's organ, and the thumping bass lines of Tallent and drumbeats of Weinberg. Springsteen says the album marks "a reinfatuation with pop music." Songs such as "Girls in Their Summer Clothes" are "straight-out big. I don't think I've written as romantically as I allowed myself to do on that song maybe since 'Born to Run.'"

On *Magic*, observed one critic, Springsteen has "rediscovered the music of his youth . . . and that revelation has freed him of the Bruce Springsteen 'man of the people' shackles and has enabled him to have some fun." Writing in *Rolling Stone*, David Fricke notes, "The arrangements, the performances and Brendan O'Brien's wall-of-surf production are mined with echoes and near-direct quotes of classic records, including Springsteen's." Indeed, the opening piano of "I'll Work for Your Love" evokes "Jungleland"; "Livin' in the Future" updates "Tenth Avenue Freeze-Out"; "Devil's Arcade," thought Ann Powers, aims for the specificity of earlier ballads such as "Meeting Across the River"; "You'll Be Coming Down" sounds "Orbisonian"; "Girls in Their Summer Clothes" is "Spectorish." "Last to Die," Fricke points out, "takes off like 'Thunder Road' but into a darkness of unknown depth."

How to return from that darkness has always been the flip side of escaping into it. The answer comes in the form of the album's masterpiece, "Long Walk Home." It opens with guitars and builds, drums and band entering for the second verse, guitar and sax solos narrating the journey after the chorus is sung the second time. The song is about a town that no longer is what it once was, a place of strangers with boarded-up stores, signs that only say "Gone." In the "deep green of summer" when "the night sky was glowin'," the narrator sees the town where he was born in the distance and begins the journey home. It will be taken alone. The song opens with what might be the end of a relationship ("You just slipped somethin' into my palm/Then you were gone"). He will try to go home, but it will be on foot. No cars, no motorcycles, no open highway. "Everybody has a reason to begin again," he sings, and he wants to begin again by trying to renew what once was but is no more.

> My father said "Son, we're lucky in this town
> It's a beautiful place to be born
> It just wraps its arms around you
> Nobody crowds you, nobody goes it alone.
> That you know flag flying over the courthouse
> Means certain things are set in stone
> Who we are, what we'll do and what we won't."

The song doesn't tell us how to go home or how to restore what the place once might have been. "A beautiful place to be born" is a far cry from "the fire we was born in" on "Backstreets." The song accepts that at one point, home had become so toxic that you had to run. It tells us it will be a long walk to return and restore. We'll get there, but don't wait up. Recall that on "Thunder Road" the narrator hoped Mary was "ready to take that long walk." The headline of a review of *Magic* in the London *Observer* put the matter simply: AN ENDLESS ROAD, A SEARCH FOR HOME: THAT'S THE AMERICAN WAY.

Speaking about the song, Springsteen said, "A guy comes back to his town and recognizes nothing and is recognized by nothing. The singer in 'Long Walk Home,' that's his experience. His world has changed. The things that he thought he knew, the people who he thought he knew, whose ideals he thought he had something in common with, are like strangers. The world that he knew feels totally alien." Springsteen added that he felt that was what had happened in America since 2000.

The song is not nostalgic; it does not romanticize the past. Rather it "looks more to the future," Springsteen offered, and invites us to wonder now "how well is the American promise kept for most American citizens." Writing in the *Nation*, David Corn took up the issue of nostalgia:

> Springsteen . . . is not wallowing in nostalgia . . . He's expressing a desire. Rock and roll has always been about yearning. In earlier days, it was about longing for sex, love, a fast car, flight. You know, "it's a death trap, it's a suicide rap," and so on. But as he surveys the horizon and sees a nation in trouble, that small town Springsteen wanted to flee as a young man doesn't look so bad now—that is, as a symbol of America's best values: community, compassion, the rule of law. So he's brought the band together and called upon the rock idiom he knows so well to share his present-day yearnings. At the age of 58, Springsteen knows that it's not about running away, it's about walking back. And though the music soars, his message is mired in realism: this walk is not going to be easy.

And so the journey continues, a journey that began more than thirty years ago when *Born to Run* was released. In 1984, Springsteen said of *Born to Run*, "I always felt that was my birthday album. All of a sudden, bang! Something happened, something crystallized and you don't even know what." The music of that album, and all the work since, A. O. Scott has shrewdly explained, is not music one grows out of: Rather, it is music one grows up to. And it is music that many listeners say defines them. But how do you calculate the influence of a song or an album in your life? How does it send you on your necessary journey or reinforce the journey you are on? We have songs that carry enormous meaning for us, songs we want played at our weddings or at our funerals, songs that every time we hear them, every single time, we pause, we remember, we smile, we sing, we ignite.

And maybe even more than that. Maybe we have music that has changed or saved our lives. It did for Springsteen: "rock 'n' roll came to my house where there seemed to be no way out. It just seemed like a dead end street, nothing I like to do, nothing I wanted to do except roll over and go to sleep or something. And it came into my house—snuck in you know, and opened a whole world of possibilities." He declared in 1984, "I know that rock and roll changed my life. It was something for me to hold on to. I had nothing. Before then the whole thing was a washout for me. It really gave me a sense of myself."

Springsteen's biographer Dave Marsh also talked about rock 'n' roll in precisely these terms when he published *Born to Run: The Bruce Springsteen Story*, a book that became a bestseller and invented the genre of rock biography. Marsh wrote, "I believe that rock and roll has saved lives, because I know it was instrumental in shaping my own. . . . We had nothing; rock lent us a sense that we could have it all." But until Springsteen emerged, the promise of rock had been broken by phoniness and commercialism. "Rock saved my life," Marsh avers, but until Springsteen, "it also broke my heart."

Springsteen's music, in particular the songs of *Born to Run,* saved or changed many a listener's life. For example, on October 6, 2007, Nishant Dahiya offered a comment on National Public Radio in which he explained how Springsteen's music affected him. A nine-year-old fourth grader in India when he first heard *Born in the U.S.A.*, he could not get the sound out of his head. A decade later, studying to be an engineer, he played Springsteen's newly released live album and heard "Thunder Road." "That incredible song, 'Thunder Road,' about life and love, about life's second chances. That night, it spoke directly to me," he says. "By the time he sang that last line, I understood the song's implicit message: that I needed to get out. That I should do what I wanted to do. That I should make my choice and take my chance. That what is life if not about taking chances—and not just for love, but for life—for real life. I can't say that that four-minute song was the only thing that set me on a different path. But that night, all alone with a textbook I didn't care about and a calculator I could have thrown against a wall, I had one of those rare moments of blinding clarity. Now, ten years later, I'm in America. I have a ticket with a seat number on it. And today, I travel to Philadelphia to see Bruce Springsteen."

Or this entry from a fan on the Web site rateyourmusic.com: "This record changed my life, it made me believe in the power of rock 'n' roll and it made me feel that no matter how small or insignificant my life was there was someone out there that understood what I was going through, someone else that could breathe the fire we was born in. Thank you Bruce."

Or this comment from Graziano Romani: "I was listening to my dad's car stereo, and I heard the song 'Born to Run.' From that moment on, my life changed. Suddenly I got into Bruce. It gave me a lot of faith, a sense of strength and emotion . . . Bruce gave me the will to start singing."

Or the reflections of Sarfraz Manzoor, who, as a sixteen-year-old Pakistani living east of London, first listened to Springsteen's music and played "Born to Run" four or five times straight. Manzoor recalls, "Being a working-class Pakistani teenager in Luton in the 80s was to live a life of itchy claustrophobia. I had drifted through adolescence experiencing few of the things that defined such times: no childhood holidays, no playing football with my dad, no family gatherings at Christmas; no sense that there was anything beyond our three-bedroom semi. I knew that there had to be some way out, but until I heard Springsteen, I did not know how."

As for me, *Born to Run* may not have changed my life, but it is central to it: The album expressed what I felt, articulated in words and music my own dream of escape and search for meaning. On first listening, I do not think I heard the darkness and despair of songs such as "Backstreets" and "Jungleland." What I heard was a primal voice that gave vent to frustration, and soaring power chords that made me want to drive faster. What I felt was that maybe I didn't have to be trapped by the American dream, and that maybe in the midst of my worst despair and fear of failure there was hope.

Springsteen did for me, eighteen years old in 1975, what Dylan had done for eighteen-year-olds in 1965 and what Presley had done for eighteen-year-olds in 1955. Springsteen once noted that Elvis freed our bodies and Dylan freed our minds. Springsteen freed our souls.

To be sure, the timelessness of *Born to Run* is that an eighteen-year-old can pick it up today and understand it, relate to it, in the same way I "got" "Like a Rolling Stone" or "Hound Dog" when I first heard them. There is permanence, of course, to potent works of art. But there is also a certain temporality. *Born to Run* came out of a historical moment that felt dislocated and stale, a time of political and social and cultural malaise. All teenagers feel trapped, but different generations feel trapped in different ways.

In 1975, I was in college and I was scared of all the things eighteen-year-olds fear—commitment, responsibility, the future. It is important to recall that mine was something of a post-heroic generation (I was born in 1957), too young to have participated fully in the cultural rebellions of the 1950s and the civil rights and anti-war movements of the 1960s, yet socialized and politicized by those movements (I had long hair, tried pot, and supported lost causes). If the nation, post-Nixon, post-Vietnam, midrecession, was in a state of national malaise, I felt deep personal ennui bordering on existential depression about the meaninglessness of life.

The extra gift of *Born to Run*, in addition to the jolt of recognition in the lyrics and music, was that Springsteen was mine—I was there from the start. Enough of my older brother bragging about seeing the Beatles at Shea or attending Woodstock. I had an artist who made me feel alive before he hit big: I was in for the long haul.

The summer of 1975, home from college, my father would ask, "What do you want to be?" I knew, of course, that he wanted me to attend law school. I took some prelaw classes, but it was history and literature that spoke to me. In 1976, I lived off campus with my girlfriend, much to the annoyance of my parents and hers. We were enacting our version of *Born to Run*, though I didn't understand that at the time. We broke up the following year, then reunited, then graduated and wondered what now.

She was in Chicago, where I had worked one summer for a lawyer, an experience that only reinforced my desire to find another profession. Still, I had applied to law school. I was accepted to some and was rejected from some, and I decided to wait a year. My parents didn't understand. Having graduated only high school, they dreamed of their son the lawyer. I dreamed of living in New York City, but doing what, I had no idea, as long as I wasn't cornered in some soul-deadening nine-to-five affair.

One summer night I called my girlfriend in Chicago. We decided we needed to figure out our relationship, so she came East and we spent a few days together. By the last day, September 15, 1978, we decided she would move to New York and we would try living together.

That night, we saw Springsteen at the Academy of Music on Fourteenth Street, or maybe it was the Palladium by then. It was her first time, my fourth or fifth. We had seats in the front of the balcony, though I do not recall sitting. The end of the set (I looked it up to confirm my memory) was "Not Fade Away" into "She's the One," "Backstreets" with the narration in the middle, "Rosalita," "Born to Run," and "Tenth Avenue Freeze-Out."

We exploded out into the city, arm in arm, exhilarated, happy, in love, feeling immortal.

That fall we broke up again.

I went to graduate school for a PhD in history. After a year apart, my girlfriend and I reunited. This time she gave me an ultimatum—marry her or move on for good. And so on July 4, 1981 (declaration of dependence, I joked), at age twenty-four (Springsteen's age when he wrote "Born to Run"), I got married. Talk about being scared that maybe you ain't that young anymore. I wanted "Born to Run" as a wedding song; I got "Can't Take My Eyes Off of You."

Springsteen's albums and concerts continued to serve as benchmarks: In Philadelphia, we went with friends to Veterans Stadium for the *Born in the U.S.A.* tour; in Los Angeles, near where I had my first job teaching American history, we attended the *Tunnel of Love* tour; in New Jersey and New York we saw him in 1992 when he toured with a different band. At some point *we*, as far as concerts went, became a lot of *me* as my wife said that while she liked Springsteen, there was only so much she could take. (She relented for front-row seats to Giants Stadium in 2003.)

In 1995 I was alone in New Brunswick for the opening of the *Tom Joad* tour. (We had moved back to New Jersey in 1992.) And in 1999, I took my son, then twelve, to his first show (the night he was born, racing to the hospital, "Thunder Road" came on the radio). I went to a concert with my brother, and then I took my wife, son, and eight-year-old daughter (the reunion tour—her first show). And then . . . let's just say it grows more obsessive from there. Multiple shows for the *Rising* tour, multiple shows alone and asking others to go for *Devils & Dust*, and multiple shows, now with students to whom I gave away extra tickets, for the start of the *Magic* tour, and tickets to all three shows at Giants Stadium at the end of the *Magic* tour in July 2008.

Granted, my behavior is a bit fanatical. But then, Springsteen may be the most dynamic live performer ever. No two shows are ever the same: Springsteen has said about performing, "You're different than you were a week ago, two weeks ago, a year ago. I'm not trying to re-create what the song was like on the record. I can do that, but there's no purpose. I'm searching for the song to be alive *now*."

The time I spend at a concert leaves me feeling renewed. For those three hours or so, only the music matters. Partially it is escape from the stresses of everyday life. Partially it is community—I walk out reconnected to certain feelings and recommitted to certain ideals. Completely it is joy.

If I am devoted to Springsteen, it must be noted that he is devoted to his audience. It's a reciprocal relationship, as it must be for any caring star and his fans, for any musician and those hearing his songs, preferably at very high decibel levels. We have aged together, Springsteen and us, marrying and having children and losing parents and going through therapy and wanting to have a good time and trying to figure out just what it means to be alive and to be an American.

I didn't become a historian, a writer, and a teacher because of Springsteen. But I have an affinity for the American themes that permeate his work. I feel nourished by them and challenged by them. What it means to be an American is a profound question for us all. And like Springsteen, as I've aged, my understanding of that problem has shifted from the romantic dream of escape to the realistic obligation of finding a place to settle down to the communitarian and spiritual duty of giving meaning to those grand abstractions: freedom, justice, equality, not to mention happiness. These, of course, are not American themes alone; they are human themes, which explain why Springsteen has a worldwide audience.

He has kept his promise: "I didn't get burned out. I didn't waste myself. I didn't die. I didn't throw away my musical values," he said in 1992.

And we as fans have kept ours. We've allowed him to grow as an artist, most of us anyhow, and have committed to the long haul. At the height of megastardom in 1984, Springsteen said, "I believe that the life of a rock 'n' roll band will last as long as you look down into the audience and can see yourself, and your audience looks up at you and can see themselves—and as long as those reflections are human, realistic ones."

This recognition has been central to my abiding affection for Springsteen. As much as he is a celebrity, as much as he is a part of the glorified culture of fame and status that is America, he appears to be just like one of us. It's possible this is an illusion, a confidence game being played on those wanting to believe that we have shared concerns. If the trick is on me, so be it. But I don't think he is a trickster. And to the extent that he is, what matters is the work, not the life: "Trust the art, not the artist." Springsteen once confessed, "I think someone can do real good work and be a fool in a variety of ways. I think my music is probably better than I am."

I believe Springsteen when he says he realized that he had to leave behind the rock 'n' roll dream that venerated a cult of personality because that was just fantasy, and he didn't want to be trapped by his own image and myth: "I think I made the mistake earlier on of trying to live within that dream, within that rock 'n' roll dream. It's a seductive choice, it's a seductive opportunity. The real world, after all, is frightening. In the end I realized that rock 'n' roll wasn't just about finding fame and wealth. Instead, for me, it was about finding your place in the world, figuring out where you belong."

There is something old-fashioned and traditional in Springsteen, something so rooted in Americana that it is almost embarrassing: his faith in hard work. He is correct when he says, "Dylan was a revolutionary. So was Elvis. I'm not that." Springsteen saw himself "as a nuts-and-bolts kind of person. I felt what I was going to accomplish I would accomplish over a long period of time, not in an enormous burst of energy or genius. To keep an even perspective on it all, I looked at it like a job—something that you do every day and over a long period of time." In its own way, this faith in the work ethic, in finding a job that you love and continuing to do it honestly and well, in embracing and living a real and not a fantasy life, makes him the most revolutionary of all rock stars.

Of course, much of this is rooted in his childhood. His parents "worked like crazy their whole lives. We weren't used to luck. That was something that happened to somebody else." And so Springsteen worked harder than anyone to make it as a guitar player, songwriter, bandleader, and performer. "I didn't see myself as some gifted genius type of person," he said, "I thought I was a hardworking guy." He only felt alive onstage, the one place where he didn't wallow in "self-loathing and self-hatred," the one place where he could prove all night how hard work paid off. It took him a long time to sort through his personal and creative obsessions. In 1992, he said, "Now I see that two of the best days in my life were the day I picked up the guitar, and the day that I learned how to put it down."

Born to Run is not just about who I was in 1975. It has remained a compass and a tool that has helped me to locate and build over the long haul. It has also been a source of inspiration. The album has continued to keep me good company on my journey, providing the soundtrack of my life, both articulating for me and helping me to articulate my dreams and fears.

At concerts, all the lights come on for "Born to Run," and everyone sings it together, pumping fists into the air. "It was a record of enormous longing, and those emotions and desires never leave you," Springsteen says. "You're dead when that leaves you. The song transcends your age and continues to speak to that part of you that is both exhilarated and frightened about what tomorrow brings. It will always do that—that's how it was built."

CODA:

In October 1975, a few weeks after his twenty-sixth birthday, Springsteen arrived in Los Angeles for a series of shows at the Roxy, a small club on the Sunset Strip. A towering billboard advertised his new album, *Born to Run*, with the headline: GET READY LOS ANGELES, HIS TIME HAS COME. Springsteen, riding in a car, looked away. He was thinking about his performance that night: "Every time you get on stage, you have to prove something. It doesn't matter if they've heard you or not. The kid on the street will make up his own mind. The music is what really matters."

As the car pulled into the lot, Springsteen heard on the radio the faint sounds of the Byrds' cover of Bob Dylan's "My Back Pages," which contains the famous couplet, "I was so much older then/I'm younger than that now." "Turn it up, turn it up," he shouted. Robert Hilburn, a music critic for the *Los Angeles Times,* was in the car: "Springsteen . . . leaned back against the seat, closing his eyes as he listened." When the song ended, he announced, 'That's one of the great ones, one of the really great ones.' "

In 1995, at age forty-six, Springsteen was asked how long he intended to play. He said that "at 60, I plan to be still doing it . . . The older you get the younger you are . . . We're moving it up as we go. It will be 80 in another five years."

We live in hope.

"Darkness." (© ERIC MEOLA, 2009)

A Q&A WITH GREIL MARCUS

Greil Marcus, a preeminent rock and cultural critic, is the author of numerous books, including the seminal *Mystery Train* (1975), *Lipstick Traces* (1989), *Invisible Republic* (1998), *Like a Rolling Stone* (2005), and *The Shape of Things to Come* (2006). He is also coeditor, with Werner Sollors, of *A New Literary History of America* (2009). Springsteen fans know him as the reviewer of *Born to Run* who in an October 1975 issue of *Rolling Stone* proclaimed that "it is a magnificent album that pays off on every bet ever placed on him." I began by asking him whether, more than thirty-five years later, the album holds up. His answer surprised me:

GM: What's interesting is I was so completely knocked out by "Born to Run" itself I had trouble at first playing the whole album. I kept playing that song over and over again. But that song has not worn all that well for me. There are other songs on that album that really grew over time, most of all "Jungleland." That's a real knockout. I remember Jon Landau telling me that when they were working on the album he kept telling Bruce "less is more, less is more." They had done rehearsal versions of that song, and then Bruce comes into the studio with a much, much cut-down version, like a two-and-a-half minute version, and Jon says "where's the rest of it?" The whole point of the song is that it goes on and on, and it builds and Bruce said "you said less is more." And Landau responded "well, not always."

LM: What you say about "Jungleland" is also true for me about "Backstreets," and in both cases part of the lasting power of those songs is Bruce's voice and its effectiveness.

GM: People are used to Bruce getting desperate and turning himself into sort of a body of pure emotion. That's what happens at the end of "Backstreets" and that's one of the reasons why it is so striking. I tend to think of Bruce as somebody who really can do so much more with less, with something like "Stolen Car" [*The River*, 1980] which is a really small song with enormous power. It's quite a black hole. The mask gets smaller and smaller and the energy gets greater and greater. A couple of lines in that song and the way that they are sung can momentarily replace his whole career, just the way the end of "Backstreets" can.

LM: The arc from "Backstreets" to "Stolen Car" is a good way to think about *Born to Run*, *Darkness on the Edge of Town*, and *The River*—as a trilogy tied together in a number of different ways. What are your thoughts on that?

GM: I think they are a trilogy of ambition, and I think his ambitions grow. He is working in a different manner. He is thinking about these albums as something that will last. The first two albums [*Greetings from Asbury Park* and *The Wild, the Innocent, and the E-Street Shuffle*] were made and they were put out. I know with *Born to Run* and *Darkness* he was continually delaying them, refusing to consider them finished. He said that one night in front of people is one night, but albums are forever. There is an attempt throughout to write songs that don't betray their inspiration, whether it is Roy Orbison or anyone else. I remember with *Darkness* feeling very disappointed that there didn't seem to be a single thing on it that really stuck. Ultimately I realized the song that did was "Darkness on the Edge of Town" which was a song that wasn't even supposed to be on the album. It was something Bruce brought in when they thought they were finished.

LM: That's fascinating because the reputation of that album seems only to have grown over time among his fans.

GM: He did a show at the Roxy [July 7, 1978] and I heard that show just a couple of days later. It was broadcast, people were taping it, someone sent me a tape of it, which turned out to be a better tape than anything I ever came across ever again. And "Racing in the Street," the version he did that night is so much greater than what he did on the album. He had not been playing these songs live, so it's only after he begins to go out and begins to play these songs in front of people that they really achieve their true form.

LM: Being located in Berkeley, you never had a chance to see Springsteen live until after he had already become something of a legend as a live performer. Do you recall the first time you saw the band?

GM: The first time I saw him was in '75 for the *Born to Run* tour at the Paramount Theatre in Oakland [October 31], which is a big old deco palace. I remember during the encores the balcony was actually shaking. But that was not actually a great show. The expectations were too high and he was performing as a national star for the first time and it just was off somehow. A couple of years later we saw him at the Berkeley Community Theatre [June 30 and 31, 1978] which is a much, much smaller place and that show was infinitely more effective. On the other hand, it was a couple of years later at the time of *The River* and he was playing stadiums, or at least he was playing the Oakland Coliseum Arena [October 27 and October 28, 1980], which is like 15,000 people, enclosed but very, very big. And he was able to achieve intimacy with very quiet delicate songs in both of those places. He had really become much more versatile as a showman or someone who could use the stage in many different ways.

LM: Fans often wonder about Springsteen the person versus Springsteen the showman. Bruce has warned us to trust the art and not the artist, but given the many opportunities you've had to get to know him off of the stage how would you describe Springsteen?

GM: I remember after the show at the Berkeley Community Theatre, which holds about 2000 people, and they made a conscious decision to bring down the size of the places he was playing, and we went backstage afterwards and I think that was the first time I had met him. Me, my wife, my brother, and a couple of other people. And Jon Landau was there, so Jon brings us into Bruce's dressing room and he leaves. And Jon is an old, old friend of mine, since the early seventies, so I was kind of surprised at that and here's Bruce who has to somehow relate to all these people he hasn't met. And I have never in my life encountered anybody with the ability to put other people at ease the way he can do it. He is a genuinely nice person, he is actually interested in other people. He likes to be recognized. He likes to be thought well of in whatever manner. Within moments we were just sitting around feeling completely comfortable and didn't feel any need to stay any longer than we might want to. That has always stayed with me and I have seen that same ability in many other situations over the years. And that is part of the way he works with his band, the way he works with an audience. It is the reason why, when during a solo tour such as the *Tom Joad* tour, he can ask the audience to be quiet because if these songs are going to work this is how it is going to work otherwise it isn't going to happen. And he can do that in a way that doesn't insult anybody.

LM: You mention Tom Joad, who of course is a seminal fictional character in American literature, the protagonist of John Steinbeck's *Grapes of Wrath*. What is your sense of Bruce's efforts to probe the contours of American culture? What happened in December 2000 when he sat in on your American Studies class, "Prophecy and the American Voice," at Princeton?

GM: Bruce is a great reader. He reads a lot and he reads well. He is self-taught, but [he also has] teachers, people like Jon Landau more importantly than anybody else both in terms of books and movies and art. Dave Marsh as well. And then whoever he might encounter. [The class] at Princeton, it was another example of his ability to work with a group of people. That can be a few people backstage or that can be ten thousand people in front of you at a concert. Getting a sense of who they are, how to win them over to your side—which means actually getting them to pay attention to what you are doing, and reaching them in a way that will have them leave and talk about what just happened.

I got a call from him asking whether he could come to my class. I said, "yes but you'll have to do the reading. It so happens the books for the next week's reading are Nick Tosches' biography of Jerry Lee Lewis, which I'm sure you already read." And he said, "Yeah, I've read that." And I said the other book is Lee Smith's novel *The Devil's Dream*. He went out and got it and read it. But then his kids got chicken pox and he had to stay home with them. So the last class, and the only class left, was on Allen Ginsberg's "Wichita Vortex Sutra." And I gave him what I gave the students, which was the text of the poem but also a recording done in 1994 where Ginsberg performed it in New York with a group of about 12 people, all different kinds of adventurous avant-garde musicians. It's a very long poem and I'm not sure Ginsberg ever performed it complete until that night. But it was an extraordinary moment where a poem written nearly thirty years before takes on, as I was saying about "Racing in the Street," takes on its real shape only much, much later.

Bruce reads the poem and listens to the tape and comes to class. I had two students who were leading the discussion and they had done a lot of work, a lot of preparation. And I told them that a friend of mine was going to be coming to the class and he was very well known. I didn't want them intimidated by it. That he was going to participate and that they should not worry about or think about it. So I walk in with Bruce and they just about fall over. But the students are totally cool. Bruce came in with an argument that he wanted to make about what the poem was about, how it got its argument across, how it worked, and he really came in with a complete argument. The way he managed to get that argument across was only to respond to something someone else said. So somebody else would say something, and he would say "just to follow up on that point." So he was able to get the argument he wanted to make out there in pieces over a three-hour seminar rather than ever saying "well, what I think this poem is about . . ." or anything like that. I think that speaks for two things. One is his ability to engage with people, but the other is to read something that he hadn't encountered before, read it deeply, and make a decision as to what it is.

LM: It's great to know Bruce is as good a student as he is a teacher. What you say about Ginsberg's poem is fascinating because it was written as an antiwar poem during the Vietnam War, yet as art, it achieved fulfillment nearly twenty years later. It leads me to think about the question of the relationship between music and the times in which it is created, particularly in regard to *Born to Run*.

GM: I think if you looked at *Born to Run*, one of the things that is missing from it is a sense of the larger world in which it appears, which is to say a post–Watergate world. The context of this album, I believe, is his career, what he has learned, where he wants to go, who he wants to become, who he thinks he is. The larger world is just not a factor. So what you are seeing in American movies at the same time—a sense of cynicism, a sense that nothing matters, nothing works, a sense that everyone is for themselves—that's not there at all. But with *Nebraska*, that's an album about the election of Ronald Reagan. Song after song is about the nihilism of Reaganite conservatism. It is so strong, and so tough, and so poetic, and so indirect in terms of addressing any of those questions that as a whole I can't imagine that record being made two years before or ten years after.

LM: And it continues to resonate because of its art. I would argue that *Born to Run* continues to resonate as well, especially because of how the album makes its listeners, both old and young, feel. But what do you make of the claim, offered in 1975, that the album in some way saved rock 'n' roll?

GM: No, I don't think so. If anything saved rock 'n' roll it was the Sex Pistols and they also, in some ways, completely invalidated it as a concept so that it became something completely different.

LM: Of course the point is to find music that may not save your life, or rock 'n' roll for that matter, but it at least makes you feel alive

GM: I went to see The New Pornographers two years ago in New York and I came out and someone said what did you think of the show, and I said it restored my faith in humanity. And I wasn't being ironic and I wasn't being funny. I said exactly what I meant. That was exactly how I felt. And I don't think I ever felt that before. But that was clearly it. That people could make such glorious sounds. That's all you want from life.

ACKNOWLEDGMENTS

My greatest debt is to Bruce Springsteen and Jon Landau Management for allowing me to quote from the songs. Their generosity makes possible the ongoing study of Springsteen's work. All lyrics have been checked against those posted at brucespringsteen.net. Special thanks must go to Mona Okada who cleared all permissions. I also appreciate the assistance provided by Alison Oscar. Garry Tallent was kind enough to discuss briefly the recording sessions with me and his insights were indispensable.

While *Runaway Dream* was in press, Springsteen released a new album. Given the title and theme of this book, I was delighted to see that he called it *Working on a Dream*.

I am overwhelmed by the support provided by Bob Crane, who heads the Friends of the Bruce Springsteen Collection housed at the Asbury Park library, and Chris Phillips, the editor of *Backstreets* magazine. Quite literally, without Bob and Chris I could not have completed this book. They tracked down and made copies of articles, facilitated introductions, and tried to answer all my questions. They exemplify the giving spirit of the community of Springsteen writers and fans. I am also grateful to Patricia La Sala at the Asbury Park Public Library.

In writing about *Born to Run*, the photographs are almost as memorable as the music. I offer my deepest thanks to Eric Meola for permission to reprint his iconic album cover, as well as several outtakes, and for allowing me to use his striking photograph titled "Darkness." I am also grateful to Barbara Pyle for her historically significant photograph, and to Timothy White for permission to reproduce his stunning portrait of Springsteen's hands playing the guitar. Thanks as well to Jim Marchese for permission to use his striking portrait of Springsteen for the book cover. I also appreciate the support provided by David Bett at Sony BMG, David Friend at *Vanity Fair*, and Daniel Wolff, who has written with passion and insight about Meola's photographs and Asbury Park.

Several current and former students assisted with research: Elise Galbo, Grace Green, Michael Klein, Erika Safir, and Nick Vasquez. I presented a version of chapter 4 to the Bruce Springsteen Symposium held at Monmouth University in 2005; I am grateful to Mark Bernhard for inviting me to participate. That paper later appeared in *Interdisciplinary Literary Studies*. In spring 2007, I taught a course on Presley, Dylan, and Springsteen. Heath Pendleton, a talented guitar-playing student, helped me understand the architecture of Springsteen's music.

A presentation to Trinity College alumni in summer 2008 clarified my thoughts about the album. I offer my thanks to Bill Jenkins for hosting the event and to Allison Boyle, Paul Raether, Ellie Shields, Aris Tzouflas, and Barrett Wilson-Murphy for an evening of stimulating conversation. My thanks as well to Rachel Ayers, Allan Feinberg, Jonathan Freedman, Sean Heffernan, Jonathan Masur, Jeff Roderman, Bryant Simon, Richard Skolnik, and Larry White.

My colleagues at Trinity College have been fully supportive of this project: Fred Alford, Zayde Antrim, Jeff Bayliss, Jen Bowman,

Jack Chatfield, Sean Cocco, Bill Decker, Rena Fraden, Cheryl Greenberg, Renny Fulco, Chris Hager, Joan Hedrick, Jimmy Jones, Kathleen Kete, Paul Lauter, Eugene Leach, Kate McGlew, Patricia McGregor, Kevin McMahon, Diana Paulin, Susan Pennybacker, Gary Reger, Dave Robbins, Ron Spencer, and Scott Tang. Sylvia DeMore, Gigi St. Peter, and Nancy Rossi have provided essential administrative support and many laughs. I wish I could list by name all the students in the American studies program—they have contributed to my work in countless ways. Special thanks to Ellen Cohn, Pam Ellis, Jessica Hart, and Julie Wheeler.

This is my second book with Peter Ginna. His good judgment and enthusiasm has supported me at every turn. Just as important, he hired Pete Beatty, a Springsteen enthusiast, as his assistant. I am grateful for their insightful readings of the manuscript. I offer my thanks as well to Mike O'Connor and Peter Miller. I am also indebted to my agent Zoe Pagnamenta and grateful for her efforts on my behalf.

Rachel Markowitz helped make this book possible. Kathy Feeley, Scott Gac, James Goodman, Douglas Greenberg, Peter Mancall, Aaron Sachs, and Thomas Slaughter read earlier versions of the manuscript and offered invaluable suggestions. They have followed the trajectory of my writing for a long time and I am fortunate for their friendship. Over the years I've gone to concerts with Dave Masur, Mark Richman, and Bruce Rossky. I hope to attend many more with them.

My in-laws Ed and Eileen Fox are a loving publicity machine for everything I do. My appreciation of music must have started with my late parents, Sarah and Seymour Masur, who enjoyed crooning Jolson and Sinatra. They thought Springsteen was Jewish, and I never bothered to correct the impression.

I knew putting headphones over Jani's pregnant belly and blasting Springsteen's songs would have good effect. Since then, Ben and Sophie have attended concerts with me and helped with research. I am counting on them to teach me how to master *Born to Run* on *Guitar Hero: World Tour*. As a family, we try to guard each other's dreams and visions.

Jani—thanks for that ultimatum all those years ago. This book is for you.

NOTES

Setting Up

1 *make the Greatest Record* Ken Tucker, "Springsteen: The Interview," *Entertainment Weekly* (February 28, 2003): 28.

3 *Rock 'n' roll has always* Patrick Humphries and Chris Hunt, *Springsteen: Blinded by the Light* (London: Plexus, 1985), 44.

3 *I'm a songwriter* Chris Phillips, ed., "*Born to Run*: The Lost Interviews: Part One," *Backstreets* 57 (Winter 1997): 25.

4 *The primary questions* Bruce Springsteen, *Songs* (New York: HarperCollins, 1998), 47.

4 *an American archetype* Lester Bangs, "Hot Rod Rumble in the Promised Land," *Creem* (November 1975), in June Skinner Sawyers, ed., *Racing in the Street: The Bruce Springsteen Reader* (New York: Penguin, 2004), 75.

4 *a true American punk* Robert Ward, "The Night of the Punk," *New Times* (September 5, 1975).

Sound Check: "The Screen Door Slams"

7 *a bold new talent* Lester Bangs, "Review of *Greetings from Asbury Park, N.J.*," *Rolling Stone* (July 5, 1973), in Editors of *Rolling Stone*, *Bruce Springsteen: The Rolling Stone Files* (New York: Hyperion, 1996), 32–33.

7 *much further along* Peter Knobler and Greg Mitchell, "Who Is Bruce Springsteen and Why Are We Saying All These Wonderful Things About Him?" *Crawdaddy* (March 1973), in June Skinner Sawyers, ed., *Racing in the Street: The Bruce Springsteen Reader* (New York: Penguin, 2004), 29–39.

7 *was important to me* Paul Williams, "Lost in the Flood," *Crawdaddy* (October 1974), in Sawyers, ed., *Racing in the Street*, 40.

7 *"I want you"—that's it* Michael Watts, "Lone Star," *Melody Maker* (November 30, 1974): 36–37, 56.

8 *Elvis, Otis Redding* Pat Knight, "Bruce Springsteen's Lone Star Promenade," *Rolling Stone* (September 12, 1974), in *Rolling Stone Files*, 37.

8 *the best thing anyone can do* Jay Cocks, "Along Pinball Way," *Time* (April 1, 1974): 80.

8 *But tonight there is someone* Jon Landau, "Growing Young with Rock 'n' Roll," *Real Paper* (May 22, 1974): 20.

10 *one of the most memorable* June Skinner Sawyers, "Introduction," in Sawyers, ed., *Racing in the Street*, ix.

10 *the kind of artist* Robert Ward, "The Night of the Punk," *New Times* (September 5, 1975).

14 *will rank among the great* John Rockwell, "The Rocky Road to Rock Stardom," *New York Times* (August 15, 1975): 74.

14 *Like only the greatest* Dave Marsh, "A Rock 'Star Is Born' Performance Review," *Rolling Stone* (September 25, 1975), in *Rolling Stone Files*, 38–39.

14 *I learnt when I was very young* Robert Crampton, "The Gospel According to Bruce," *Times Magazine* (London) (July 27, 2002): 21.

14 *is everything that has been claimed* Marsh, "A Rock 'Star is Born,'" in *Rolling Stone Files*, 39.

15 *discrepancy between the impact* Rockwell, "The Rocky Road to Rock Stardom," *New York Times* (August 15, 1975): 37.

15 *I like the classic idea* Neil Strauss, "Human Touch," *Guitar World* (October 1995): 60.

15 *We were ready to be booted* PRX Radio, "Bruce Springsteen: The Story of *Born to Run*" (November 10, 2005): http://www.prx.org/pieces/7067.

15 *We got a band* Paul Williams, "Lost in the Flood," in Sawyers, ed., *Racing in the Street*, 42.

15 *To me, the idea* Robert Hilburn, "Springsteen: Out in the Streets," *Los Angeles Times* (October 19, 1980), in Sawyers, ed., *Racing in the Street*, 95.

Chapter 1: Before *Born to Run*

17 *Springsteen was seven* Most accounts, following Springsteen's recollection, say he was nine. For example, Springsteen said in concert on August 20, 1981, "I remember when I was nine years old and I was sitting in front of the TV set and my mother had Ed Sullivan on and on came Elvis." But the dates do not match. There is no question he recalls seeing Elvis, so he must have been seven.

17 *Elvis Presley was the big bang* Jimmy Iovine, "American Icons: Elvis Presley, Bob Dylan, and Bruce Springsteen," *Rolling Stone* (May 15, 2003): 74.

18 *I couldn't imagine anyone* Johanna Pirttijärvi, Stage Introduction to "Glory Days," Cincinnati (July 6, 1984) from Storyteller, http://www .brucebase.org.uk/story.htm.

18 *I wanted to be a baseball player* Dave Marsh, *Two Hearts* (New York: Routledge, 2004), 27. This volume combines his two previous Springsteen biographies, *Born to Run* (1979) and *Glory Days* (1987), with some new material.

18 *It reached down* Paul Nelson, "Springsteen Fever," *Rolling Stone* (July 13, 1978), in Editors of *Rolling Stone, Bruce Springsteen: The Rolling Stone Files* (New York: Hyperion, 1996), 69.

18 *We had a very eccentric* Joe Levy, "Bruce Springsteen: The *Rolling Stone* Interview," *Rolling Stone* (November 1, 2007): 56.

18 *One of Springsteen's earliest memories* Bruce Springsteen, *Songs* (New York: HarperCollins, 1998), 136.

19 *I hated school* Peter Knobler, "Bruce Springsteen's Rites of Passage," *Crawdaddy* (October 1978): 48.

20 *I was raised Catholic* Robert Duncan, "Lawdamercy: Springsteen Saves," *Creem* (October 1978): 41.

20 *We're Democrats* Jann Wenner, "Bruce Springsteen: We've Been Misled," *Rolling Stone* (September 22, 2004): 38.

20 *Just like Superwoman* Jay Cocks, "Rock's New Sensation: The Backstreet Phantom of Rock," *Time* (October 27, 1975), in June Skinner

Sawyers, ed., *Racing in the Street: The Bruce Springsteen Reader* (New York: Penguin, 2004), 68.

20 **In 1998, he described her** Charlie Rose, Interview with Bruce Springsteen (November 20, 1998). Asked in 1975 what he would do if he ever got wealthy, Springsteen answered, "Get my mother to quit working." (Ray Coleman, "Springsteen: It's Hard to Be a Saint," *Melody Maker* [November 15, 1975]: 41).

20 **I always remember my mother** National Public Radio, "Bruce Springsteen on a 'Magic' Campaign," *Morning Edition* (March 5, 2008).

21 **My father struggled very hard** National Public Radio, "Bruce Springsteen on a 'Magic' Campaign."

21 **I remember when I was a kid** Pirttijärvi, Stage Introduction to "Independence Day," Rotterdam (April 29, 1981).

21 **perhaps that kind of action** Patrick Humphries and Chris Hunt, *Springsteen: Blinded by the Light* (London: Plexus, 1986), 13.

22 **I grew up in a house** Charlie Rose, Interview with Bruce Springsteen (November 20, 1998). Also see Gavin Martin, "Hey Joad, Don't Make It Sad," *New Musical Express* (March 9, 1996): 30.

22 **of having a dialogue** CBS News, "Springsteen Interview with Ed Bradley," *60 Minutes* (January 21, 1996).

22 **When I was really young** Pirttijärvi, Stage Introduction to "I'm on Fire," Los Angeles (October 10, 1985).

22 **When I got to be about sixteen** Pirttijärvi, Stage Introduction to "Independence Day," Paris (April 18, 1981) and Barcelona (April 21, 1981).

23 **I couldn't ever remember** Fred Schruers, "Bruce Springsteen and the Secret of the World," *Rolling Stone* (February 5, 1981), in *Rolling Stone Files*, 112.

23 **one of the best times** Kurt Loder, "The *Rolling Stone* Interview: Bruce Springsteen," *Rolling Stone* (December 6, 1984), in *Rolling Stone Files*, 163. For the story of being bought his guitar, see Patrick Humphries, "Springsteen: Interview," *Record Collector* (February 1999): 27; and Robert Hilburn, "Seasoned Springsteen: He's Older,

Happier, But Is He Still the Boss?," *Washington Post* (August 25, 1992): D1.

23 *Everything from then on* Peter Knobler and Greg Mitchell, "Who Is Bruce Springsteen and Why Are We Saying All These Wonderful Things About Him?," *Crawdaddy* (March 1973), in Sawyers, ed., *Racing in the Street*, 33.

23 *I was someone* Robert Hilburn, "Springsteen Off and Running," *Los Angeles Times* (September 28, 1975): V1.

24 *Music saved me* Cocks, "Rock's New Sensation," p. 68

24 *once I found the guitar* Knobler, "Bruce Springsteen's Rites of Passage," 50.

24 *The first day* Maureen Orth, "Making of a Rock Star," *Newsweek* (October 27, 1975), in Sawyers, ed., *Racing in the Street*, pp. 56–57.

24 *Rock 'n' roll was the only* "Out in the Streets: Bruce Springsteen Interviewed by Robert Hilburn, October, 1980," in Charles Cross, ed., *Backstreets: Springsteen: the Man and His Music* (New York: Harmony Books, 1989), p. 79.

24 *Onstage I talk a lot* David Hepworth, "Springsteen: The Interview," *Q Magazine* (August 1992).

24 *I was lucky* Pirttijärvi, Stage Introduction to "Independence Day," Gothenburg, Sweden (May, 3, 1981).

25 *My pop, he used to* Pirttijärvi, Stage Introduction to "It's My Life," New York (October 28, 1976).

26 *I couldn't stand reading* Joseph Rose, "Lightning Strikes on Thunder Road," *Hit Parader* (April 1976): 26.

26 *stretch it out into a story* National Public Radio, "Bruce Springsteen Discusses His Music," *Fresh Air* (November 15, 2005).

27 *The* next *night* Marsh, *Two Hearts*, 30.

27 *The first time I heard Bob Dylan* Bruce Springsteen, Rock and Roll Hall of Fame Induction Speech for Bob Dylan (January 2, 1988).

28 *there was something special* Christopher Connelly, "Still the Boss," *Rolling Stone* (September 26, 1985), in *Rolling Stone Files*, 183.

28 *used to tell me* Pirttijärvi, Stage Introduction to "The River," Los Angeles (October 2, 1985).

29 *We were scared going up* Loder, "The Rolling Stone Interview: Bruce Springsteen," in *Rolling Stone Files*, 153.

29 *What happened?* Pirttijärvi, Stage Introduction to "The River," Los Angeles (October 2, 1985).

29 *I had this habit* Pirttijärvi, Stage Introduction to "My Father's House," Los Angeles (November 16, 1990).

30 *My mother said they went* Will Percy, "Rock and Read: Will Percy Interviews Bruce Springsteen," *DoubleTake* (Spring 1998), in Sawyers, ed., *Racing in the Street*, 310–11.

30 *a real Hendrix/Cream* Bill Flanagan, "Ambition, Lies, and the Beautiful Reward," *Musician* (November 1992): 68.

31 *The Upstage became* Rebecca Traister, "Farewell from Asbury Park, NJ," *Salon* (January 3, 2006): http://www.salon.com/mwt/feature/2006/01/03/asbury_park.

31 *Hey guys, there's some kid* Joseph Dalton, "Bruce Springsteen Made in the U.S.A.," *Rolling Stone* (October 10, 1985), in *Rolling Stone Files*, 186.

32 *just had this enormous appetite* Anders Martensson and Jorgen Johansson, *Local Heroes: The Asbury Park Music Scene* (New Brunswick: Rutgers University Press, 2005, 2008), 95.

32 *When I walked in the first night* Mark Hagen, "The Midnight Cowboy: Interview," *Mojo* (January 1999): 84.

32 *the resin from the surfboards* Humphries, "Springsteen: Interview," 27.

32 On the riots, see Daniel Wolff, *4th of July, Asbury Park: A History of the Promised Land* (New York: Bloomsbury, 2005), 164–90.

33 *The riots changed the economics* Traister, "Farewell from Asbury Park, NJ."

33 *After the riots* Martensson and Johansson, *Local Heroes*, 63.

33 *Bruce didn't want to do* Ibid., 62.

33 *We would have been happy* Wolff, *4th of July*, 198.

33 *one day Bruce was gone* Martensson and Johansson, *Local Heroes*, 86.

33 *I had some personal problems* Hagen, "The Midnight Cowboy: Interview," 73.

34 *Through West, Springsteen met* The relationship would eventually disintegrate and result in a bitter lawsuit. For differing accounts, see Marc Eliot with Mike Appel, *Down Thunder Road: The Making of Bruce Springsteen* (New York: Simon & Schuster, 1992) and Marsh, *Two Hearts*. Also see Fred Goodman, *The Mansion on the Hill* (New York: Vintage, 1997), 287–98.

34 *I just said, "Hell"* Robert Hilburn, *Springsteen* (New York: Rolling Stone Press, 1985), 44–46.

34 *It was a big, big day* Hagen, "The Midnight Cowboy: Interview," 72.

36 *What did you change* Humphries, "Springsteen Interview," 27.

36 *I figured if I could get* Mark Kmetsko, "Paying the Price of Genius," *The Scene* (January 24–30, 1974): 5.

36 *I wanted a rhythm section* Hagen, "The Midnight Cowboy: Interview," 74.

36 *twisted autobiographies* Springsteen, *Songs*, 7.

36 *I never wrote* "Say Hello to Last Year's Genius," *Zoo World* (March 14, 1974): p. 14.

37 *I wrote like a madman* "Was Bob Dylan the Previous Bruce Springsteen?," *New Musical Express* (October 6, 1973): 16.

37 *a considerable new talent* Lester Bangs, "Review of *Greetings from Asbury Park, N.J.*," *Rolling Stone* (July 5, 1973), in *Rolling Stone Files*, 32–33.

37 *in an era of diminishing* Bruce Pollack, "Springsteen Celebrates Street Life," *New York Times* (December 16, 1973): 186.

37 *was my "getting out of town"* Springsteen, *Songs*, 26–27.

38 *goodbye to my adopted* Ibid., 25.

38 *I really don't want* "Say Hello to Last Year's Genius," 14.

38 *Songs are not literally* Neil Strauss, "Springsteen Looks Back but Keeps Looking On," *New York Times* (May 7, 1995): H1.

39   *There ain't a note*   Fred Schruers, "Bruce Springsteen and the Secret of the World," *Rolling Stone* (February 5, 1981), in *Rolling Stone Files*, 112.

Chapter 2: The Making of *Born to Run*

41   *I don't want to have*   Edwin Miller, "The Rock 'n' Roll Kid in Jungleland," *Seventeen* (December 1975): 115.

41   **Born to Run *was the first time***   Mark Hagen, "The Midnight Cowboy: Interview," *Mojo* (January 1999): 76.

41   *We were working on a*   Trevor Dann, "Bruce Springsteen on Writing 'Born to Run,'" BBC Radio 2, http://www.bbc.co.uk/radio2/soldon song/songlibrary/borntorun.shtml.

42   *it was a sixteen-track*   "Top 100 Singles of the Last Twenty-Five Years," Editors of *Rolling Stone, Bruce Springsteen: The Rolling Stone Files* (New York: Hyperion, 1996), p. 274.

42   *You couldn't relax*   Ibid.

42   *It was more*   Ibid.

42   *I wanted to make one of the greatest*   CBS News, "Born to Run: Recalling the Making of Bruce Springsteen's Album 'Born to Run'" (November 13, 2005).

42   *That was the most horrible*   Robert Duncan, "Bruce Springsteen Is Not God (And Doesn't Want to Be)," *Creem* (January 1976): 35.

42   *Suddenly, I was the future*   James Peterson, "The Ascension of Bruce Springsteen," *Playboy* (March 1976): 169

42   *It was* the *most intense*   Peter Knobler, "Running on the Backstreets with Bruce Springsteen," *Crawdaddy* (October 1975): 42.

43   *When I went into the studio*   Bruce Springsteen, Rock and Roll Hall of Fame Induction Speech for Roy Orbison (January 21, 1987).

44   *I want to get girls*   "Bruce Under the Boardwalk," *Sounds* (March 16, 1974): 12.

45   *I'm still fiddling*   Jerry Gilbert, "Bruce Springsteen: It's Hard to Be a Saint in the City," *Zig Zag* 45 (1974): 12.

45 *The alternate mixes* For a survey of *Born to Run* session recordings available on bootleg, see "On the Tracks 4.0—Born to Run," www .brucebase.org.uk/5.htm.

46 *When we rehearsed* Anders Martensson and Jorgen Johansson, *Local Heroes: The Asbury Park Music Scene* (New Brunswick: Rutgers University Press, 2005, 2008), 87.

46 *There's a lot of stuff* Paul Williams, "Won't You Come Home Bruce Springsteen," *Gallery* (August 1975): 36.

47 *Spontaneity* Dave DiMartino, "Bruce Springsteen Takes It to the River," *Creem* (January 1981): 60.

47 *Over Bruce's bed* For an analysis that develops the Peter Pan–Wendy connection, see Randall E. Auxier, "An Everlasting Kiss: The Seduction of Wendy," in Randall Auxier and Doug Anderson, eds., *Bruce Springsteen and Philosophy* (Chicago: Open Court, 2008), 103–18.

47 *song sounded huge* Knobler, "Running on the Backstreets," 40.

47 *is better than anything* Dave Marsh, "Walk Tall . . . or Don't Walk at All," *Creem* (October 1974): 35.

48 *'Born to Run' was the essence* Martensson and Johansson, *Local Heroes*, 139.

49 *was as close to jazz* Author interview with Garry Tallent, October 8, 2008.

50 *he included the following titles* "Spare Parts: Springsteen's Studio Sessions, 1966–88," Charles Cross, ed., *Backstreets: Springsteen: the Man and His Music* (New York: Harmony Books, 1989), 154.

51 *been coming along* Williams, "Lost in the Flood," in June Skinner Sawyers, ed., *Racing in the Street: The Bruce Springsteen Reader* (New York: Penguin, 2004), 46.

51 *I went to the bathroom* Phil Sutcliffe, "The Fairytale Album," *Mojo* (January 2006): 84.

52 *people were near tears* Knobler, "Running on the Backstreets," 40.

52 *The biggest thing Landau did* Ibid., 40.

52 *That was a nightmare* Jon Pareles, "'Born to Run' Reborn 30 Years Later," *New York Times* (November 15, 2005): E1.

52 *on the last day* Ashley Kahn, "Springsteen Looks Back on 'Born to Run,'" *Wall Street Journal* (November 10, 2005): D7.

53 *Sometime in February, Landau* See Landau's testimony in Marc Eliot with Mike Appel, *Down Thunder Road: The Making of Bruce Springsteen* (New York: Simon & Schuster, 1992): 128.

54 *a big help to me* Paul Nelson, "Springsteen Fever," *Rolling Stone* (July 13, 1978), in *Rolling Stone Files*, 69.

54 *Springsteen is one of the hardest* "Bruce's Right-Hand Men," *Melody Maker* (November 15, 1975): 39–43.

54 *It was really hard* "The Top 100: The Best Albums of the Last Twenty Years," *Rolling Stone* (August 27, 1987), in *Rolling Stone Files*, 230.

55 *If you have a good line* Dave Marsh, *Two Hearts* (New York: Routledge, 2004), 121.

55 *Writing it was very difficult* Hagen, "The Midnight Cowboy: Interview," 82.

56 *took a different approach* Knobler, "Running on the Backstreets," 40–42.

56 *It was on the keyboard* Bruce Springsteen, *Songs* (New York: HarperCollins, 1998), 46.

56 *my whole problem* Sutcliffe, "The Fairytale Album," 84.

57 *We were recording epics* "The Top 100: The Best Albums of the Last Twenty Years," 230.

57 *I was hanging around the studio* Van Zandt tells the story in Gary Graff, "Little Big Man," *Guitar World* (October 1995): 196. Other colorful versions appear in "The Runaway American Dreamer," *Uncut* (November 2005): 78, and Sutcliffe, "The Fairytale Album," 84.

58 *He'd say, 'Hang on'* Andrew Tyler, "Bruce Springsteen and the Wall of Faith," *New Musical Express* (November 15, 1975): 25–27.

58 *There was a monster* CBS News, "Born to Run: Recalling the Making."

58 *The release date* Marsh, *Two Hearts*, 133.

58 *I had this* **horrible** *pressure* Duncan, "Bruce Springsteen is Not God," 35.

58 *What about you?* Williams, "Won't You Come Home Bruce Springsteen," 36.

58 *what made the record so hard* Duncan, "Bruce Springsteen Is Not God," 35.

59 *Bruce would spend eight hours* Robert Hilburn, "The Music Industry Titans," *Los Angeles Times* (November 26, 2006): F1.

59 *Every day, before I'd go* Duncan, "Bruce Springsteen Is Not God," 35.

59 *I just lean my head* Ibid., 73.

60 *I bled dry on that thing* Ray Coleman, "Springsteen: It's Hard to Be a Saint in the City," *Melody Maker* (November 15, 1975): 40.

60 *We mixed the album* "The Top 100: The Best Albums of the Last Twenty Years," 230.

61 *It's the scariest thing* Chris Phillips, ed. "*Born to Run*: The Lost Interviews: Part Two," *Backstreets* 58 (Spring 1998): 29.

61 *"Is it over?"* Ibid.

62 *scared me off a bit* John Rockwell, "New Dylan from New Jersey? It Might as Well Be Springsteen," *Rolling Stone* (October 9, 1975), in *Rolling Stone Files*, 46.

62 *After it was finished?* Duncan, "Bruce Springsteen Is Not God," 73.

62 *Look, you're not supposed* Marsh, *Two Hearts*, 137.

62 *There's something he is not saying* Williams, "Won't You Come Home Bruce Springsteen," 36.

Chapter 3: The Songs of *Born to Run*

64 *"Thunder Road" opens the album* Bruce Springsteen, *Songs* (New York: HarperCollins, 1998), 43–47.

64 *There is something about the [piano] melody* Brian Hiatt, "'Born to Run' Turns Thirty," *Rolling Stone* (November 17, 2005): 17.

67 *it was the hokiest* Bruce Springsteen, *VH1 Storytellers* (April 2005).

67 *there are a lot of ascending*   Bob Doerschuk, "Roy Bittan: Riding America with the Boss," *Keyboard* (December 1986): 69–70.

68 *it just felt all-inclusive*   Neil Strauss, "Human Touch," *Guitar World* (October 1995): 65.

69 *begins, in effect*   Nick Hornby, *Songbook* (New York: Riverhead, 2003), 7–14. In the bibliography, Hornby tells readers where to find his album selections. For "Thunder Road," he simply says, "You know where to get this."

71 *A rainy, windy night it was*   Mary Jude Dixon, "Clarence Clemons: The Big Man Behind the Boss," *Suite 101*, http://www.suite101.com/ article.cfm/bruce_springsteen/27772.

72 *the barrier to the outside world*   Daniel Wolff, *4th of July, Asbury Park: A History of the Promised Land* (New York: Bloomsbury, 2005), 209.

76 *I hate being called "Boss"*   Dave DiMartino, "Bruce Springsteen Takes It to the River," *Creem* (January 1981): 26.

76 *Eventually, Bruce would write*   Mark Hagen, "The Midnight Cowboy: Interview," *Mojo* (January 1999): 86.

76 *I live by night*   Robert Hilburn, "Springsteen: Out in the Streets," *Los Angeles Times* (October 19, 1980), in June Skinner Sawyers, ed., *Racing in the Street: The Bruce Springsteen Reader* (New York: Penguin, 2004), 97.

80 *a misfit in my own town*   Judy Wieder, "Bruce Springsteen: The *Advocate* Interview," *Advocate* (April 2, 1996), in Sawyers, ed., *Racing in the Street*, 211–20.

84 *take place in the space*   Greil Marcus, "Springsteen's Thousand and One American Nights," *Rolling Stone* (October 9, 1975), in Editors of *Rolling Stone, Bruce Springsteen: The Rolling Stone Files* (New York: Hyperion, 1996), p. 49.

85 *I knew it was gonna happen*   Hilburn, "Out in the Streets," 95.

86 *Now "Born to Run"*   Chet Flippo, "Bruce Springsteen Interview," *Musician* (November 1984): 54.

86 *This is a song*   Johanna Pirttijärvi, Stage Introduction to "Born to Run," Los Angeles (April 27, 1988) from Storyteller, http://www.brucebase .org.uk/story.htm.

90 *stories inspired by the haunting* Jessica Kaye and Richard J. Brewer, eds., *Meeting Across the River* (New York: Bloomsbury 2005), xi.

90 *In the past, when he would try* Doerschuk, "Roy Bittan: Riding America with the Boss," 69–70.

93 *on* Born to Run *there was the hope* Peter Knobler, "You Want It, You Take It, You Pay the Price," *Crawdaddy* (October 1978): 54.

95 *I used a narrative folk voice* Springsteen, *Songs*, 101.

96 *You can't just be a dreamer* Patrick Humphries and Chris Hunt, *Springsteen: Blinded by the Light* (London: Plexus, 1986), 44.

96 *is about confronting one's own death* Springsteen, *Songs*, 101.

96 *are best treated as a trilogy* In his review in *Rolling Stone*, Paul Nelson treats the three albums as a trilogy. "Review of *The River*," *Rolling Stone* (December 11, 1980), in *Rolling Stone Files*, 104–8.

Chapter 4: The Geography of *Born to Run*

97 *The only concept that was around* Peter Knobler, "Running on the Backstreets with Bruce Springsteen," *Crawdaddy* (October 1975): 35–43.

97 *I really went towards the band* Chris Phillips, ed., "*Born to Run*: The Lost Interviews: Part One," *Backstreets* 57 (Winter 1997): 22.

98 *Whatever I hear, I digest* Ibid., 23.

98 *the strain of the whole album* Knobler, "Running on the Backstreets," 44.

99 *less eccentric and less local* Bruce Springsteen, *Songs* (New York: HarperCollins, 1998), 47.

99 *remarkably specific sense* Dave Marsh, *Two Hearts* (New York: Routledge, 2004), 140.

99 *allows [place] to take shape* Bob Crane, *A Place to Stand: A Guide to Bruce Springsteen's Sense of Place* (Baltimore: Palace Books, 2002), 1.

99 *I began to write* Robert Crampton, "The Gospel According to Bruce," *Times Magazine* (London) (July 27, 2002): 21.

99 *I was going to have a song* Knobler, "Running on the Backstreets," 43.

102 *I wanted something* Eric Meola, *Born to Run: The Unseen Photos* (San Rafael: Insight Editions, 2006). Also see "Meola on Springsteen,"

PDN Online (2000): http://pdngallery.com/legends/legends4/lastplaces/video.html.

102 *I set the pose up*   Anne Rodgers, "Clarence Clemons," *Palm Beach Post* (November 13, 2005): 4J.

107 *Elvis is my religion*   Lee Hudson Teslik, "Love Him Tender: The King Is Back," *Harvard Crimson* (April 26, 2002).

107 *you could make an argument*   Will Percy, "Rock and Read: Will Percy Interviews Bruce Springsteen," *DoubleTake* (Spring 1998), in June Skinner Sawyers, ed., *Racing in the Street: The Bruce Springsteen Reader* (New York: Penguin, 2004), 316.

108 *used to wonder*   Johanna Pirttijärvi, Stage Introduction to "Can't Help Falling in Love," Los Angeles (September 25, 1985) from Storyteller, http://www.brucebase.org.uk/story.htm.

108 *I do not believe that the essence*   Mikal Gilmore, "Bruce Springsteen Q&A," *Rolling Stone* (November 5–December 10, 1987), in Editors of *Rolling Stone, Bruce Springsteen: The Rolling Stone Files* (New York: Hyperion, 1996), 246.

109 *When the screen door slams*   Springsteen, *Songs*, 47.

112 *What's happened in the '70s*   Phillips, ed. *"Born to Run*: The Lost Interviews: Part One," 25.

112 *The thing people tend to forget*   National Public Radio, "Bruce Springsteen Discusses His Music and Performs," *Morning Edition* (April 26, 2005).

115 *there's that searchin' thing*   Kurt Loder, "The *Rolling Stone* Interview: Bruce Springsteen," *Rolling Stone* (December 6, 1984), in *Rolling Stone Files*, 155.

Chapter 5: The Reception of *Born to Run*

119 *among the great rock experiences*   John Rockwell, "The Rocky Road to Rock Stardom," *New York Times* (August 15, 1975): p. 74.

120 *in the studio, Bruce was astigmatic*   Paul Nelson, "Is Bruce Springsteen Worth the Hype?," *Village Voice* (August 25, 1975): 94.

120 *should be all [Springsteen] needs* John Rockwell, "Springsteen's Rock Poetry at Its Best," *New York Times* (August 29, 1975): 11.

121 *inspires the sort of pandemonium* Charles Michener with Eleanor Clift, "Bruce Is Loose," *Newsweek* (September 1, 1975): 43.

121 *Now we have someone* "Springsteen Off and Running," *Los Angeles Times* (September 28, 1975): VI. Also see Robert Hilburn, "Springing Springsteen—Too Fast?," *Los Angeles Times* (October 18, 1975): B5, and "Rock 'n' Roll: What'll He Do for an Encore," *Los Angeles Times* (November 9, 1975): P62.

122 **Born to Run** *breathed* Robert Hilburn, *Springsteen* (New York: Rolling Stone Press, 1985), 68.

122 *bits and pieces from so many rock* John Rockwell, "New Dylan from New Jersey? It Might as Well be Springsteen," *Rolling Stone* (October 9, 1975), in Editors of *Rolling Stone, Bruce Springsteen: The Rolling Stone Files* (New York: Hyperion, 1996), 41–47.

124 *You take what you find* Greil Marcus, "Springsteen's Thousand and One American Nights," *Rolling Stone* (October 9, 1975), in *Rolling Stone Files*, 48–51.

125 *filtered through Sixties songs* Bangs, "Hot Rod Rumble in the Promised Land," in June Skinner Sawyers, ed., *Racing in the Street: The Bruce Springsteen Reader* (New York: Penguin, 2004), 74–77.

125 *Someone convinced Springsteen* Jon Pareles, "Pop Top" *Record Buyers Guide* (October 1975).

126 *Just how much American myth* Robert Christgau, "Review of *Born to Run*," *Village Voice* (September 22, 1975): 122.

126 *to become a victim* David McGee, "The Power and Urgency of Bruce Springsteen," *Record World* (October 25, 1975).

127 *If Brecht and Weill* "Review," *Gallery* (November 1975): 35.

127 **Born to Run** *just may be* Mary Mook, "Sounds in the Sun," *Co-Ed* (December 1975): 62.

127 *would not have been won* Stephen Holden, "Springsteen Paints His Masterpiece," *Circus Raves* (December 1975): 52.

128　*virtually the only type of rock*　Frank Rose, "Bruce Springsteen: A Rebel, A Doo-Wop King," *Circus* (January 20, 1976): 16.

129　*which should be played if anyone*　Joe Edwards, "Springsteen's 'Born to Run': A One-Dimensional Disappointment," *Aquarian* (October 7, 1975). I am indebted to Bob Crane for bringing this review to my attention and providing a brief history of the newspaper.

129　*He nurtures the look*　Jay Cocks, "Rock's New Sensation: The Backstreet Phantom of Rock," *Time* (October 27, 1975), in Sawyers, ed., *Racing in the Street*, 64–73.

131　*Springsteen's verse is one*　Letters to the Editor, *Time* (November 17, 1975).

131　*rocketed to million-dollar gold*　Maureen Orth, "Making of a Rock Star," *Newsweek* (October 27, 1975), in Sawyers, ed., *Racing in the Street*, 53–63.

132　*Is Springsteen really the Rock Messiah*　Henry Edwards, "If There Hadn't Been a Bruce Springsteen, Then the Critics Would Have Made Him Up," *New York Times* (October 5, 1975): 125.

132　*irritating review*　"Letters: Springsteen—Born to Stir Up Controversy," *New York Times* (October 19, 1975): 133.

133　*That bothered me a lot*　Robert Hilburn, "Springsteen: Out in the Streets," *Los Angeles Times* (October 19, 1980), in Sawyers, ed., *Racing in the Street*, 93.

133　*Recounting Columbia's strategy*　"Springsteen: The Merchandising of a Superstar," *BusinessWeek* (December 1, 1975): 53.

133　*The word "hype"*　"The Selling of Springsteen," *Melody Maker* (October 25, 1975): 3. Also see Chris Welles, "Born to Get 'Itchy Excited,'" *MORE* (Fall 1975): 10–14.

133　*The fact remains*　John Rockwell, "'Hype' and the Springsteen Case," *New York Times* (October 24, 1975): 34.

134　*One writer described the showy*　Andrew Tyler, "Bruce Springsteen and the Wall of Faith," *New Musical Express* (November 15, 1975): 25.

134　*If he survives all the publicity*　Robin Denselow, "The Importance of Springsteen," *Guardian* (December 5, 1975): 10.

134 *for one of the things I did want* Tyler, "Springsteen and the Wall of Faith," 25.

134 *What am I doing on the cover* Hilburn, "Springing Springsteen," B5.

134 *There was a point* Hilburn, "Out in the Streets," 93.

135 *was a very big mistake* "Smash Hit Springsteen," *Melody Maker* (November 15, 1975): 39.

135 *People keep telling me* Ray Coleman, "Springsteen: It's Hard to Be a Saint in the City," *Melody Maker* (November 15, 1975): 41.

135 *I felt that—that it was insulting* Bob Costas, "Bruce Springsteen Talks About His Music and His Career," *Today* (December 7, 1998).

135 *If you're lucky he'll finish* Chris Charlesworth, "Springsteen Turns on the Heat," *Melody Maker* (February 9, 1974): 14.

136 *everyone was expecting something* Simon Frith, "Casing the Promised Land," *Creem* (March 1976): 26, 72.

137 *Springsteen mesmerized the audience* "On Stage," *Arnold Bocklin* (December 1975): 29.

137 *still an impressive performance* "Review" *Guardian* (November 20, 1975): 12.

137 *turns out to be is the leader* David Hancock, "Born to Lean," *Record Mirror* (November 29, 1975): 24.

137 *feed directly off their audience* Michael Watts, "Caught in the Act: Springsteen Delivers the Goods," *Melody Maker* (November 29, 1975): 28.

138 *uses his guitar like Charlie Chaplin* Robert Ward, "The Night of the Punk," *New Times* (September 5, 1975).

138 *Chaplinesque sense of humour* Denselow, "The Importance of Springsteen," 10.

138 *one of the few '70s performers* Dave Seal, "Bruce Springsteen: The Next Best Thing?" *Arnold Bocklin* (November 1975): 2–3.

139 *grown to love it* Jerry Gilbert, "Bruce Brilliance Still There," *Sounds* (November 13, 1975): 16.

139 *You can't jive the kid* "Smash Hit Springsteen," 39–43.

139   *skillful portrayal of the stereotype*   Roy Carr, "Roy Orbison Makes Big Comeback," *New Musical Express* (September 6, 1975): 16.

140   *ponderous mock-Spector arrangements*   Charles Murray, "The Sprucing of the Springbean," *New Musical Express* (October 11, 1975): 26–27.

140   *friends tell me this grows*   Charlie Gillett "Single File," *New Musical Express* (November 29, 1975): 28.

141   *This album is fantastic*   *Extra Nouvelle Series* 6 (November 1975): 65.

141   *a lively and convincing work*   *Sounds* (Germany) (November 1975): 60.

141   *In America he is poised*   *New Music Magazine* (Japan) (November 1975): 135. For translation from the French, German, and Japanese, I am indebted to Sarah Blanks, Joahannes Evelein, and Jeffrey Bayliss.

141   *It marks the transition* James Wolcott, "A Future Hero, Or Is Bruce Springsteen Last of a Breed?," *Circus Raves* (November 1975): 46–47.

141   *pale-colored poetry*   Ibid., 47.

142   *shuffled behind the Boss*   James Wolcott, "The Hagiography of Bruce Springsteen," *Vanity Fair* (December 1985), in Sawyers, ed., *Racing in the Street*, 126–29.

142   *both the relative unanimity*   Robert Christgau, "Yes, There Is a Rock Establishment (But Is That Bad for Rock?)," *Village Voice* (January 26, 1976): http://www.robertchristgau.com/xg/rock/critics-76.php.

142   *The story that had been missed*   In 1988, John Lombardi built on Christgau's analysis to offer a stern critique of Springsteen's popularity, arguing that "Bruce was a 'rock critic's' dream, a means of rationalizing nostalgic feelings of 'rebellion' and blue-collar sympathy with comfortable middle-aged incomes and 'life-styles.'" See John Lombardi, "The Sanctification of Bruce Springsteen and the Rise of Mass Hip," *Esquire* (December 1988): 139–54.

143   *a rich if somewhat silly period*   Christgau, "Yes, There Is a Rock Establishment."

145   *I'd written "Born to Run"*   "Bruce Has the Fever: Ed Sciaky Interviews Bruce Springsteen, August 1978," in Charles Cross, ed., *Backstreets: Springsteen: the Man and His Music* (New York: Harmony Books, 1989), 71.

145 *It got so where, if I wrote a book* Peter Knobler, "Bruce Springsteen's Rites of Passage," *Crawdaddy* (October 1978): 52. For an account of the lawsuit, see David McGee, "Bruce Springsteen Claims the Future of Rock & Roll," *Rolling Stone* (August 11, 1977), in *Rolling Stone Files*, 59–66, and Marc Eliot with Mike Appel, *Down Thunder Road: The Making of Bruce Springsteen* (New York: Simon & Schuster, 1992), 200. According to the deposition included in Eliot's book, Springsteen said, "I have been cheated. I wrote 'Born to Run,' every line of that fucking song is me and no line of that fucking song is his. I don't own it. I can't print it in a piece of paper if I wanted to. I have been cheated."

145 *I loved the album the first time* Tony Parsons, "Blinded by the Hype," *New Musical Express* (October 9, 1976): 22–23.

Chapter 6: *Born to Run* Thirty Years On

147 *Neither Bette Midler* Robert Christgau, "Yes, There Is a Rock Establishment (But Is That Bad for Rock?)," *Village Voice* (January 26, 1976): http://www.robertchristgau.com/xg/rock/critics-76.php.

148 *is obviously not a Francis Scott Key* Richard Lee, "New Jersey Opinion in Support of a Proposal for a State Anthem," *New York Times* (June 15, 1980): Section 11, p. 22.

149 *I think it is only fit* "Letters to the New Jersey Editor," *New York Times* (June 29, 1980): Section 11, p. 27, and July 6, 1980, Section 11, p. 22.

149 *the message of this song* "The Legislature May be Off and 'Running' with Springsteen's Song," *Star Ledger* (May 20, 1980): 19.

151 **Nebraska** *comes as a shock* Steve Pond, "*Nebraska* Album Review," *Rolling Stone* (October 28, 1982), in Editors of *Rolling Stone*, *Bruce Springsteen: The Rolling Stone Files* (New York: Hyperion, 1996), 131. Also see Robert Palmer, "Bruce Springsteen Fashions a Compelling, Austere Message," *New York Times* (September 26, 1982): Section 2, p. 21, and Stephen Holden, "When the Boss Fell to Earth, He Hit Paradise," *New York Times* (August 9, 1992): H1.

152 *You're very conscious* Joe Levy, "Bruce Springsteen: The *Rolling Stone* Interview," *Rolling Stone* (November 1, 2007): 54.

153 *I just started to read* Johanna Pirttijärvi, Stage Introductions to "Independence Day," Paris (April 19, 1981), Brussels (April 26, 1981), and Rotterdam (April 29, 1981). Also see Dave Marsh's discussion in *Bruce Springsteen on Tour* (New York: Bloomsbury, 2006): 132–34.

154 *In 1984, nearly ten years after* For an insightful discussion of the album, see Geoffrey Himes, *Born in the U.S.A.* (New York: Continuum, 2005).

157 *offstage, Mr. Springsteen apparently* Robert Palmer, "Springsteen's Music Hits Chord of America," *New York Times* (August 6, 1985): C13.

158 *for all the exhilaration* Stephen Holden, "Springsteen Scans the American Dream," *New York Times* (May 27, 1984): H19.

158 *after a decade of rock stardom* Palmer, "Springsteen's Music Hits Chord of America," C13.

158 *an old-fashioned populist* Jon Pareles, "Bruce Springsteen—Rock's Popular Populist," *New York Times* (August 18, 1985): H1.

159 *has become a brooding* Richard Harrington, "Springsteen's Wrong Turn: He's Back on the Same Old Roads," *Washington Post* (June 10, 1984): H1.

159 *a place where crumbling towns* Bill Barol, "There's Magic in the Night," *Newsweek* (August 27, 1984): 64.

159 *I went through a very confusing* Mans Iverson, "Born Again," *Beats* (August 1992): 8.

160 *I just kind of felt "Bruced"* James Henke, "Bruce Springsteen: The *Rolling Stone* Interview," *Rolling Stone* (August 6, 1992), in *Rolling Stone Files*, 321.

160 *Here's a song I played* Pirttijärvi, Stage Introduction to "Born to Run," London (June 25, 1988) from Storyteller, http://www.brucebase.org.uk/story.htm.

161 *He also went into therapy* Henke, "The *Rolling Stone* Interview," 319.

162 *is a delight* Chris DaFoe, "Has the Boss Lost His Touch?," *Globe and Mail* (March 28, 1992).

162 *in 1974, I was a* Holden, "When the Boss Fell to Earth," H1.

163 *the guy in "Living Proof"* Mans Iverson, "Born Again," 8.

163 *After* **Born to Run**, *it was, O.K.* Nicholas Dawidoff, "The Pop Populist," *New York Times Magazine* (January 26, 1997), in June Skinner Sawyers, ed., *Racing in the Street: The Bruce Springsteen Reader* (New York: Penguin, 2004), 246–65.

164 *the twang of hand-picked guitars* Jon Pareles, "Springsteen: An Old Fashioned Rocker in a New Era," *New York Times* (March 29, 1992): H1.

164 *I wanted to write about things* Neil Strauss, "Springsteen Looks Back but Keeps Looking On," *New York Times* (May 7, 1995): H1.

164 *a great rock & roll* Henke, "The *Rolling Stone* Interview," 332.

164 *I remember thinking that's what* Dawidoff, "Pop Populist," 251.

165 *I believe that your politics* David Corn, "Bruce Springsteen Tells the Story of the Secret America," *Mother Jones* (March/April 1996): 22–25.

166 *Well, what is my costume?* National Public Radio, "Bruce Springsteen on His Music, Life, and New Solo Tour," *Morning Edition* (April 27, 2005).

167 *into the abyss* Strauss, "Springsteen Looks Back but Keeps Looking On," H1.

167 *Bruce Springsteen, you always knew* Bono, "Bono's Speech at the 1999 Hall of Fame Induction Ceremony," http://www.u2station.com/news/archives/1999/03/bonos_speech_at_1.php.

168 *unlike a politician* Pareles, "Bruce Springsteen—Rock's Popular Populist," H1.

168 *Springsteen is singing against* Jack Newfield, "Can Springsteen Ignite Political Passion?," *Village Voice*, quoted in Melvin Maddocks, "Bruce Springsteen—the Pied Piper as Populist," *Christian Science Monitor* (September 27, 1985): 23.

169 *none more so than Springsteen* Maddocks, "Bruce Springsteen—the Pied Piper as Populist," 23.

169 *that much about politics* Robert Hilburn, "The Politicization of Bruce Springsteen," *Los Angeles Times* (October 25, 1984): K1.

169 *I want people to find* Robert Hilburn, "Rock 'n' Roll Rites of Springsteen: Emotions, Illusions," *Los Angeles Times* (August 4, 1974): H58.

169 *I don't come out and promote* Holden, "When the Boss Fell to Earth," H1.

169 *I heard a political message* Corn, "Bruce Springsteen Tells the Story," 22–25.

170 *I read in the* Press *this morning* Dawidoff, "Pop Populist," 261.

170 *That's part of my job* Jon Pareles, "His Kind of Heroes, His Kind of Songs," *New York Times* (July 14, 2002): A1.

170 *I found those to be very* Josh Tyrangiel, "Reborn in the USA," *Time* (July 27, 2002): 52–59.

170 *It's something we do once* Robert Crampton, "The Gospel According to Bruce," *Times Magazine* (London) (July 27, 2002): 19–21.

171 *Like* Born in the U.S.A. *before it* Kurt Loder, "Review," *Rolling Stone* (August 22, 2002): 81.

171 *Since* Born to Run, *the album* A. O. Scott, "The Poet Laureate of 9/11," *Slate* (August 6, 2002): http://www.slate.com/id/2069047/.

172 *All people have is hope* Pareles, "His Kind of Heroes, His Kind of Songs," A1.

172 *Our goal is to change* Bruce Springsteen, "Chords for Change," *New York Times* (August 5, 2004): A23.

173 *had an enormous effect* Phil Sutcliffe, "You Talkin' to Me?: Interview with Bruce Springsteen," *Mojo* (January 2006): 88.

173 *We remain a land* Pirttijärvi, Stage Introduction to "Born to Run," Philadelphia (October 1, 2004).

174 *As a Springsteen fan* Scott Galup, "Springsteen's Political Ballad," *Washington Times* (November 5, 2004): D1.

174 *We support Bruce* Damien Cave, "For Fans at Springsteen Concert the Music Seems to Matter More than the Message," *New York Times* (October 14, 2004): B6.

174 *On* Born to Run, *there's that* Ashley Kahn, "Springsteen Looks Back on 'Born to Run,'" *Wall Street Journal* (November 10, 2005): D7.

175 *There's a part of the singer* CBS News, "Bruce Springsteen Discusses

His Music, New Album and Tour with E Street Band," *60 Minutes* (October 7, 2007).

175 *It's personal and political* John Aizlewood, "Banned by Starbucks is Kind of Fun at 55," *Evening Standard* (London) (May 25, 2005): 10.

176 *The first thing that strikes you* Pirttijärvi, Stage Introduction to "Jesus Was an Only Son," Atlantic City, New Jersey (November 13, 2005).

177 **Born to Run** *was a spiritual record* Chet Flippo, "Bruce Springsteen Interview," *Musician* (November 1984): 54. Also see Chet Flippo, "Blue-Collar Troubadour," *People* (September 3, 1984): 73.

177 *got a lot less defensive* Jon Pareles, "Bruce Almighty," *New York Times* (April 24, 2005): A1.

178 *Everything I knew* Larry McShane, "Springsteen Reflects on 'Born to Run,'" Associated Press (November 11, 2005).

178 *"to" was always, Where do I live?* National Public Radio, "Bruce Springsteen Discusses His Music," *Fresh Air* (November 15, 2005).

179 *People took that music* Nick Hornby, "A Fan's Eye View," *Observer Music Monthly* (July 17, 2005): http://www.guardian.co.uk/music/2005/jul/17/popandrock.springsteen.

179 *a local sensation* Jon Pareles, "'Born to Run' Reborn Thirty Years Later," *New York Times* (November 15, 2005): E1.

179 *Wired with poetic precision* Kahn, "Springsteen Looks Back on 'Born to Run,'" D7.

179 *The biggest problem with Bruce* Robert Christgau, "Re-Run," *Blender* (January–February 2006): http://www.robertchristgau.com/xg/cdrev/springsteen-ble.php.

179 *What Springsteen represents* Clayton Purdum, "*Born to Run* (30th Anniversary Edition) Reissue," *Coke Machine Glow* (January 12, 2006): http://www.cokemachineglow.com/record_review/1013/bruce springsteen.

180 *If ever a song desperately* Barry Schwartz, "Bruce Springsteen, *Born to Run* 30th Anniversary Edition," *Stylus* (January 8, 2006): http://www.stylusmagazine.com/reviews/bruce-springsteen/born-to-run-30th-anniversary-edition.htm.

180 *the worst time to go through* Eric Alterman, "Tramps Like Us," *Nation* (September 5, 2005).

181 *many of Mr. Springsteen's* Harlan Coben, "Rock and a Hard Place," *New York Times* (November 25, 2005): A39.

181 *Bruce Springsteen is an American* Lester Bangs, "Hot Rod Rumble in the Promised Land," *Creem* (November 1975), in Sawyers, ed., *Racing in the Street*, 73.

181 *in what it means to live* CBS News, "Springsteen Discusses His Music."

182 *The greatest pop music* ABC News, "Interview with Ted Koppel," *Nightline* (September 1, 2003).

Encore: "What Else Can We Do Now?"

184 *Well, there it is* CBS News, "Springsteen: Silence Is Unpatriotic," *60 Minutes* (October 7, 2007): http://www.cbsnews.com/stories/2007/10/04/60minutes/main3330463.shtml.

185 *My songs, they're all about* Joe Levy, "Bruce Springsteen: The *Rolling Stone* Interview," *Rolling Stone* (November 1, 2007): 54.

185 *I'm interested in what it means* CBS News "Bruce Springsteen Discusses His Music, New Album and Tour with E Street Band," *60 Minutes* (October 7, 2007).

185 *In a way, Springsteen* National Public Radio, "Bruce Springsteen on a 'Magic' Campaign," *Morning Edition* (March 5, 2008).

186 *has sailed away on a bloody* CBS News, "Springsteen Discusses His Music."

187 *a reinfatuation with pop* A. O. Scott, "In Love with Pop, Uneasy with the World," *New York Times* (September 30, 2007): E1

187 *straight-out big* Levy, "Bruce Springsteen: The *Rolling Stone* Interview," 53.

187 *The arrangements, the performances* David Fricke, "Review of *Magic*," *Rolling Stone* (October 18, 2007): 119–20.

187 *aims for the specificity* Ann Powers, "Springsteen Sings for the Believers," *Los Angeles Times* (September 30, 2007): F14.

189 *AN ENDLESS ROAD* Tim Adams, "An Endless Road, A Search for Home: That's the American Way," *Observer* (London) (October 14, 2007): 64.

189 *A guy comes back to his town* Scott, "In Love with Pop," E1.

189 *looks more to the future* National Public Radio, "Bruce Springsteen on a 'Magic' Campaign."

189 *Springsteen . . . is not wallowing* David Corn, "Springsteen's *Magic*: Darkness in the Center of Town," *Nation* (October 2, 2007): http://www.thenation.com/blogs/capitalgames/239190/springsteen_s_i_magic_i_darkness_in_the_center_of_town posted 10/02/2007.

190 *I always felt that was my birthday* Chet Flippo, "Bruce Springsteen Interview," *Musician* (November 1984): 55.

190 *The music of that album* Scott, "In Love with Pop," E1.

190 *rock 'n' roll came to my house* Robert Duncan, "Lawdamercy: Springsteen Saves," *Creem* (October 1978): 64.

190 *I know that rock and roll* Chet Flippo, "Blue-Collar Troubadour," *People* (September 3, 1984): 73.

190 *I believe that rock and roll* Dave Marsh, *Two Hearts* (New York: Routledge, 2004), 4. It should come as no surprise that many authors of works on Springsteen confess that, like Eric Alterman, "*Born to Run* exploded in my home and my mind and changed my life." See *It Ain't No Sin to Be Glad You're Alive: The Promise of Bruce Springsteen* (New York: Little, Brown and Company, 1999), 73–74.

191 *That incredible song* National Public Radio, "Finding a New Path in Springsteen's 'Thunder Road,'" *Weekend All Things Considered* (October 6, 2007).

192 *I was listening to my dad's* Phil Kuntz, "In Europe, Uncle Sam Isn't So Popular, but the Boss Rocks," *Wall Street Journal* (October 18, 2002): A1.

192 *Being a working-class Pakistani* Sarfraz Manzoor, "The Boss and Me," *Guardian* (August 7, 2002). Also see *Greetings from Bury Park: A Memoir* (New York: Vintage, 2007) and Pico Ayer, "Born to Run Away," *Time International* (June 25, 2007): 100.

193 *In 1975, I was in college*   This paragraph draws on my essay "The Long Run with Springsteen," *Chicago Tribune* (August 21, 2005): 3.

195 *You're different than you were*   Cal Fussman, "Bruce Springsteen: It Happened in Jersey," *Esquire* (August 2005): 92.

196 *I didn't get burned out*   James Henke, "Bruce Springsteen: The *Rolling Stone* Interview," *Rolling Stone* (August 6, 1992), in Editors of *Rolling Stone, Bruce Springsteen: The Rolling Stone Files* (New York: Hyperion, 1996), 328.

196 *I believe that the life*   Kurt Loder, "The *Rolling Stone* Interview: Bruce Springsteen," *Rolling Stone* (December 6, 1984), in *Rolling Stone Files*, 161.

197 *I think someone can do real good work*   Ibid., 163.

197 *I think I made the mistake*   Mikal Gilmore, "Twentieth Anniversary Special: Bruce Springsteen Q&A," *Rolling Stone* (November 5–December 10, 1987), in *Rolling Stone Files*, 246.

197 *Dylan was a revolutionary*   Ibid., 240.

198 *worked like crazy their whole lives*   CBS News, "Ed Bradley Interviews Bruce Springsteen," *60 Minutes* (January 21, 1996).

198 *I didn't see myself as some gifted genius*   *The History of Rock 'n' Roll* (New York: Time-Life Video, 1995).

198 *Now I see that two of the best*   Henke, "The *Rolling Stone* Interview," 323.

198 *It was a record of enormous longing*   Brian Hiatt, "'Born to Run' Turns Thirty," *Rolling Stone* (November 17, 2005): 17.

199 *Springsteen . . . leaned back against*   Robert Hilburn, "Springing Springsteen—Too Fast?," *Los Angeles Times* (October 18, 1975): B5.

199 *at 60, I plan to be*   Neil Strauss, "Springsteen Looks Back but Keeps Looking On," *New York Times* (May 7, 1995): H1.

SELECTED BIBLIOGRAPHY

Alterman, Eric. *It Ain't No Sin to Be Glad You're Alive: The Promise of Bruce Springsteen*. New York: Little, Brown and Company, 1999.

Auxier, Randall and Doug Anderson. *Bruce Springsteen and Philosophy*. Chicago: Open Court, 2008.

Bernhard, Mark, Kenneth Womack, and Jerry Zolton, editors. "Glory Days: A Bruce Springsteen Celebration." *Interdisciplinary Literary Studies* 9 (Fall 2007): 1–206.

Cavicchi, Daniel. *Tramps Like Us: Music and Meaning Among Springsteen Fans*. New York: Oxford University Press, 1998.

Coles, Robert. *Bruce Springsteen's America*. New York: Random House, 2003.

Crane, Bob. *A Place to Stand: A Guide to Bruce Springsteen's Sense of Place*. Baltimore: Palace Books, 2002.

Cross, Charles, editor. *Backstreets: Springsteen: the Man and His Music*. New York: Harmony Books, 1989.

Cullen, Jim. *Born in the U.S.A.: Bruce Springsteen and the American Tradition*. New York: Harper, 1997.

Editors of *Rolling Stone*, *Bruce Springsteen: The Rolling Stone Files*. New York: Hyperion, 1996.

Eliot, Marc with Mike Appel. *Down Thunder Road: The Making of Bruce Springsteen*. New York: Simon & Schuster, 1992.

Gilmore, Mikal. "Bruce Springsteen's America," in Gilmore, *Night Beat: A Shadow History of Rock 'n' Roll*, 211–26. *New York*: Anchor, 1998.

Goodman, Fred. *The Mansion on the Hill*. New York: Vintage Books, 1997.

Guterman, Jimmy. *Runaway American Dream: Listening to Bruce Springsteen*. Cambridge, MA: Da Capo, 2005.

Hilburn, Robert. *Springsteen*. New York: Rolling Stone Press, 1985.

Himes, Geoffrey. *Born in the U.S.A.* New York: Continuum, 2005.

Humphries, Patrick and Chris Hunt. *Bruce Springsteen: Blinded by the Light*. London: Plexus, 1985.

Kaye, Jessica and Richard Brewer, editors. *Meeting Across the River*. New York: Bloomsbury, 2005.

Kirkpatrick, Rob. *The Words and Music of Bruce Springsteen*. Westport, CT: Praeger, 2006.

Marsh, Dave. *Bruce Springsteen on Tour, 1968–2005*. New York: Bloomsbury, 2006.

————. *Two Hearts*. New York: Routledge, 2004.

Martensson, Anders and Jorgen Johansson. *Local Heroes: The Asbury Park Music Scene*. New Brunswick, NJ: Rutgers University Press, 2005, 2008.

Meola, Eric. *Born to Run: The Unseen Photos*. San Rafael, CA: Insight Editions, 2006.

Sandford, Christopher. *Springsteen: Point Blank*. Cambridge, MA: Da Capo, 1999.

Santelli, Robert. *Greetings from E Street: The Story of Bruce Springsteen and the E Street Band*. San Francisco: Chronicle Books, 2006.

Sawyers, June Skinner, editor. *Racing in the Street: The Bruce Springsteen Reader*. New York: Penguin, 2004.

Smith, Larry David. *Bob Dylan, Bruce Springsteen, and American Song*. Westport, CT: Praeger, 2002.

Springsteen, Bruce. *Songs*. New York: HarperCollins, 1998.

"Symposium: The Lawyer as Poet Advocate: Bruce Springsteen and the American Lawyer," *Widener Law Journal* 14 (2005).

Symynkywicz, Jeffrey. *The Gospel According to Bruce Springsteen: Rock and Redemption from* Asbury Park *to* Magic. Louisville: Westminster John Knox Press, 2008.

Wolff, Daniel. *4th of July Asbury Park: A History of the Promised Land*. New York: Bloomsbury, 2005.

LYRIC CREDITS

INDEX